eBAY®
QuickSteps
Second Edition

JOHN CRONAN

CAROLE MATTHEWS

New York Chicago San Francisco
Lisbon London Madrid Mexico City
Milan New Delhi San Juan
Seoul Singapore Sydney Toronto

The McGraw·Hill Companies

Cataloging-in-Publication Data is on file with the Library of Congress

McGraw-Hill books are available at special quantity discounts to use as premiums and sales promotions, or for use in corporate training programs. For more information, please write to the Director of Special Sales, Professional Publishing, McGraw-Hill, Two Penn Plaza, New York, NY 10121-2298. Or contact your local bookstore.

eBAY® QUICKSTEPS, SECOND EDITION

1234567890 CCI CCI 01987

ISBN: 978-0-07-148559-3
MHID: 0-07-148559-7

SPONSORING EDITOR / Roger Stewart

EDITORIAL SUPERVISOR / Jody McKenzie

PROJECT MANAGER / Samik Roy Chowdhury

SERIES CREATORS AND EDITORS / Martin and Carole Matthews

ACQUISITIONS COORDINATOR / Carly Stapleton

TECHNICAL EDITORS / Carole Matthews, John Cronan

COPY EDITOR / Lisa McCoy

PROOFREADER / Joette Lynch

INDEXER / Valerie Perry

PRODUCTION SUPERVISOR / Jean Bodeaux

COMPOSITION / International Typesetting and Composition

ILLUSTRATION / International Typesetting and Composition

SERIES DESIGN / Bailey Cunningham

ART DIRECTOR, COVER / Jeff Weeks

COVER DESIGN / Patti Lee

As we have used eBay and focused our attention on the vast community it serves, we have become aware of the profound changes in how we buy and sell in this global economy. eBay represents a shift in tangible and intangible ways. Not only are millions of people conducting business at some level (from online garage sales to huge, global companies), but also we are thinking about the world in a very different way. No longer is that buyer in England a stranger or that seller of silk in Cambodia an unattainable source. We don't know whether our seller is tall, male or female, color-blind, or a soccer fan, but we do know whether he or she conducts business in an honorable way. What is this thing that combines materialism with such a sense of the essence of who we are? With that question in mind, we would like to dedicate this book to the millions of eBay users who have helped to transform the age-old practices of buying and selling into this vital and dynamic global economy.

—John Cronan and Carole Matthews

About the Authors

John Cronan has more than 25 years of computer experience and has been writing and editing computer-related books for more than 15 years. His recent books include *Microsoft Office Excel 2007 QuickSteps*, *Microsoft Office Access 2007 QuickSteps*, and *eBay Business QuickSteps*. John and his wife Faye operate an antiques business in Washington state and frequent area auctions in search of merchandise they can "bring back to life." An eBay member since 1999, John couples his in-depth experience in writing books on software products with his familiarity of antiques and eBay use to bring a unique perspective to *eBay QuickSteps*. John and Faye (and cat Little Buddy) reside in the historic mill town of Everett, WA.

Carole Boggs Matthews has more than 30 years of computing experience. She has authored or co-authored more than 60 books, including *Microsoft Office PowerPoint 2007 QuickSteps*, *PhotoShop CS2 QuickSteps*, and *eBay Business QuickSteps*. Prior to her writing career, she co-founded and operated a computer business, developing tools to help others use computers in their businesses. An eBay user since 1998, Carole now applies that experience and many years of writing to *eBay QuickSteps*, bringing both business and computer knowledge to the book. Carole lives in Washington state with her husband Marty, son Michael, two cats, and the family dog.

Contents at a Glance

Contents

5

6

9

10

Acknowledgments

Although this book has only two names on the cover, it was really produced by a fantastic team of truly talented people. This team, the QuickSteps backbone, has again pulled together to produce a really great book in an incredibly short time. They did this by putting in endless hours, working selflessly with each other, and applying a great amount of skill. In particular, we wish to thank Roger Stewart as our acquisitions editor, Carly Stapleton for overall coordination, Jody McKenzie for tracking the project, Valerie Perry for indexing, Lisa McCoy for copy editing, and Samik Roy Chowdhury for project management.

To the many eBay users and businesses we contacted while writing this book who shared their experiences, suggestions, listing data, and other materials. In particular, we'd like to thank Vicki Detwiler (dvdet), eBay PowerSeller, eBay Store owner (Vicki's Goodies), and Trading Assistant for her support as well as Carol McGeehan (luvantiqs), art and antiques dealer, eBay PowerSeller, and Trading Assistant.

Thanks to all for helping to make this a better book!

How to...

Chapter 1
Stepping into eBay

eBay is the world's largest *online* market, made up of sellers and buyers from all over the planet, not just your friendly neighborhood stores. You have the world at your fingertips—where almost anything can be bought and sold, at exactly the right price. You can buy goods from businesses or individuals anywhere—or sell them—and all from your own computer. eBay is both an exciting adventure for a novice buyer or seller and a place where business is conducted. It is easily accessible to all who have a computer and a sense of what to do.

This book provides an understanding of how a purchase or sale transaction works, from the seller getting the item on eBay to the buyer purchasing the item. You will learn to navigate around eBay, and how to buy and sell items. Finally, you will learn how to protect yourself. First off is a walk around eBay and finding your way around.

Walk Through an eBay Transaction

The path of a transaction within eBay (Figure 1-1) illustrates the roles of the buyer and seller as they interact with eBay and each other. Sally, the seller, may be listing her item as an auction item or as an item to be sold at a fixed price. Bob, the buyer, and Sally may never meet, but through business transactions, they will know each other in a way that even their neighbors don't know each of them!

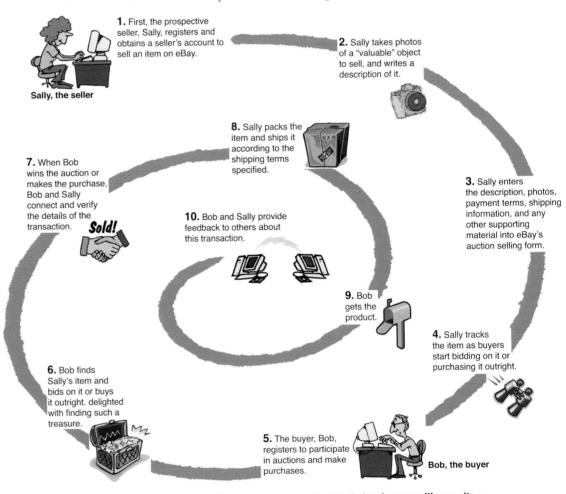

1. First, the prospective seller, Sally, registers and obtains a seller's account to sell an item on eBay.

Sally, the seller

2. Sally takes photos of a "valuable" object to sell, and writes a description of it.

8. Sally packs the item and ships it according to the shipping terms specified.

7. When Bob wins the auction or makes the purchase, Bob and Sally connect and verify the details of the transaction. **Sold!**

10. Bob and Sally provide feedback to others about this transaction.

3. Sally enters the description, photos, payment terms, shipping information, and any other supporting material into eBay's auction selling form.

9. Bob gets the product.

4. Sally tracks the item as buyers start bidding on it or purchasing it outright.

6. Bob finds Sally's item and bids on it or buys it outright. delighted with finding such a treasure.

5. The buyer, Bob, registers to participate in auctions and make purchases.

Bob, the buyer

*Figure 1-1: **A walk through an eBay transaction shows important steps in buying or selling an item.***

Find Your Way Around eBay

Navigating around eBay can be confusing. The home page, shown in Figure 1-2, is crammed with visual enticements, all screaming to be looked at. These are continually changing. However, you'll find that eBay is organized in a fairly convenient way, and once you can see this, you will never get lost. Here are some of the most important links on the home page.

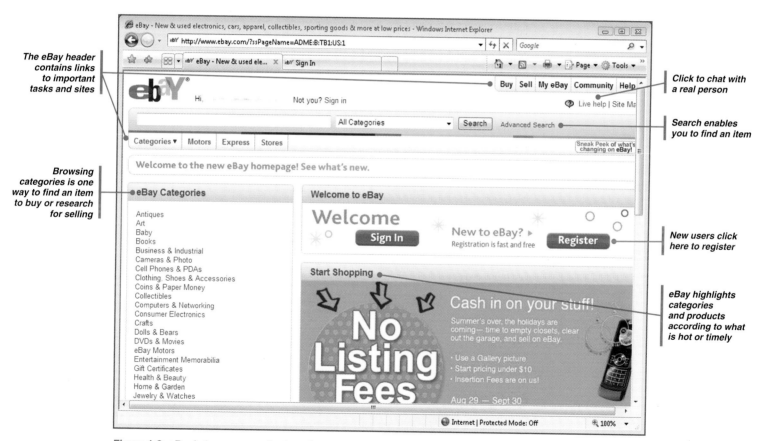

The eBay header contains links to important tasks and sites

Click to chat with a real person

Search enables you to find an item

Browsing categories is one way to find an item to buy or research for selling

New users click here to register

eBay highlights categories and products according to what is hot or timely

Figure 1-2: *eBay's home page displays links to its many destinations.*

Browse eBay's Home Page

Your first stop is the home page, your base of operations when you start using eBay. From here, you can access any other location in eBay, get registered, and do anything else you need to do to get started. To get to the home page:

1. Open your browser.

2. Type www.ebay.com in the address bar, and press **ENTER**. The window displayed in Figure 1-2 opens.

3. When you register and log on, the home page displays additional information, as seen in Figure 1-3. You can track your activity from the home page. To register and then log on, see "Register as an eBay Member" in this chapter.

Identify the Primary Header Links Bar

On the upper right of the eBay header, you will see the primary header links bar. By clicking one of the links you can: | Buy | Sell | My eBay | Community | Help |

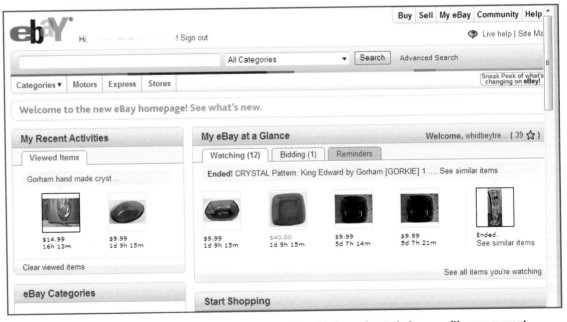

Figure 1-3: **When you log on, the home page contains additional information to help you with your current activity and recent watching, selling, and other alerts.**

- Point to **Buy** to open a menu displaying options to browse categories, get help with bidding and buying for the first time, look at buyer tools (such as instant messaging, desktop shortcuts to eBay, the eBay Toolbar, and more), and see reviews for items being sold and guides for learning about a variety of topics. (See Chapter 4 for more information.)

- Point to **Sell** to select from a menu to actually sell an item, get started with how to sell, decide what to sell, review seller tools and eBay Stores, and get information about shipping from the Shipping Center. (See Chapter 8 for more information on shipping items.)

- Point to **My eBay** to open a menu so that you can select which page in My eBay you want to see: the Summary page, which items you are watching, which items you are bidding on, your selling activity, and your Favorites. See Chapters 1 and 2 for information on working with My eBay.

- Point to **Community** to connect to various community components: news about eBay and the site; the Answer Center, where you can learn from other eBayers; workshops and discussion forums, where eBay teachers are available; eBay blogs and groups; and eBay Giving Works, where you can support your favorite charity. (See the "Connecting with the eBay Community" QuickFacts later in this chapter.)

- Point to **Help** for a menu of aids provided by eBay. (See "Find Help Topics" later in this chapter.)

Also on the eBay header you will see another links bar with frequent destinations:

- Click **Categories** to begin searching for items you want to sell or buy. (see "Explore Categories" later in this chapter.)

- Click **Motors** to display links to buying and selling everything from boats, motorcycles, autos, all-terrain vehicles (ATVs), and airplanes, to parts and accessories for them. Figure 1-4 shows the initial window.

- Click **eBay Express** to quickly shop for new items at a fixed price. You will be able to see competitive prices for extraordinary shopping possibilities.

- Click **eBay Stores** to find a store or create your own store in eBay. eBay Stores offer the same opportunities that are available on the regular eBay (or ebay.com) that is, auctions, Buy It Now fixed-price sales, and combo auctions with Buy It Now features (see Table 1-1). This is where you can find deals, if you are a buyer, or can create a storefront to list less expensive items, if you are a seller. Since fees are lower for

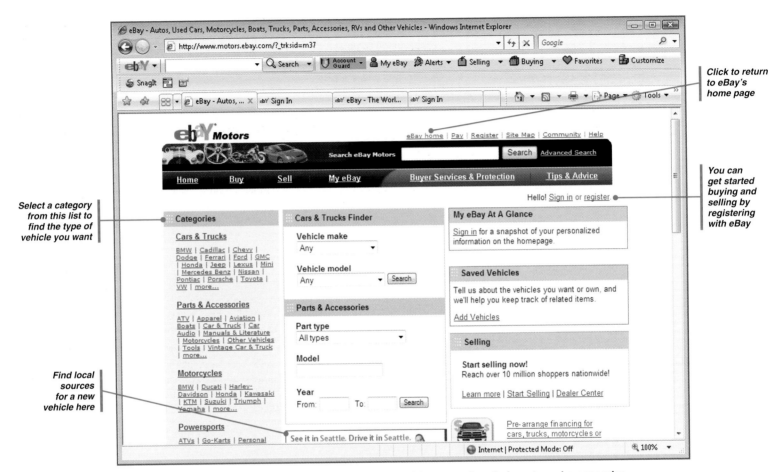

Click to return to eBay's home page

Select a category from this list to find the type of vehicle you want

Find local sources for a new vehicle here

You can get started buying and selling by registering with eBay

Figure 1-4: On the Motors page, you can buy all types of vehicles, as well as their parts and accessories.

stores, the items are usually listed at lower prices than those on regular eBay. To open a store, you have to have sold and had feedback on at least 20 items, or be ID Verified (a way to guarantee to the buyer that you are who you say you are), or have a PayPal account in good standing. Statistics seem to bear out that the eBay Stores sites get more traffic and higher-volume sales than the regular eBay items, especially with the links from items offered by the store in the regular sites and cross-promotion services that eBay offers. Chapter 10 talks more about eBay Stores.

TRANSACTION	DESCRIPTION	SELLER'S REQUIREMENTS
Standard auction	Follows a common auction format where a seller offers an item for sale and buyers bid on it. The highest bidder wins the right to purchase the item. There are variations on this format. For instance, a seller may require a hidden, minimum amount to be bid, known as a *reserve price*.	You must obtain a seller's account.
Dutch auctions (also known as a multiple-item auction)	Allows you to sell multiple items that are the same. You can sell them in an online auction format, where each buyer has to bid higher than the others, but all get it at the same lowest-bid price, or in a fixed-price format, where all items are sold for the same price.	You must be ID Verified or have a feedback rating of at least 30 and be registered for at least two weeks. If you have a PayPal account, you only need a feedback rating of 15.
Private auction	Allows the buyer to bid without revealing his or her user ID. Only the seller knows who the bidder is. This is usually done when the buyer might be embarrassed by the bid, such as with adult items or pharmaceutical products. (To access mature items, buyers need to provide verification data to ensure that they are at least 18 years old.)	You must obtain a seller's account. (If the option is not showing on the Sell Your Item form, click **Show/HIde Options**, click Format, and then click **Private Listing**.)
Buy It Now (Auction)	A combination auction that offers the item for a fixed price. If a buyer agrees to pay that price, the sale is made. If a buyer offers a lower price, however, the Buy It Now price is replaced with a normal auction format.	You must be ID Verified or have a feedback rating of at least 10 to offer a Buy It Now item. Feedback requirement is only 5 if you have a PayPal account. (To sell multiple Buy It Now items, see the requirements for a Dutch auction.)
Buy It Now (Fixed Price)	Offers the item for a given price, and there is no auction.	You must have a feedback rating of at least 10 for a single item or be ID verified (or, for more than one item, have a feedback rating of 30 (15 with a PayPal account) or be ID Verified and be a registered user for at least 14 days. (To sell multiple Buy It Now items, see the requirements for a Dutch auction.)

Table 1-1: Types of Transactions

Explore Categories

1. Each item is identified as belonging to a *category*. A category is simply a system of names, within which an item may be found. For example, a diamond ring will probably be found in the broad category Jewelry & Watches. In that category, however, are many other possibilities, such as Antique, Fashion, Gold or Silver, etc. How well you can nail down the category for your item is really important—either to buy or sell it. There are thousands of categories that are constantly being revised, so it is both very easy and very hard to find the category you want to use; many categories are

NOTE

Many items have a specialized Search feature found on the left sidebar to help you locate the exact match. For instance, to narrow down the search for a ring, you can search by Band, Wedding & Anniversary, Cubic Zirconia, Diamond Bridal Ring Sets, Gemstone Rings, and more. Chapter 2 talks more about the overall Search feature.

Narrow Your Results

Rings
Bands, Wedding & Anniversary (18834)
Cubic Zirconia & Moissanite (34626)
Diamond Bridal Ring Sets (1881)
Diamond Engagement/ Annivers. (12999)
Diamond Right-Hand Rings (6377)
Gemstone Rings (46281)
Metal Fashion Rings (8223)
Other (8335)

eBay Categories

Antiques
Art
Baby
Books
Business & Industrial
Cameras & Photo
Cell Phones & PDAs
Clothing, Shoes & Accessories
Coins & Paper Money
Collectibles
Computers & Networking
Consumer Electronics
Crafts
Dolls & Bears
DVDs & Movies
eBay Motors
Entertainment Memorabilia
Gift Certificates
Health & Beauty
Home & Garden
Jewelry & Watches
Music
Musical Instruments
Pottery & Glass
Real Estate
Specialty Services
Sporting Goods
Sports Mem, Cards & Fan Shop

*Figure 1-5: **Categories start you on your way to finding the item you want.***

available, but the exact one may be harder to identify. On the home page, using either the header link bar or the eBay Categories sidebar, find the overall category that contains your item. Click the link. (Using the diamond ring example, you would most likely click **Jewelry & Watches**). Figure 1-5 shows the categories on the home page sidebar.

2. On the next level, find the category that most closely matches what you want. Click that link. In our example, rings can be found in several subcategories, such as Body Jewelry; Ethnic, Tribal Jewelry; and Pins, Brooches. (In our example, clicking Rings | Diamond Engagement/Anniversary yields a screen displaying the beginning of close to 13,000 items.)

3. Continue to explore the categories until you find what you want. You may have to back up and start again or refine your browsing.

Explore Meet Our Family

If you scroll down the home page, you'll see a Meet Our Family sidebar. Here you will see other eBay companies. Particularly useful ones include the following:

- Click **Half.com** to find new and used books, textbooks, music, DVDs, and games at reduced prices. These items are offered at fixed prices rather than auction prices, so it is more like shopping in a regular store. This is particularly nice for folks who don't want to bother with auctions.

- Click **Kijiji** to view or post a free classified ad. The ads are posted for over 200 cities in 50 states.

- Click **PayPal** to register on PayPal or check your account. When you are actively buying or selling items on eBay, you'll find that PayPal is essential to your transactions.

- Click **ProStores**, if you are a seller, to establish your own branded storefront with a separate Web site, domain name, and store identity.

- Click **Rent.com** to list or search for apartments and homes to rent. You can also find roommates, get quotes from moving companies, and get help managing apartment listings. To search, specify the city and state, when you want to move, the rental price range, and the type of housing for which you're looking. If you lease a property here, Rent.com will pay you $100.

- Click **Shopping.com** for comparison shopping. If you are a serious shopper, this link will let you search for and compare products.

- Click **Skype** (pronounced skiipe) to call others using a headphone and your computer. This makes long distance calls inexpensive and efficient. You also can track your transactions without a browser. When you use Skype, eBay posts an icon identifying you as available using Skype access

- Click **StubHub** to buy or sell tickets to sporting events, Broadway and other theater shows, concerts, and other events.

- Click **StumbleUpon** to surf the Internet, finding new Web sites, discovering what others are talking about, or just connecting with others who share your passions.

ACCESS GLOBAL eBAY SITES

To access eBay sites in other countries:

1. Scroll down the home page to the Meet Our Family sidebar.

2. Under Global Sites, click the **Choose Country** down arrow.

3. Click the name of the country that you want to see. The eBay Web site for that country, using its own language if not English, will be displayed.

Find What's Hot or Timely

You'll find that the home page hones in on what consumers are buying right now. Often, categories of products will be featured.

1. On the home page under Start Shopping, click a category that appeals to you. You see a page with all the items in that category displayed.

2. Use the Product Finder on the left sidebar to narrow your search.

Look Through Featured Items

As a buyer, you can quickly see items, usually more highly priced items, that are being promoted by sellers. Sellers pay an added fee to have their items featured on eBay's pages. As a seller, using the Featured Items listings increases your visibility within eBay. This feature separates items from the mass of eBay's offerings and shows the item in a special Featured Items list on high-traffic pages.

QUICKFACTS

USING A USER ID AND PASSWORD

To register with eBay, you must have both a User ID and a password.

CREATE A USER ID

The User ID is the name by which others on eBay do business with you and come to recognize you over time. To be more effective as a seller, your User ID can be one that identifies your business or products. As a buyer, you don't have the same considerations to worry about. In any case, it is your eBay name, so it ought to be one you like. You can have more than one User ID, but you need a separate e-mail address for each one.

Your User ID must follow these rules:

- Must be more than one character long
- Must contain letters or numbers (but not "eBay" or the letter "e" followed by numbers)
- Cannot contain @, &, ', < or >, or more than one _ (underscore)
- Cannot contain spaces or tabs (but can contain a hyphen as long as it's not at the beginning)
- Cannot be an e-mail address or Web site, or contain any Uniform Resource Locators (URLs)
- Must be unique in the eBay system

CREATE A PASSWORD

You will be asked to enter a password that verifies you are the valid user of your User ID. Since this password is an important one, you will want to follow these guidelines:

- Use a unique password for eBay. That is, do not use the same password that you use for other Web sites or for your e-mail.
- Do not share the password with others.

There are restrictions for some items, such as adult items. Chapter 6 contains additional information on how to use this feature. To find featured items to buy or research:

1. On the home page, scroll down until From Our Sellers is displayed. You'll see a few items that are currently being displayed on the home page. The selection of items displayed here changes regularly.

From our Sellers	
• CHARLOTTE BOBCATS Website Doma...	• SPRINT MOGUL PPC6800SP BUNDLED...
• Land Acres Waterfront Hunting ...	• SCREENPRINTING BUSINESS OPPORT...
• Framed Photo of Trevi Fountain...	• WHOLESALE COMPUTER COMPANY 4 S...

See all featured items

2. Click **See All Featured** Items to display all featured items, not just the ones that have been rotated to the home page.

Register as an eBay Member

Before you register, you need:

- A valid e-mail address
- A User ID, which you create
- A password, which you enter
- To be at least 18 years of age

Register for eBay

To register to buy or sell items (there is an additional step to establish a seller's account in order to sell—see Chapter 6):

1. From the home page, click **Register**. You will see the Register: Enter Information window, as shown Figure 1-6.

2. Enter your name and address information, phone number, and e-mail address (enter it twice to confirm it) into the text boxes, pressing **TAB** to advance to the next box.

New to eBay? ▶
Registration is fast and free   **Register**

Secret question
Pick a suggested question... ▾
Pick a suggested question...
What street did you grow up on?
What is your mother's maiden name?
What is the name of your first school?
What is your pet's name?
What is your father's middle name?
What is your school's mascot?

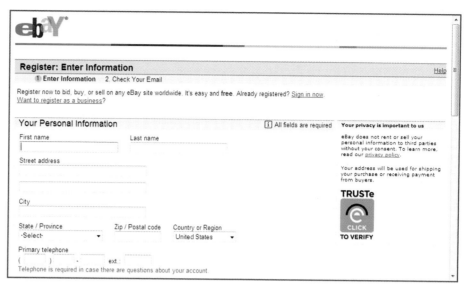

Figure 1-6: *When you register for eBay, your first task is to enter your personal name and address information.*

3. Enter the following additional information, as shown in Figure 1-7:

   ● Enter your new User ID (see the "Using a User ID and Password" QuickSteps). Click **Check Availability Of User ID** to see if the User ID you want is available. When you have found a valid User ID, press **TAB**.

   ● Enter your password in the **Create Password** box, press **TAB**, and enter the password again. Press **TAB**.

   ● Click the **Secret Question** down arrow to see the list of questions eBay may ask to verify your identity in case you forget your password or need to change it. Select the question you want to be your identifying one. Press **TAB**.

   ● Under Secret Answer, type your answer to the question you chose. Press **TAB**.

   ● Click the **Date Of Birth** down arrow, and choose the month and day of your birthday. Type the year. Press **TAB**.

   ● After reading the user agreement (seen in Figure 1-8) and privacy policy by clicking the links, click the **I Agree To The Following** check box. See "Read the User Agreement/eBay Policies" later in the chapter for additional information.

   ● Click **Continue**.

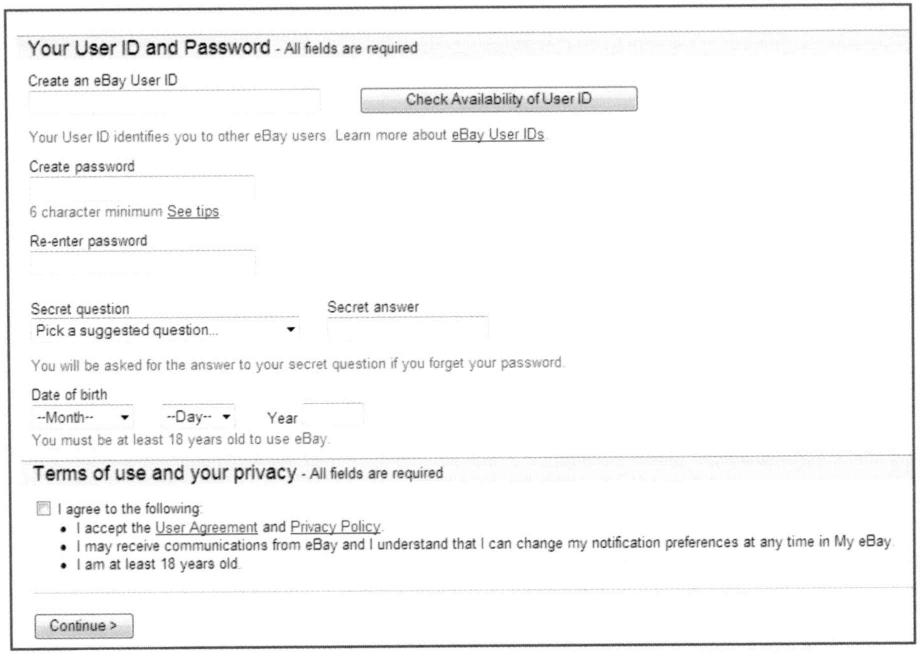
Your User ID and Password - All fields are required
Create an eBay User ID
Check Availability of User ID
Your User ID identifies you to other eBay users. Learn more about eBay User IDs.
Create password
6 character minimum See tips.
Re-enter password
Secret question
Pick a suggested question...
Secret answer
You will be asked for the answer to your secret question if you forget your password.
Date of birth
--Month--
--Day--
Year
You must be at least 18 years old to use eBay.
Terms of use and your privacy - All fields are required
I agree to the following:
I accept the User Agreement and Privacy Policy.
I may receive communications from eBay and I understand that I can change my notification preferences at any time in My eBay.
I am at least 18 years old.
Continue >

Figure 1-7: ***Your User ID and password are entered during the registration process, along with a question to verify your identity.***

NOTE

If you have not entered a required field, if your entry does not match the rules, or if your User ID has been used or reserved, you will receive an error message telling you that you must correct the information before continuing. Reenter the incorrect information and continue.

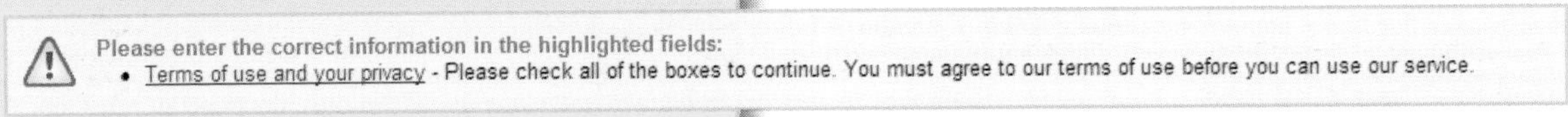
Please enter the correct information in the highlighted fields:
Terms of use and your privacy - Please check all of the boxes to continue. You must agree to our terms of use before you can use our service.

4. On the Register: Confirm Identity page, enter this information (if you already have successfully registered or been ID Verified under another User ID, you may not need to supply confirmation identification. In this case, you will be taken directly to the Registration: Check E-mail page):

   - Enter your credit card number, including the three-digit number on the back of the card. Then enter the expiration date. Click **Continue**. The screen shown in Figure 1-9 will be displayed.

5. Click **Continue To *name* E-mail**. You will receive an e-mail from eBay. To be able to buy and sell on e-Bay, you will need to click the **Activate Your eBay Membership** link. (To sell, you'll need to complete the additional step of opening a seller's account. Chapter 6 describes how to obtain a seller's account.)

Your registration is confirmed. You are now armed and ready to sally forth deeper into eBay.

QUICKSTEPS

RESTORING YOUR PASSWORD

If you forget your password, or if you just want to change it, you can get a new password by changing it to a new one.

CHANGE YOUR PASSWORD

1. From the home page, click **My eBay** on the eBay header. (You may have to enter your password.) The My eBay window opens.

2. In the My eBay Views sidebar, under My Account, click the **Personal Information** link.

3. Click **Edit** next to Password. (You may need to re-enter your password.) The Change Your Password window opens, as seen in Figure 1-10.

4. Type your password in the Old Password text box. Press **TAB**.

5. Type your new password in the New Password text box. Press **TAB**.

6. Retype the new password.

7. Click **Submit Changes**. Your new password is activated.

FORGET YOUR PASSWORD?

When you are prompted to enter your password and you have forgotten it:

1. Under the Password text box, click the **Forgot Your Password?** link. You are taken to the Forgot Your Password? page.

2. Enter your eBay User ID in the text box, and click **Continue**.

3. On the Forgot Your Password: Verify Identity page, type the answer in the text box to the question that you specified when you first registered, such as your pet's name or the name of the street where you grew up.

Continued . . .

Your User Agreement

The following describes the terms on which eBay offers you access to our services.

Introduction

Welcome to eBay. By using the services on the eBay websites (eBay.com and other related websites where this agreement appears) (the "Sites"), you are agreeing to the following terms, including those available by hyperlink, (the "Agreement" or "User Agreement") with eBay Inc. and the general principles for the websites of our subsidiaries and international affiliates. If you reside outside of the United States, you are contracting with one of our international eBay companies: In countries within the European Union, your contract is with eBay Europe S.à r.l.; in all other countries, your contract is with eBay International AG. If you have any questions, please refer to the Help section on the Sites.

Before you may become a member of eBay, you must read and accept all of the terms and conditions in, and linked to, this User Agreement and the Privacy Policy. We strongly recommend that, as you read this User Agreement, you also access and read the linked information. By accepting this User Agreement, you also agree that your use of some eBay-branded websites or websites we operate may be governed by separate user agreements and privacy policies. The agreement that applies on any of our domains and subdomains is always the agreement that appears in the footer of each website.

This Agreement is effective on July 9, 2007, for current users, and upon acceptance for new users. The previous amendment to this Agreement was effective for all users on February 1, 2006.

Using eBay

While using the Sites, you will not:

- post content or items in an inappropriate category or areas on the Sites;
- violate any laws, third party rights, or our policies such as the <u>Prohibited and Restricted Items</u> policies;
- use the Sites if you are not able to form legally binding contracts, are under the age of 18, or are temporarily or indefinitely suspended from our Sites;
- fail to deliver payment for items purchased by you, unless the seller has materially changed the item's description after you bid, a clear typographical error is made, or you cannot authenticate the seller's identity;

*Figure 1-8: **The user agreement must be agreed to before you can register with eBay.***

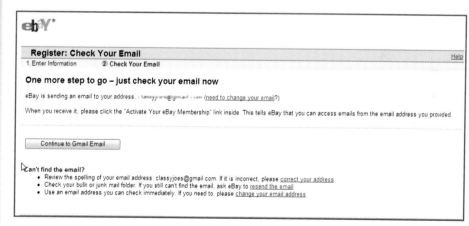

*Figure 1-9: **The final page of the registration, Register: Check E-mail, is where you activate your eBay account using an e-mail sent to you by eBay.***

QUICKSTEPS

RESTORING YOUR PASSWORD

(Continued)

4. Enter your ZIP code and telephone number (If you have moved, these may be different from your current ZIP and telephone number, unless you have updated that information), and your date of birth, and click **Continue**.

5. The Confirmation Step window opens, and you are notified that an e-mail has been sent.

Forgot Your Password: Confirmation Step

You're almost done

An email has been sent to the email address you have on file in My eBay

To complete the process of changing your password:

1. Check your email account.
2. Click the link or button in the email.

If you no longer have access to this email account, please go Register again with eBay.

---

6. Check your e-mail, and click the link in it that sends you to the Change Password window in eBay.

7. Enter your User ID, and click **Continue**. You are taken to the procedure for changing your password, as described previously.

8. You may be asked if you want to display nonsecure items on the page. Click **Yes** or **No**. In the New Password text box, type your new password. Press **TAB**.

9. Reenter the password, and click **Submit Changes**. You will see an acknowledgement that your new password is activated.

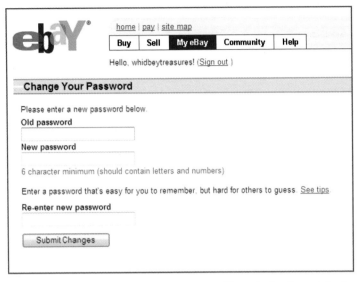

Figure 1-10: *You can change your password by entering the original one and the new one two times to verify that you have entered it correctly.*

Review the Rules and Policies

Before you register, you may want to take some time and review the user agreement and privacy policy. They are fairly long, and you may be tempted to skip them altogether. However, I would encourage you to read them, or at least scan them, since they are binding legal contracts that you will be agreeing to. In addition, there are several other policies that you might be interested in, such as Rules for Buying and Rules for Selling.

Read the User Agreement/eBay Policies

The user agreement outlines the terms and conditions under which you will interact with eBay. It describes the rules you will follow and what eBay's responsibilities are to you. It describes how misunderstandings and complaints are handled, among other issues.

QUICKSTEPS

SIGNING IN "PERMANENTLY"

You can be signed in automatically when you go to eBay by performing certain steps when you are asked to sign in:

1. Enter your eBay User ID.

2. Enter your password.

3. Click **Keep Me Signed In On This Computer For One Day, Unless I Sign Out**.

    Sign In Securely >

    ☑ Keep me signed in on this computer for one day, unless I sign out.

4. Click **Sign In Securely**.

NOTE

From the Rules and Policies page, you can also read the many other policies, such as Rules for Buyers and Rules for Sellers, How eBay Protects Intellectual Property (VeRO), Rules for Everyone, and more.

1. From the home page, scroll down to the second links bar on the eBay footer, and click **Policies**. The Rules and Policies page, as displayed in Figure 1-11, opens.

    Security Center | Policies
    c. All Rights Reserved Desig

2. Click **Your eBay User Agreement**.

3. Click **Home** on the links bar beneath the eBay header to return to the home page.

Review Restricted Items

Certain items cannot be sold on eBay. These include alcohol, most animals, counterfeit or unauthorized replicas, tobacco, fireworks—the list goes on, as is partially seen in Figure 1-12.

1. From the home page, scroll down to the second links bar in the eBay footer, and click **Policies**.

2. Click **Rules For Sellers**.

3. Click **Prohibited And Restricted Items And Services**.

4. Select the category containing the item in which you are interested.

5. Click **Home** in the links bar beneath the eBay header to return to the home page.

Rules and Policies

Top Questions about Rules and Policies

1. How can I report an item that appears to be violating eBay rules and policies?

2. Why was my account suspended?

3. What are the rules and policies for listing items for sale on eBay?

4. I sold an item and have not yet received payment. What can I do?

5. What is VeRO and why was my item ended because of it?

eBay Rules and Policies - Overview

Trust and Safety Tutorials

Rules for Everyone
Rules for Everyone - Overview | Misuse of eBay Email
Forwarding System
Transaction Interference | more...

Rules for Buyers
Rules for Buyers - Overview | Unwelcome and Malicious
Buying Policy
Unpaid Item Policy | more...

Your eBay User Agreement

How eBay Protects Intellectual Property (VeRO)

Rules about Feedback
Feedback Policies - Overview | Feedback Manipulation
Feedback Abuse, Withdrawal and Removal | more...

Rules for Sellers
Rules for Sellers - Overview | Shill Bidding
About Me Page Guidelines | more...

| Security Center | Policies | Site Map | Help

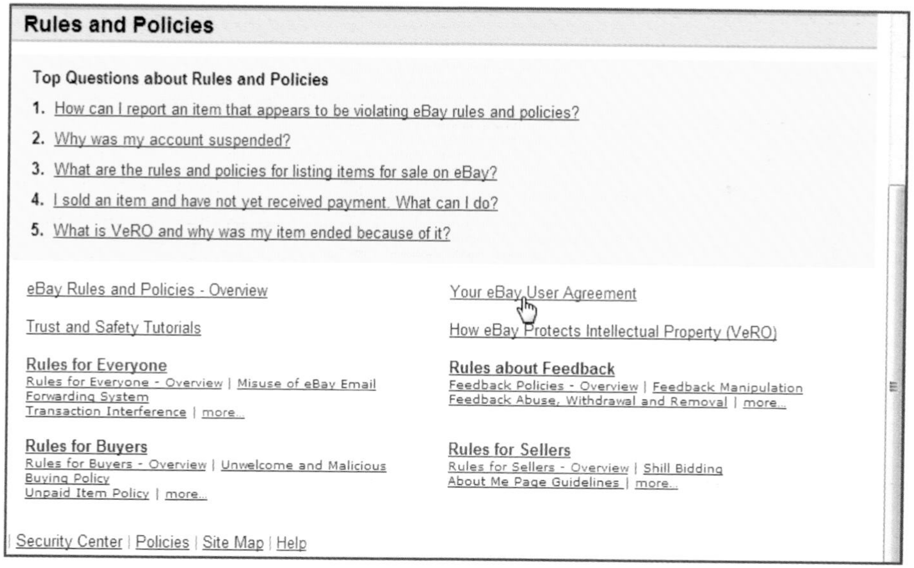

Figure 1-11: Policies are issued to provide consistency and security to users.

NOTE

At the time this book was going to the printer (fall 2007), a major makeover was planned for the My eBay page and its several views.

Prohibited and Restricted Items and Services	
Prohibited and Restricted Items - Overview	Alcohol
Animals and Wildlife	Artifacts
Catalytic Converters	Cell Phone (Wireless) Service Contracts
Charity or Fundraising Listings	Contracts
Counterfeit Currency and Stamps	Credit Cards
Describing Drugs or Drug-Like Substances	Drugs & Drug Paraphernalia
Electronic Surveillance	Electronics Equipment
Embargoed Goods and Prohibited Countries	Encouraging Illegal Activity
Event Tickets	Firearms, Weapons and Knives
Food	Gift Cards
Government and Transit Documents	Government and Transit Uniforms
Government IDs and Licenses	Hazardous, Restricted, and Perishable Items
Human Remains	Importation of Goods into the United States
International Trading	Lockpicking
Lottery Tickets	Mailing Lists and Personal Information

Figure 1-12: *The Prohibited and Restricted Items list contains those items that cannot be sold on eBay.*

Customize My eBay

The one part of eBay that is totally your domain, and where you interact with eBay both in buying and selling, is My eBay. You can customize how eBay interacts with you and the information it displays. For instance, you can change the views offered, or you can change information, such as your User ID, e-mail address, address information, shipping information, password, and About Me page.

Go to My eBay

From the home page, point to **My eBay** on the eBay header. Click the page you want to see from the drop-down menu, such as **Summary**. You may be asked to sign in, and then the My eBay page will be displayed, as shown in Figure 1-13.

This is a list of the views available in My eBay

This summarizes a display of your selected views

This fairly new user has a feedback rating of 39

Click here to customize the My Summary view

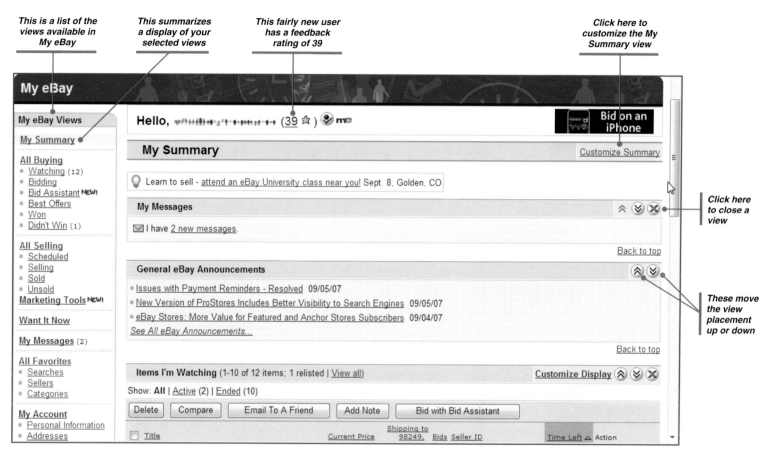

Click here to close a view

These move the view placement up or down

Figure 1-13: My eBay is where you find information and customize views within eBay.

Customize the My Summary View

To select the views to display in My Summary:

1. Click **Customize Summary** on the My Summary title bar. The Customize My Summary dialog box appears, as shown in Figure 1-14.

2. In the Available Views box, click the view you want to see in My Summary. Click the right-pointing arrow to move the selection to the Views To Display box.

UICKSTEPS

WORKING WITH MY eBAY VIEWS

When you are looking at a view, you can use it or change it in several ways.

SORT A VIEW

- To change the way items listed in a view are sequenced, click a column heading.
- To reverse the sort, click the column again.

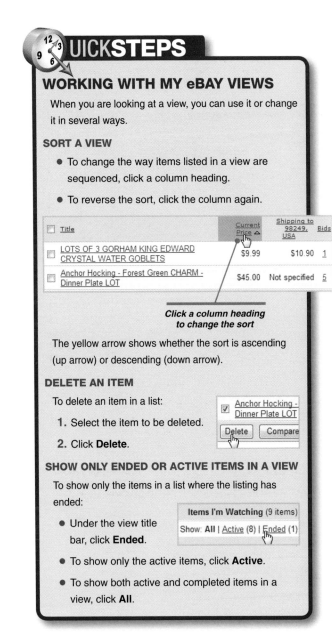

Click a column heading to change the sort

The yellow arrow shows whether the sort is ascending (up arrow) or descending (down arrow).

DELETE AN ITEM

To delete an item in a list:

1. Select the item to be deleted.

2. Click **Delete**.

SHOW ONLY ENDED OR ACTIVE ITEMS IN A VIEW

To show only the items in a list where the listing has ended:

- Under the view title bar, click **Ended**.
- To show only the active items, click **Active**.
- To show both active and completed items in a view, click **All**.

Select an available view to include in My Summary

Select a displayed view to remove it from My Summary

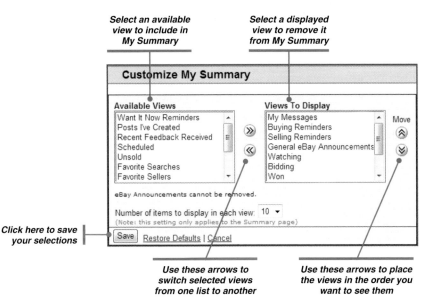

Click here to save your selections

Use these arrows to switch selected views from one list to another

Use these arrows to place the views in the order you want to see them

Figure 1-14: *You can change the views displayed in My Summary by switching between Available Views and Views To Display.*

3. If there are views in the Views To Display box that you don't want in My Summary, select them and then click the left-pointing arrow.

4. Arrange the views by clicking the up and down arrows.

5. Click **Save** to save your changes.

Customize a My eBay View

You can change the columns in a My eBay view to place them in the order you want to see them and also select which columns to include in the view.

1. Click **Customize Display** in the view title bar. The Customize *viewname* dialog box shown in Figure 1-15 will appear.

2. Select from among these options to customize the view:

- To add a column from the Available Columns list, select a column name, and click the right-pointing arrow to move it to the Columns To Display list.
- To remove a column from the view, select a column from the Columns To Display list, and click the left-pointing arrow.

UICKSTEPS

ADDING NOTES TO LISTINGS ON A VIEW

In several views, you can add comments to selected items that are only visible to you.

ADD A NOTE

1. On a view displaying listing details, scroll to the listing, and select the check box to the left of the item title.

2. Click **Add Note** at bottom of the view table.

3. In the Add Note To Item area, type the note and click **Save**. Your text displays below the item as a *My Note*.

HIDE MY NOTES AND eBAY NOTES

1. On a view displaying listing details, scroll to the listing whose notes you want to hide (not all views have associated notes).

2. Click **Customize Display** in the view's title bar.

3. In the Display area, select or clear the **My Notes** and **eBay Notes** check boxes.

4. Click **Save**.

Click a column title to select it to be added to the view display

Click a column title to select it to be removed from the view

Click these arrows to place the columns in the order you want to view them

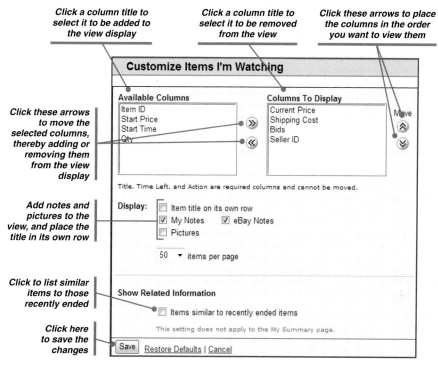

Figure 1-15: *Your My eBay views can be customized to contain the columns you want to see in the desired order.*

- To re-order the columns on the view, click the up and down arrows under Move.
- To show the item title above the details, select **Item Title On Its Own Row**.
- To display notes with the items, select **My Notes**.
- To display eBay notes, select **eBay Notes**.
- To display pictures on the seller's form, select **Pictures**.
- Click the **Items Per Page** down arrow, and select a number.

3. Click **Save** to save your view changes.

Set Your Personal Information and Preferences

You can change personal information, such as your account User ID, password, secret question, and About Me page. Personal information also includes your

NOTE

Chapter 3 contains additional information on using My eBay to help manage your bidding activities. Chapter 7 helps you organize My eBay from a seller's perspective.

e-mail and contact information and financial information, such as checking account or credit card numbers. You can also set your preferences, such as when and where you are notified of buying, selling, or other transactions and newsletters you want to receive. You can also set selling preferences and member-to-member communication preferences, such as whether you use Skype.

SET YOUR PERSONAL INFORMATION

My Account
- Personal Information
- Addresses
- Preferences
- Feedback
- PayPal Account
- Half.com Account
- Seller Account
- Subscriptions

1. From the My eBay Views sidebar, scroll down to My Account, and click the **Personal Information** link.

2. From this page, you will be able to review and change the following:

   - **Your account information:** account type (individual or business), User ID, password, secret question, and About Me page

   - **Your e-mail and contact information:** e-mail address, name and address, mobile phone number, or instant messenger provider

   - **Your financial information:** checking account and credit card information

SET MY eBAY PAGE PREFERENCES

You can vary several aspects of how eBay interacts with you, for example, the opening My eBay page, how time is displayed, whether you want to retrieve removed items, or how Help content is displayed in My eBay.

My Account
- Personal Information
- Addresses
- Preferences
- Feedback

1. From the My eBay Views sidebar under My Account, click **Preferences**.

2. Scroll to General Preferences, and click the **Show** link for My eBay.

3. Change the options as follows:

   - To change the opening page displayed, select the view you want to see when My eBay is displayed.

   - Select whether you want to see time displayed as Time Left or End Time/Date.

   - To see Help content, select **Yes** next to Display Help Content In My eBay.

   - Click **Yes** to show personalized picks (where eBay displays items based on your recent picks), your favorite searches on the home page search area, and suggested favorite sellers based on your buying history.

4. Click **Apply** to accept your changes.

5. To hide your changes, click **Hide** on the My eBay title bar.

Use ID Verify

eBay offers a service to verify that its U.S. (and U.S. territories) buyers and sellers are who they say they are. This gives others confidence that they are dealing with a real person, not a cyberspace phantom. To use ID Verify, you pay $5 to a third-party company (Equifax, only available in the U.S.) whose business it is to verify identities. You supply some personal information (credit card account information and driver's license number, for instance) and, once verified, you receive an ID Verify icon that is placed in your feedback profile.

1. Click **Sell** on the eBay header. Scroll down to the bottom of the page, and click **Selling Resources** in the first links bar.

2. Under Third Party Services, click **ID Verify**. The ID Verify page is displayed.

> **Third Party Services**
> eBay Solutions Directory
> SquareTrade Dispute Resolution
> Consulting/Professional Services
> Product Recalls
> Warranty Services
> ID Verify
> Escrow Services

3. Click **Sign Up Now** to start the process.

4. On the ID Verify: Accept Terms page, click **I Agree** after you read and agree to three conditions:

   - To pay $5 if you are granted an ID Verify designation (you don't pay if you don't pass)
   - Not to provide false information
   - Not to change your contact information for 30 days

5. Sign in with your User ID and password. Click **Secure Sign In**.

6. On the Verify Account Information page, verify that your contact information is correct. You also need to supply your date of birth and driver's license number. Click **Continue** when finished.

7. Verify your information by scanning the Verify Account Information page. If the information is correct, click **Continue**. If it is incorrect, click **Back** and correct it.

8. You are asked some questions that only you know the answers to, including filling in credit card numbers, a past street address, and perhaps a mortgage amount. Click **Continue** when finished.

9. Review and verify your information.

10. After signing in one more time, you are informed that your ID Verify procedure is successful, as shown in Figure 1-16.

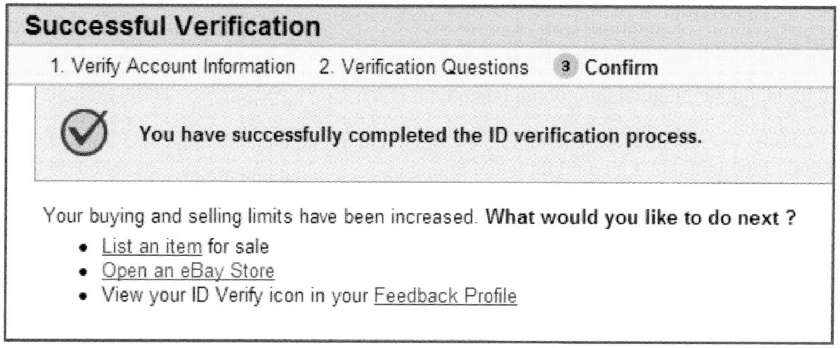

Successful Verification

1. Verify Account Information   2. Verification Questions   ③ Confirm

✓ You have successfully completed the ID verification process.

Your buying and selling limits have been increased. **What would you like to do next ?**
- List an item for sale
- Open an eBay Store
- View your ID Verify icon in your Feedback Profile

*Figure 1-16: **The ID Verify Successful page immediately lets you know that you have passed the ID Verify procedure.***

CONNECTING WITH THE eBAY COMMUNITY

The eBay Community connects you to five main avenues of communication with other eBay users, as shown in Figure 1-17:

- **Feedback** connects you to the Feedback Forum, where you can learn all there is to know about feedback and find feedback for people with whom you're thinking about doing business.

- **Connect** provides for creating your own eBay My World page and a number of links for connecting to discussion boards, groups (such as collectors or regional eBay groups), eBay blogs, chat rooms, and the Answer Center.

- **News** provides general announcements, calendar events, and a newsletter, *The Chatter*.

- **Education** lists where you can find workshops, mentors, and more.

- **More Community Programs** allows you to connect with other community and group agendas, such as eBay Giving Works (the charity outlet), eBay Government Relations for getting involved in legislative activity, and other vents; and People for finding eBay Groups, reading about eBay Community Values, and learning about other members who have earned recognition.

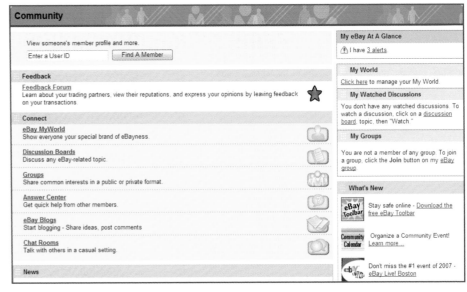

Figure 1-17: *The eBay Community offers several ways of connecting with other eBay users.*

11. Click **Feedback Profile** to see that the icon has been placed in your Member Profile.

12. Click **Home** in the links bar beneath the eBay header to return to the home page.

Learn About eBay Help and the eBay Community

You can find help about eBay by clicking the Help link. You can search for the information you need alphabetically or by topic. The eBay Community is considerable, and you can find discussions, blogs, and groups by type of item, by type of buyer or seller, or by almost any other category.

Find Help Topics

eBay Help comes in several varieties. You can search for Help topics alphabetically, type a question, or search by broad category, such as How Do I Sell An Item?

FIND ANSWERS BY TYPING THE TOPIC

1. Open the Help page by clicking **Help** on the eBay header.

2. In the Search Help text box, type the topic for which you want to search.

Search the Help pages (Does not search for items or products)

Example: 'payment methods'   Search Help Pages   Tips

3. Click **Search Help Pages**.

4. Select the topic in the resulting list.

BROWSE TOPICS

Beneath the Help title bar on the Help page, you will see several links to the most common questions asked. Click one of the **Top Questions About eBay** links to find your most common answers.

Another way you can browse topics is to find topics alphabetically or by subject.

- In the eBay Help sidebar, click **A-Z Index**, for the alphabetic Help topics.

  –Or–

- Click one of the other Help Topics or Related Links to read about one of the listed topics.

Contact eBay

You can contact eBay by sending an e-mail (after verifying that your question is not already answered somewhere else) or by talking to someone via a chat program.

SEND AN E-MAIL

To contact eBay for help from the Help menu, you first must walk through a series of questions and topics to make sure that the answer is not already in the system. After you have gone through that, you can send an e-mail asking your question.

1. Click **Help** on the eBay header.

2. Under the eBay Help sidebar, click **Contact Us**. A list of categories is displayed. Click the category that most closely matches your question. Click **Continue**.

3. Within the topic you have selected, click a subtopic.

Contact Us

| 1. Select a Category | 2. Select a Subtopic | ③ Review Help and Email Us |

These related Help pages may answer your question:

- Providing identification for registration
- About the registration process
- If you are already registered

Contact Customer Support

✉ Email us with your question or concern.

4. When you click it, you may be presented with another level of subtopic. Continue with the refining of your question. When you are at the closest level to your question, click **Continue**.

5. You will see some suggested Help topics. If the suggested topic does not help you, click **E-mail Us** under Contact Customer Support.

6. An e-mail form is displayed with an e-mail topic as selected by you. If the topic is different, click **Select A New Subject.**

7. When the topic is as accurate as you can get, type your question under Enter Your Question/Concern, and click **Send**. Allow 24 to 48 hours to receive an answer.

LIVE ONLINE HELP

To get immediate online help while you are playing or working with eBay, use the Live Help feature.

1. On the eBay home page, click the **Live Help** link on the eBay header. Determine if any of the suggested Help topics will answer your question. If not, continue with the following steps to contact an eBay agent.

2. In the Chat window, scroll down and type your e-mail address or eBay User ID.

3. Click the **Subject** down arrow, and select a subject that most closely mirrors your question. Click **Send**. A Chat window will open, and you will see a two-box window.

4. An eBay agent will sign on, identifying herself or himself by name and asking for your question. Simply type your question and click **Send**. The agent will then respond, and then the two of you can communicate back and forth until you have reached some resolution. A sample query is shown in Figure 1-18.

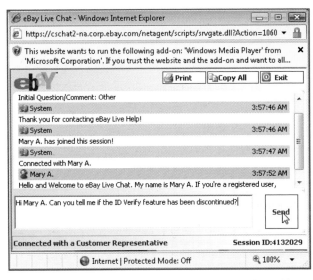

*Figure 1-18: **Use Live Help to carry on a conversation with a live person in a Chat window.***

Chapter 2

Researching on eBay (Buyers or Sellers)

Part of doing a good job in buying or selling an item on eBay is doing your homework and finding out everything you can about the item you want to buy or sell. This includes researching the actual item and comparing such things as price, components or parts available, possible conditions (such as with coins or antiques), identification markings, and so on. You can also research the seller you are buying from. Does the seller have a history on eBay? Is the feedback mostly favorable to the seller? Where is he or she located—will they require shipping internationally, for instance?

This chapter leads you through searching for and identifying the item you want to buy or sell, starting with how you can use eBay to help you find out about items.

QUICK**FACTS**

IDENTIFYING MY EBAY ICONS

My eBay uses icons to distinguish the type and status of listings. These icons are located on the right of the listing row. You can click the icon at the head of each column to sort the items by that icon:

- Auction format 🔨
- Fixed-price item ▥
- eBay Store inventory 🏠
- Ad, such as for real estate 🏢
- Checkout is complete 🛒
- Item has been paid for $
- Item has been shipped 📦
- You have left feedback for this item ☆
- You have received positive feedback for this item ⊕
- You have received negative feedback for this item ⊖
- You have received neutral feedback for this item ◯
- Item has been relisted ↺
- The item is ending ◷
- You are outbid ✕
- Best Offer Only format 💲
- Second Chance Offer 🐾
- Cross promote with another item 📇

TIP

The lowest-level item or category is referred to as the "listing category."

Use Tools Available in eBay

A handy way to see what is happening in your favorite categories is to establish Favorite lists in My eBay. You can also establish Favorite lists for your most common searches and your most regularly accessed sellers or stores. Further aids include the use of icons and the Search feature.

Set Up Your Favorite Categories, Searches, and Sellers

You can set up your favorite categories, searches, and sellers in My eBay. This allows you to quickly find what you are looking for with ease.

1. Point to **My eBay** in the eBay header. Click **Favorites**.

2. Type your password, and click **Sign In**. The My eBay All Favorites page is displayed, as shown in Figure 2-1. You will see all your favorite searches, sellers, and categories currently available.

Save Favorite Categories

When you save your favorite categories in My eBay, you can quickly see items currently for sale, items newly listed, auctions ending soon, and completed auctions in these categories. You can establish favorite categories for up to four categories.

1. On the My eBay Views sidebar in My eBay, find All Favorites and click **Categories**. If prompted, type your password and click **Sign In**.

All Favorites
- Searches
- Sellers
- Categories

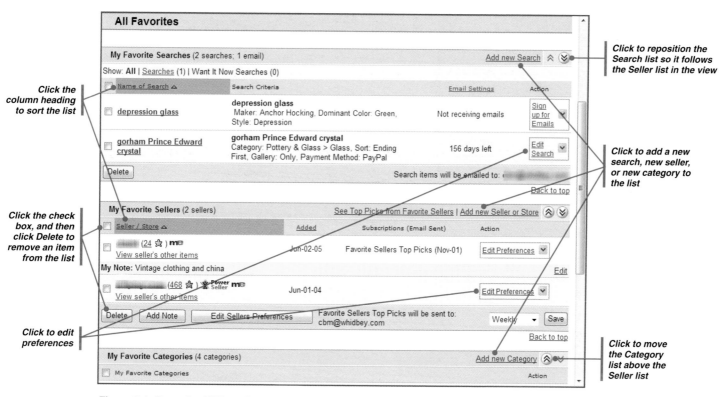

All Favorites

My Favorite Searches (2 searches; 1 email)　　　　　　　　　　　　　　Add new Search ⊗ ⊗

Click to reposition the Search list so it follows the Seller list in the view

Show: **All** | Searches (1) | Want It Now Searches (0)

Click the column heading to sort the list

☐ Name of Search △	Search Criteria	Email Settings	Action
☐ depression glass	**depression glass** Maker: Anchor Hocking, Dominant Color: Green, Style: Depression	Not receiving emails	Sign up for Emails ▾
☐ gorham Prince Edward crystal	**gorham Prince Edward crystal** Category: Pottery & Glass > Glass, Sort: Ending First, Gallery: Only, Payment Method: PayPal	156 days left	Edit Search ▾

Delete　　　　　　　　　　　　　　　　　　Search items will be emailed to:

Click to add a new search, new seller, or new category to the list

Back to top

My Favorite Sellers (2 sellers)　　　　See Top Picks from Favorite Sellers | Add new Seller or Store ⊗ ⊗

Click the check box, and then click Delete to remove an item from the list

☐ Seller / Store △	Added	Subscriptions (Email Sent)	Action
☐ ▓▓▓ (24 ☆) m℮ View seller's other items	Jun-02-05	Favorite Sellers Top Picks (Nov-01)	Edit Preferences ▾

My Note: Vintage clothing and china　　　　　　　　　　　　　　　　　　　　　Edit

| ☐ ▓▓▓▓ (468 ☆) ⭐Power Seller m℮ View seller's other items | Jun-01-04 | | Edit Preferences ▾ |

Click to edit preferences

Delete　　Add Note　　Edit Sellers Preferences　　Favorite Sellers Top Picks will be sent to: cbm@whidbey.com　　Weekly ▾　Save

Back to top

My Favorite Categories (4 categories)　　　　　　　　　　　　　　　Add new Category ⊗ ⊗

Click to move the Category list above the Seller list

☐ My Favorite Categories			Action

Figure 2-1: *From the All Favorites page, you can see the searches, sellers, and categories you like to track.*

CAUTION

If you select more than four categories as favorites, you will have to delete one before you can add another.

⊕ You have reached your maximum number of Favorite Categories (4).
　To save a new category, delete an existing category from your list below and try again.

2. The My Favorite Categories view is displayed. Click **Add New Category**. You will see a selection box containing categories you can select. Figure 2-2 shows an example of how a category, Books, has been selected.

Add new Category
🖑 Action

3. To set up a new category, click a category in the first box. The next level of items contained in the selected category is displayed to the right. Continue to click the desired category until you have found the lowest-level item. A message informing you that you have finished selecting a category appears.

4. Click **Save This Category** to add or change your favorite categories.

5. Repeat steps 3 and 4 for up to three more categories.

TIP

If you want to use a previous method to save a favorite category rather than the new "multi-box" approach, click **Here** at the end of the following sentence: If You Prefer To Use The Old-Style Method Of Choosing A Category, Click **Here**. You can scroll to the category you want and click it.

If you prefer to use the old-style method of choosing a category, click here.

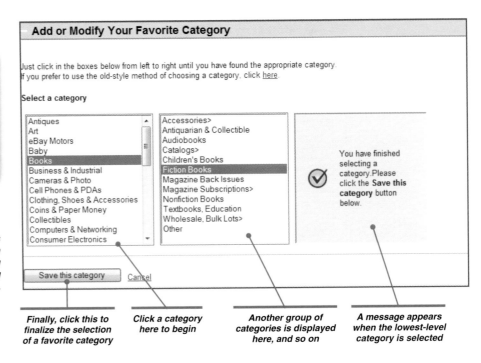

Add or Modify Your Favorite Category

Just click in the boxes below from left to right until you have found the appropriate category. If you prefer to use the old-style method of choosing a category, click here.

Select a category

Antiques	Accessories>
Art	Antiquarian & Collectible
eBay Motors	Audiobooks
Baby	Catalogs>
Books	Children's Books
Business & Industrial	Fiction Books
Cameras & Photo	Magazine Back Issues
Cell Phones & PDAs	Magazine Subscriptions>
Clothing, Shoes & Accessories	Nonfiction Books
Coins & Paper Money	Textbooks, Education
Collectibles	Wholesale, Bulk Lots>
Computers & Networking	Other
Consumer Electronics	

You have finished selecting a category. Please click the **Save this category** button below.

Save this category   Cancel

*Figure 2-2: **To select categories for your Favorite list, scroll through the list clicking the categories you want until a message informing you to save this category appears.***

Finally, click this to finalize the selection of a favorite category

Click a category here to begin

Another group of categories is displayed here, and so on

A message appears when the lowest-level category is selected

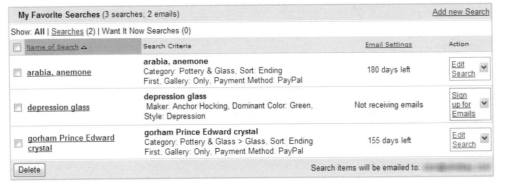

My Favorite Searches (3 searches; 2 emails)   Add new Search

Show: **All** | Searches (2) | Want It Now Searches (0)

Name of Search △	Search Criteria	Email Settings	Action
arabia, anemone	**arabia, anemone** Category: Pottery & Glass, Sort: Ending First, Gallery: Only, Payment Method: PayPal	180 days left	Edit Search
depression glass	**depression glass** Maker: Anchor Hocking, Dominant Color: Green, Style: Depression	Not receiving emails	Sign up for Emails
gorham Prince Edward crystal	**gorham Prince Edward crystal** Category: Pottery & Glass > Glass, Sort: Ending First, Gallery: Only, Payment Method: PayPal	155 days left	Edit Search

Delete   Search items will be emailed to:

Save Your Favorite Searches in My eBay

Saving your favorite searches in My eBay allows you to quickly see the results of up to 100 searches. You can receive e-mail notifying you of new actions for specific items.

1. Click **My eBay** on the eBay header.

2. In the My eBay Views sidebar, under All Favorites, click **Searches**. The My Favorite Searches view is displayed.

3. Click **Add New Search**. The form in Figure 2-3 is displayed.

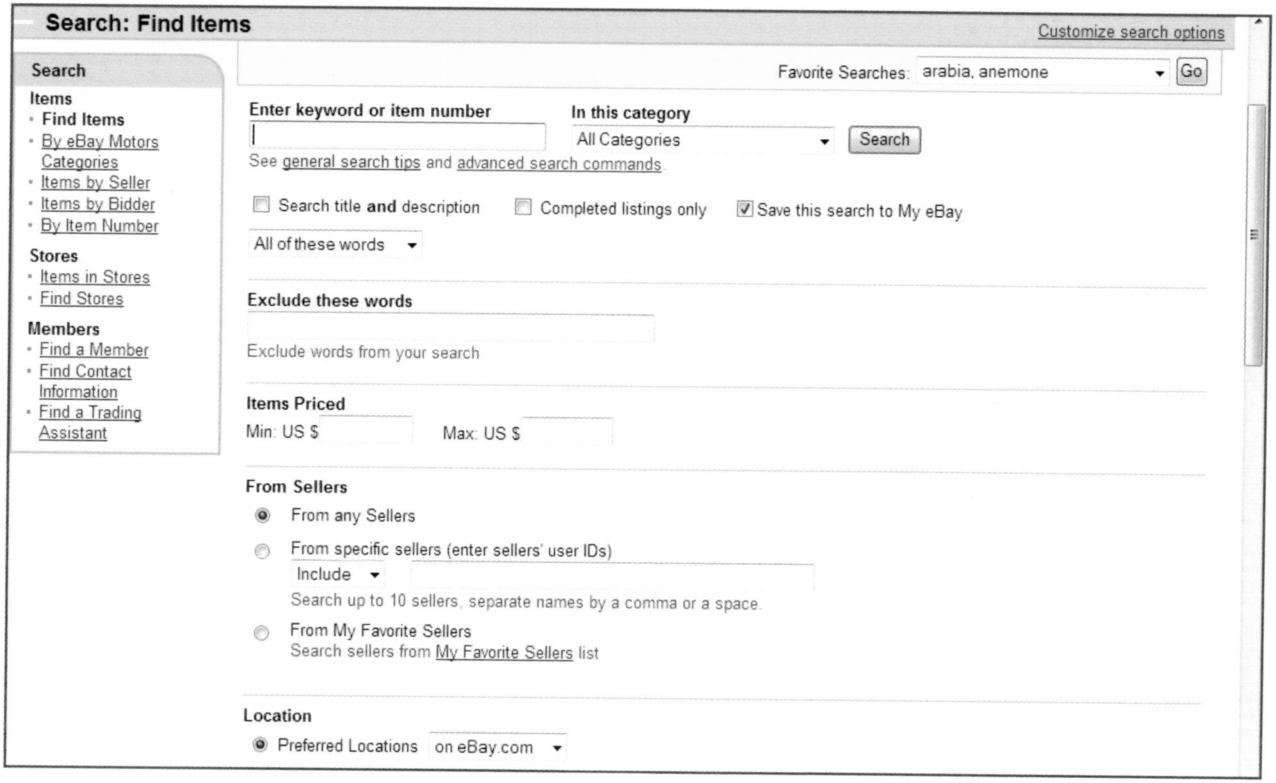

Figure 2-3: *Fill in the form, and click Search to save your favorite searches for quick access later.*

4. First, enter the keyword or item number of the item for which the search is to be saved. This is the only required search entry:

- Click **General Search Commands** to get hints for how to make your keywords more effective in finding what you want.

- Click **Advanced Search Commands** to see how you can enter text and punctuation to get more precise searches. See the "Using Search Variations" QuickFacts to see a summary of these options.

5. Click the **In This Category** down arrow to select a category within which the keywords will be found.

QUICKFACTS

USING FAVORITE CATEGORY LISTS

Once you have saved your favorite categories, you can use them to display only the items you're interested in seeing. For each category, you will see a line of links that connects you to a sub-search for these items:

- **All Active** displays all active items meeting your category selection.
- **Starting Today** displays only the new items listed today.
- **Ending Today** displays only the items ending their auctions today.
- **Ending Within 5 Hours** displays a list of the items ending their auctions within five hours.

☐ Coins & Paper Money:Coins: Ancient:Other
All Active | Starting Today | Ending Today | Ending Within 5 Hours

TIP

To change or refine your saved favorite search, click **Edit Search** in the My Favorite Searches view on the My eBay page (you might need to click the **Action** column down arrow if Edit Search is not displayed). On the Save As Favorite Searches dialog box, select the criteria you now want for your search. Then click **Save** to save the change.

Edit Search ▾

TIP

You can also access up to three of your most recently added favorite searches on the home page under the Search box.

---

6. You can click **Search** at this point and get a successful search. The item titles and descriptions will be searched for active items only. If you want to tighten your search parameters, complete any other optional choices, as described in the sections "Use the Basic Search" and "Use Advanced Search."

7. Click **Search** when you have filled in any search parameters you want. Over the search results, you will see a Save As Favorite Search message box.

- Type a name in the **Name This Search** text box.
- Click **Email Me Daily When New Items Match My Search For** if you want to track all activity in this search. Accept or change the duration by clicking the down arrow and selecting an option.

8. Click **Save** to save the search.

9. Later, in My eBay, on the My Favorite Searches page, click the search link listed to display the latest results for your search.

Save Links to Your Favorite Sellers and Stores

You can save up to 30 favorite sellers or eBay Stores.

1. Click **My eBay** on the eBay header.

2. On the My eBay Views sidebar, beneath All Favorites, click **Sellers**.

3. Click **Add New Seller Or Store**. The form in Figure 2-4 is displayed.

4. Type the seller's User ID or Store name, and click **Continue**.

5. The Add To My Favorite Sellers And Stores page will be displayed. You can add a note to yourself about the seller and sign up to receive e-mails related to him or her. Click **Save** to save the seller as one of your favorites.

USING SEARCH VARIATIONS

You can use special characters and combine text in new ways to get more precise searches. Some of the ways include the following:

- To list keywords that may be in titles, just type the words with a space between them.

- To list specific keywords in a specific order, type the words with quotation marks around them. This finds only items matching the text between the quotes.

- To delete items from the search that contain a certain word, type a minus sign (–) with no space before each word. To delete any items with several words in the title, you can also place the words within parentheses with a comma separating them, and with a minus sign without a space immediately before the left parenthesis, such as –(used, old, antique).

- To find items with either one word or another, place both words in parentheses separated by commas, such as (green,blue).

- To find words starting with certain characters, follow the characters with an asterisk, such as org*. This finds all words beginning with "org."

TIP

To delete a favorite category, search, seller, or Store from your Favorite list, select the check box next to the name, and click **Delete**. To delete all items, select the check box in the column heading bar, and click **Delete**.

My Favorite Sellers (2 sellers)

☑ Seller / Store ▲

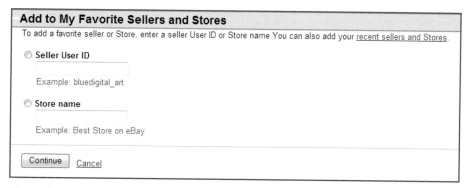

Add to My Favorite Sellers and Stores

To add a favorite seller or Store, enter a seller User ID or Store name. You can also add your recent sellers and Stores.

○ **Seller User ID**

Example: bluedigital_art

○ **Store name**

Example: Best Store on eBay

[Continue] Cancel

*Figure 2-4: **Add a new seller or Store to your Favorite list by typing the User ID or Store name and clicking Continue.***

Use the Basic Search

The Search feature, found in the eBay header, can quickly narrow your quest for information. By defining a good search, you can either get right to the item in question or close to it. To perform a basic search:

1. On the home page (or on just about any eBay page), in the eBay header, type the keywords for which you want to search.

2. Click the **Categories** down arrow, and click the category you want. An example is shown in Figure 2-5.

3. Click **Search**. You will either be shown a listing of items or given an opportunity to refine your search by specifying additional category information.

Bob, the buyer, is searching for antique hatpins from Bali. It may be a short list!

![eBay screenshot: Buy Sell My eBay Community Help. Hello, (Sign out). Site Map. Search box with "depression glass", category "Pottery & Glass", Search button, Advanced Search.]

*Figure 2-5: **The Basic Search page allows you to scan the universe of items in a particular category for those you want to see.***

QUICK**FACTS**

IDENTIFYING ICONS IN LISTINGS

eBay uses icons to identify certain characteristics of listed items. Some of the most common icons you will see in a listing are as follows:

- The item has a fixed price, so you can buy it directly from the seller without bidding in an auction. `Buy It Now`

- You can either pay a fixed price or start a negotiation with the seller with a best offer. `Buy It Now or Best Offer`

- A picture is contained in the detailed listing. 📷

- The seller accepts PayPal. 🅿

- The item would make a good gift for someone. 🎁

- The item has been listed within the past 24 hours. ☀

- The item is featured in the eBay Gallery, so you will see the photo in browsing and search results. 🖼

- The item is in the eBay Live Auctions. 🔨

NOTE

A gift item is really just a listing upgrade a seller has paid extra for to get the Gift icon in their listing—everything on eBay would be good gift for someone!

Use Advanced Search

The Advanced Search feature allows you to widen your search parameters using several additional criteria.

1. On the eBay header, click **Advanced Search**. The page shown in Figure 2-6 is displayed.

2. Identify the item you are searching for by typing a keyword or item number in the Enter Keyword Or Item Number text box.

3. Click the **In This Category** down arrow, and click a category.

4. Enter the following information:

   - To search the description in addition to the title for your keyword(s), select the **Search Title And Description** check box.

   - To search only the listings that have ended, select the **Completed Listings Only** check box.

   - To save this search as a favorite search in My eBay, select the **Save This Search To My eBay** check box.

   - Click the **All Of These Words** down arrow, and choose **All Of These Words, Any Of These Words, Exact Phrase**, or **Exact Match Only**.

   - To identify items to be excluded from the search, type the words in the **Exclude These Words** textbox. Listings containing these words will be excluded from the search results.

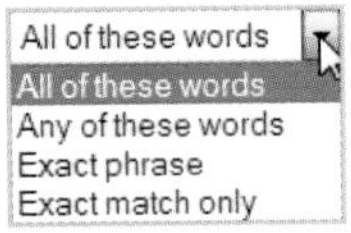

   - To limit the price, under Items Priced, type a price range in the Min and Max text boxes.

Search: Find Items

Customize search options

Search

Items
- **Find Items**
- By eBay Motors Categories
- Items by Seller
- Items by Bidder
- By Item Number

Stores
- Items in Stores
- Find Stores

Members
- Find a Member
- Find Contact Information
- Find a Trading Assistant

Favorite Searches: Frankoma Pottery ▼ Go

Enter keyword or item number

In this category

All Categories ▼ Search

See general search tips and advanced search commands.

☐ Search title **and** description ☐ Completed listings only ☐ Save this search to My eBay

All of these words ▼

Exclude these words

Exclude words from your search

Items Priced

Min: US $ Max: US $

From Sellers

◉ From any Sellers

◯ From specific sellers (enter sellers' user IDs)
  Include ▼
  Search up to 10 sellers, separate names by a comma or a space.

◯ From My Favorite Sellers
  Search sellers from My Favorite Sellers list

Location

◉ Preferred Locations on eBay.com ▼

◯ Items located in United States ▼

Figure 2-6: *The Advanced Search page allows you to refine your search in additional ways and to consider international items.*

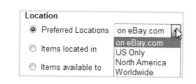

- Under From Sellers, click the button to select which sellers you want included in the search: all sellers, only specific sellers (for whom you include the Sellers' User IDs), or the sellers in your Favorite Sellers list.

- From the Location entry, click the **Preferred Locations** down arrow, and select where in the world you want the search to include. Click the **Items Located In** down arrow, and select the country where you want the item to be located. Click the **Items Available To** down arrow, and click the country to which the seller will ship the item.

TIP

Try to be precise about what you are searching for, naming the article, color, size, brand name, and so on. Keeping in mind that typos are not uncommon in the listings, use typical *misspellings* in addition to correct spellings for more results.

CAUTION

eBay includes common words, such as "and," "or," and "the," in its search, so it will only find items that have those exact words. For example, if you specify "mug or cup," it will find only "mug or cup" items, not any mugs *or* any cups, as you might expect.

- To find an item close to your location, click the **Items Within _Miles Of** check box, and then click the miles from the drop-down menu. Type the ZIP or postal code, or click a city using the **Select A Popular City** down arrow.

- To specify which currency you want to pay in, click the **Currency** down arrow, and click your choice.

- To view multiple identical items sold per listings, click the **Multiple Item Listings** down arrow and choose **At Least, Exactly**, or **At Most**. Type the number of items you want to buy. Click **Items Listed As Lots** if you want to include items made up of lots (groups).

- Under Show Only, click the check boxes defining the items that you want included in the search. If you select Listings, click the down arrow and select the start or end times, and then click the time down arrow and click the hours or days. You can change the timing to be a date range by clicking **Change To Date Range**.

- To search for items having bids currently in process, under Number of Bids, type the minimum number of bids in the Min text box and the maximum number of bids in the Max text box.

- To include Really Simple Syndication (RSS) feeds that can track changes to an item, click **Show** to the right of Affiliate Tracking Information, click the **Provider** down arrow, and choose a provider for the RSS feeds.

- To select how you want the items sorted in the search results listing, click the **Sort By** down arrow, and click a sort sequence. Click the **View Results** down arrow, and click whether you want to see all items in the search results listing, those items featured in the Gallery (that is, items with pictures in the listings), or to show the item numbers. Click the **Results Per Page** down arrow to choose a number of items in the search results listing.

5. When the search criteria are as you want, click **Search**.

Search for a Member's Information

The following sections explain how to find information about a member, perhaps to find what items are being sold by a specific seller.

Search: Find a Member

| Search |

1 exact match and 4 close matches for member:

User ID	Member for	Location	About Me
Exact Match:			
(595 ★)	6 years 10 months	NY, United States	
Close Matches:			
(73 ★)	4 years 10 months	Germany	
(28 ☆)	2 years 11 months	Belgium	
(0)	1 year 10 months	Spain	
(2)	1 year 9 months	AZ, United States	

*Figure 2-7: **You will find exact or close matches to your search on a User ID.***

Search: Items by Seller

Search

Items
* Find Items
* By eBay Motors Categories
* **Items by Seller**
* Items by Bidder
* By Item Number

Stores
* Items in Stores
* Find Stores

Members
* Find a Member
* Find Contact Information
* Find a Trading Assistant

Enter seller's User ID

Find items offered by a particular seller.

☐ Include completed listings   Last 30 days ▼

☐ Include bidders' and buyers' email addresses
(Only available if you are the seller of the listed items.)

☑ Show close and exact User ID matches

Sort by   **Results per page**
Time: ending soonest ▼   50 ▼

| Search |

*Figure 2-8: **You can find items sold by a specific seller and limit the items displayed by completion or by timing.***

FIND AN INDIVIDUAL MEMBER'S PROFILE

To find a member's feedback rating and items being sold:

1. On the eBay header, click **Site Map**.

2. On the Site Map page, find the Connect section on the right, and click **Find A Member**. The Search: Find A Member page will be displayed.

Connect
* About Me
* Chat Rooms
* Discussion Boards
* eBay Blogs
* eBay My World
* eBay Wiki
* Find a Member
* Find Contact Information

3. Type a member's User ID or e-mail address in the text box.

4. Click **Search**. The exact or closest matches for your User ID will be displayed, as shown in Figure 2-7:

   * Click the feedback number to view the Member Profile, which includes the feedback score and ratings, the feedback itself, and links to other information, such as the ID history.

   * Click **Seller's Items** to view the items for sale by the seller. See "Find Seller's Items" for more precise identification of items.

   * Click the User ID to see the eBay My World page, which includes the feedback information.

FIND SELLER'S ITEMS

To find items sold by a specific seller, you can either search by items or by the seller's User ID.

1. Using the previous instructions, click **Site Map** on the eBay header. Under Connect, click **Find A Member**. The page shown earlier in Figure 2-7 is displayed.

2. In the Search sidebar, click **Items By Seller**, and the page shown in Figure 2-8 will be displayed.

3. In the **Enter Seller's User ID** text box, type the User ID.

4. You have these options:

   * To only search for listings that have ended, click the **Include Completed Listing** check box, and click the down arrow to select a time period for completed items.

Sally, the seller, is researching items sold by her competitors. She has an edge!

Search
Items
* Find Items
* By eBay Motors Categories
* Items by Seller
* Items by Bidder
* By Item Number

QUICKSTEPS

FINDING A MEMBER'S CONTACT INFORMATION

To find a bidder's or seller's contact information, you must be involved in a transaction with them.

1. On the eBay header, click **Advanced Search**.

2. On the Search: Find Items page, on the Search sidebar, click **Find Contact** under Members. The page in Figure 2-9 is displayed.

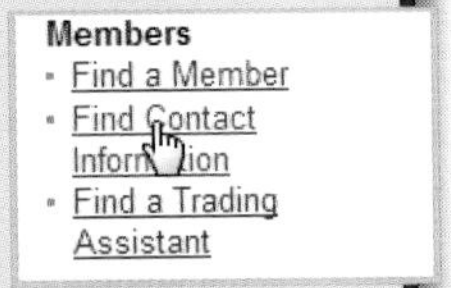

   Members
   · Find a Member
   · Find Contact Information
   · Find a Trading Assistant

3. Type the User ID in the **Enter User ID Of Member** text box.

4. Type the item number in the **Item Number Of The Item You Are Trading With The Above Member** text box. You will find the item number to the right of the listing name in My eBay.

5. Click **Search**. If you qualify, the contact information will be e-mailed to you. Your information will also be sent to the other member, according to the privacy policy.

- To include the bidder's and buyers' e-mail addresses, select the relevant checkboxes. This feature will be unavailable if you are not the seller of the items listed.

- To include both User IDs that exactly match and those that are similar, click the **Show Close And Exact User ID Matches** check box. (It may be set that way as the default, in which case, you leave the check mark to select the option.)

- To sort the listings, click the **Sort By** down arrow, and click your choice. Click **Results Per Page** to determine how many listings you want per page.

Sort by
Time: ending soonest
Time: oldest first
Time: newly listed
Time: ending soonest
Price: lowest first
Best Match

5. Click **Search** when you are satisfied with your search criteria.

Find a Bidder's Activity

To find items a bidder is interested in:

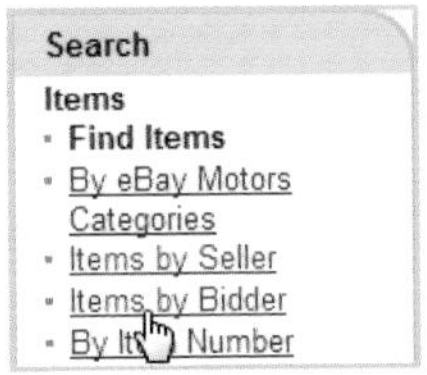

1. On the eBay header, click **Advanced Search**.

2. On the Search sidebar, click **Items By Bidder**. The Search: Items By Bidder page is displayed.

3. In the Enter Bidder's User ID text box, type the User ID. You have these options:

   - Click the **Include Completed Items** check box to see items the bidder has won or bought in the last 30 days.

   Search
   Items
   · Find Items
   · By eBay Motors Categories
   · Items by Seller
   · Items by Bidder
   · By Item Number

- If you are only interested in looking at all of the bidder's items, even when he or she was not the winner, click the **Even If Not The High Bidder** button.

- If you are only interested in looking at this bidder's high bids, click the **As High Bidder Only** button.

- Click the **Results Per Page** down arrow, and choose the number of results you want displayed on a page.

4. Click **Search**. An example of what you may see is shown in Figure 2-10.

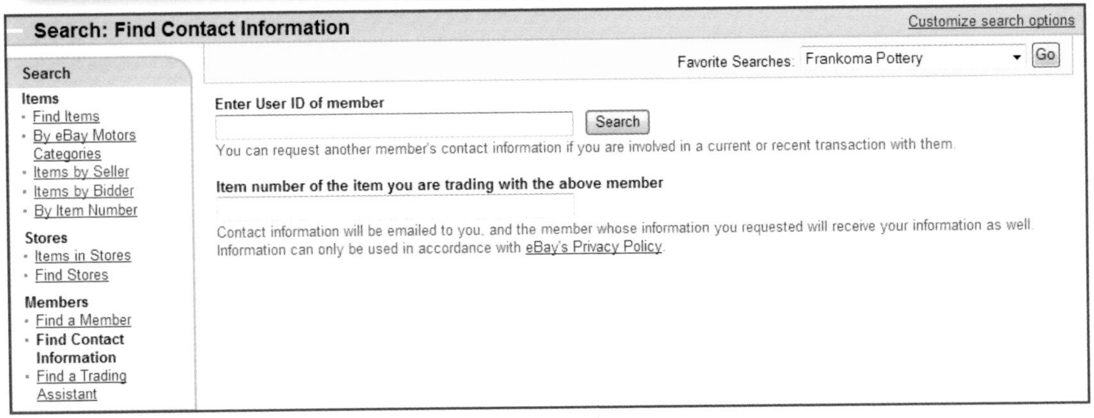

Search: Find Contact Information

Customize search options

Search

Items
· Find Items
· By eBay Motors Categories
· Items by Seller
· Items by Bidder
· By Item Number

Stores
· Items in Stores
· Find Stores

Members
· Find a Member
· **Find Contact Information**
· Find a Trading Assistant

Favorite Searches: Frankoma Pottery [Go]

Enter User ID of member

[   ] [Search]

You can request another member's contact information if you are involved in a current or recent transaction with them.

Item number of the item you are trading with the above member

[   ]

Contact information will be emailed to you, and the member whose information you requested will receive your information as well. Information can only be used in accordance with eBay's Privacy Policy.

*Figure 2-9: **You can get a member's contact information only if you have an active transaction with them.***

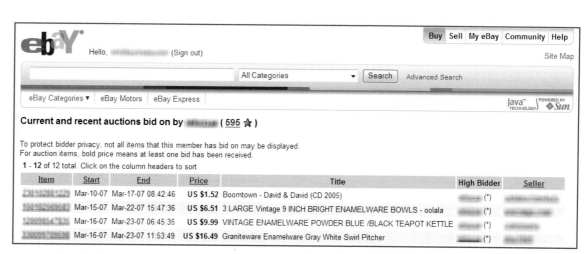

Figure 2-10: A bidder's activity shows details of the listed items the bidder is/has been attempting to buy.

NOTE

To get personal contact information about another eBay member, you must be involved in a transaction with him or her, and you can only use the information to resolve problems or to complete a transaction that you have with this person. For example, you may be trying to find a winning bidder to send the item to him or her, or want to ask a seller a question about an item. Or, you may be trying to resolve a conflict. Sellers can get contact information for bidders in an active auction and for the winning bidder/buyer after the listing is closed. A bidder can get information about a seller during an auction, or after, if he or she is the winning bidder. The information disclosed includes the contact information for both the buyer and seller, and an e-mail is also sent to both participants. That is, the person for whom you are requesting information will receive an e-mail disclosing that you want his or her contact information and disclosing yours.

Find a Store

To find a particular eBay Store, you can use the Search feature to find either the Store by name or by keywords identifying the merchandise it sells.

1. Click **Advanced Search** on the eBay header.
2. On the Search sidebar, under Stores, click **Find Stores**.
3. Type the Store name or keywords for the types of merchandise sold by the Store.
4. Select between searching for other Stores that may have the same items and searching by Store name only.
5. Click **Search**.

Stores
- Items in Stores
- Find Stores

Search Stores for Items

Searches using the basic or advanced search do not include eBay Store items (with a few exceptions, as noted in Chapter 10). To search for items by eBay Store:

1. On the eBay header, click **Advanced Search**. The Search: Find Items page will be displayed.

eBay QuickSteps   *Researching on eBay (Buyers or Sellers)*   **37**

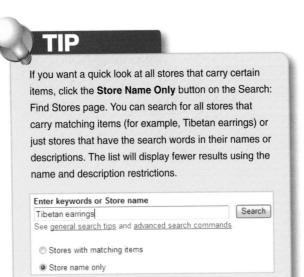

TIP

If you want a quick look at all stores that carry certain items, click the **Store Name Only** button on the Search: Find Stores page. You can search for all stores that carry matching items (for example, Tibetan earrings) or just stores that have the search words in their names or descriptions. The list will display fewer results using the name and description restrictions.

> Enter keywords or Store name
>
> Tibetan earrings | Search
>
> See general search tips and advanced search commands.
>
> ○ Stores with matching items
> ● Store name only

2. On the Search sidebar, under Stores, click **Items In Stores**. An example of this page can be seen in Figure 2-11.

> Stores
> · Items in Stores
> · Find Stores

3. In the **Enter Keyword Or Item Number** text box, type the item keyword(s) or item number.

4. Click the **In This Category** down arrow, and choose which category you want the search to include.

5. Click the **Search Title And Description** check box to include the description in addition to the title in a search.

6. Click **Completed Listings Only** to include only items that have already ended.

7. Click **Save This Search To My eBay** to reuse this search again as one of your favorite searches.

8. By selecting the **Search Store Inventory Items Only** check box, you can restrict your search to items that may not be in listings but that are in eBay Store inventories. These items may be priced lower in order to move them. eBay Store sellers have store-only items that may not appear in regular searches and, possibly, regular auction items. Without selecting this option, you will get both types of listings.

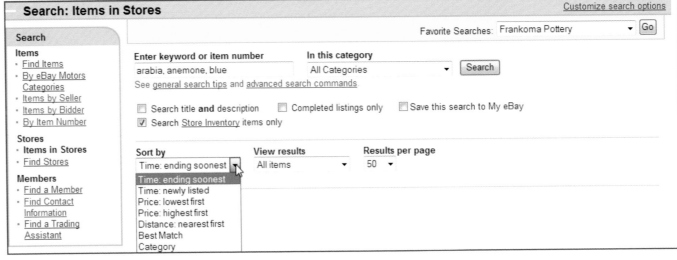

Figure 2-11: *Searching for items in eBay Stores can show inventory that might not easily be found otherwise.*

IDENTIFYING ICONS FOR eBAY USERS

Here are some of the most common icons identifying attributes of users:

- About Me link me
- PowerSeller (someone who sells a high volume of items while maintaining 98 percent positive feedback ratings) Power Seller
- Link to seller's Store
- ID Verified
- User ID has changed within the last 30 days
- New user within the last 30 days

NOTE

You can also find a seller's About Me page from the listing for an item. In this case, click the item link to display the item description. Then, in the Meet The Seller area, click the **About Me** icon.

Meet the seller

Seller: _____ (2692 ⭐) Power Seller me
Feedback: **99.7% Positive**
Member: since Jan-26-99 in United States
About Me

---

9. Click the **Sort By** down arrow, and choose how you want the results sorted.

10. Click **View Results** and select whether you want all items found, items with a Gallery picture, or whether the item number should be shown.

View results
All items
All items
Picture Gallery
Show item numbers

11. Click **Search** when the criteria are as you want them.

Find Someone's About Me Page

To display an eBay member's About Me page:

1. From the eBay header, click **Advanced Search**.

2. On the Search sidebar, under Members, click **Find A Member**.

3. In the **Enter User ID Or Email Address Of Member** text box, type the User ID or e-mail address, and click **Search**. A list of members whose User IDs or e-mail addresses match or are close to the one you entered will be displayed.

4. If the member has an About Me page, click the **About Me** icon and the page will be displayed.

____ (8)	4 years 4 months	IL, United States
____ (24 ⭐) me	7 years 9 months	WA, United States About Me
____ (11 ⭐)	7 years 3 months	KY, United States

Find Someone's ID History

A user may have had more than one User ID. Many users had previously used an e-mail address for their User ID. This is no longer allowed, so changing User IDs is not uncommon, nor is it something negative. Perhaps the user has a new business or a different sense of what he or she wants to use as an ID. However, a user might be trying to hide a negative rating by changing User IDs. Be particularly careful if an ID has changed recently. To find out what other User IDs have been used by an eBay member:

1. From the eBay header, click **Advanced Search**. Under Members, click **Find A Member**.

2. Type the User ID or e-mail address, and click **Search**.

3. In the member's information area, click **ID History** and you'll see a listing of the User IDs the member has used. (If you do not see the member's information area, click the feedback number to get it.)

> Member since: May-24-01
> Location: United States
> - ID History
> - Items for Sale

Research an Item

You may find yourself searching for special items, such as completed items, gift items, or Buy It Now items, or, perhaps, cars or real estate, where the item is more expensive and not necessarily an auction at all. There are unique ways to search for these items, as you'll find in this section.

Find Completed Items

To search for items on which the auctions have been completed so that you can compare prices:

1. From the eBay header, click **Advanced Search**. The Search: Find Items page is displayed.

2. Type the keyword(s) for the item you want to find or the item number.

3. Click the **In This Category** down arrow, and select a category.

4. Click **Completed Listings Only**. Your screen may look something like Figure 2-12.

5. Click **Search**. A listing of all the items is displayed.

Figure 2-12: *To find items on which the auctions have been completed, use the Advanced Search feature.*

TIP

A completed auction does not necessarily mean that an item has been sold. Many auctions, regardless of format, simply run out of time with no bids being placed.

NOTE

If you have just performed a search, or if you have a list of items that you would like to refine, you may be able to find what you want without using the Search feature. The Search Options sidebar is displayed to the left of the list of items. You can refine the search by location, PayPal items, completed items, Buy It Now items, gift items, items priced in a certain range, or auctions for items ending soon. Select the options you want, and click **Show Items**.

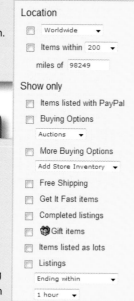

TIP

If you want to customize the Search Options sidebar, click **Customize Options Displayed Above** at the bottom of the sidebar. The Customize Your Search page is displayed. You can add items to the sidebar by clicking an item in the Available Search Options list box and clicking the right-pointing arrow. Remove items from the sidebar by clicking an item in the Options You Want Displayed list box and then clicking the left-pointing arrow. Click **Apply Changes** to redisplay the sidebar with the changes.

NOTE

You can also use eBay Express or Want It Now to find items you don't want to bid on.

Find Buy It Now or Gift Items

At times, you might be in a hurry to get an item. Or, perhaps you are not interested in participating in auctions. In these cases, eBay has fixed-price items that you can buy without going through the auction process.

1. From the eBay header, click **Advanced Search**. The Search: Find Items page is displayed.

2. Type the keyword(s) for the item you want to find or the item number.

3. Click the **In This Category** down arrow, and select a category.

4. Scroll to the Show Only section:

   - Click **Buying Options** and click the down arrow to select **Buy It Now Items** to find something you can buy right now.

   - Click **Gift Items** to find an item for a gift.

5. Click **Search**. The results are displayed.

Understand the Lingo

eBay has a vocabulary all its own. For example, if you read, "BTW, the CM diamond ring is TDF, and the SH is Free," you might be left scratching your head, wondering what you are buying! Interpretation: "By the way, the customized diamond ring is to die for, and the shipping and handling is free." How can you let a potential buyer know what attributes your item has without being too wordy? Tables 2-1 through 2-4 contain some examples of common word usages for describing the conditions of an item, common auction terminology, shipping descriptions, and "chit chat" acronyms that communicate in a shorthand way.

A RUN of 1925 Peace dollars NGC MS 64 NEAR GEM!
THese puppies are NEAR GEM!!! $140 each in GEM!

ACRONYM	WHAT IT STANDS FOR
AO	All Original
AUTO	Autographed
BU	Brilliant Uncirculated (coins)
CM	Customized
CU	Crisp Uncirculated
EC	Excellent Condition
EF	Extra File Condition
EX	Excellent Condition/Exceptional
EUC	Excellent Used Condition
FC	Fine Condition
FOR	Forgery
G/GD	Good Condition
Gently Used	Item shows little wear
GU/GW	Gently Used/Gently Worn (clothing)
HIC/HIL	Hole In Cover/Hole In Label
HTF	Hard To Find
LSW	Label Shows Wear
MCU	Might Clean Up
MIJ	Made in Japan
MIMB/MIMP/MIOP/ MIP/MNB	Mint In Mint Box/Mint In Mint Package/ Mint In Opened Package/Mint In Package/Mint No Box
Mint, MS	Mint Condition, Mint State
NARU	Not A Registered User
NBW	Never Been Worn

ACRONYM	WHAT IT STANDS FOR
NC	No Cover
NGC	Numismatic Guarantee Company (coins)
NIB/NIP/NIMSP	New In Box/New In Package/New In Manufacturer's Sealed Package
NM	Near Mint
NRFB/NRFSB	Never Removed From Box/Never Removed From Sealed Box
NW	Never Worn (clothing)
NWOT/NWT	New Without Tags/New With Tags
NR	No Reserve Price
OB/OF	Original Box/Original Finish
OOP	Out Of Print
P/PC	Poor Condition (coins)/Poor Condition
PF/PR	Proof Coin/Poor Condition Proof
RARE	This can be a subjective assessment
SR	Slight Ring Wear
SW	Slight Wear
UPI	Unpaid Item
VF/VFC	Very Fine Condition
VG/VGC	Very Good Condition
VHTF	Very Hard To Find
VR	Very Rare (this can also be a subjective assessment)
WOB/WOC/WOF/ WOR	Writing On Back/Writing On Cover/ Writing On Front/Writing On Record

Table 2-1: *Conditions Describing an Item*

QUICKFACTS

AWARDING SELLER STARS

Stars are awarded to eBay participants based on their feedback points. The longer a buyer or seller has been on eBay, the more points he or she will have. A user gets +1 point for good feedback, 0 points for neutral feedback, and –1 for negative feedback. Feedback from repeat buyers or sellers gives one point, not one per transaction. Users with a negative feedback of –4 are not allowed to bid or sell on eBay. After ten feedback ratings, a yellow star is awarded:

10 to 49 points	Yellow Star	☆
50 to 99 points	Blue Star	★
100-499 points	Turquoise Star	☆
500 to 999 points	Purple Star	★
1000 to 4999 points	Red Star	★
5000 to 9999 points	Green Star	☆
10,000 to 24,999 points	Yellow Shooting Star	⛤
25,000 to 49,999 points	Turquoise Shooting Star	⛤
50,000 to 99,999 points	Purple Shooting Star	⛤
100,000 or higher points	Red Shooting Star	★

AKA	Also Know As
BIN	Buy It Now
FB	Feedback
FOR	Forgery
FVF	Final Value Fee
NR/NORES	No Reserve
NARU	Not A Registered User
NPB	Non-Paying Buyer
S/O	Sold Out

*Table 2-2: **Auction Acronyms***

ASAP	As Soon As Possible
DOA	Dead On Arrival (item is damaged when delivered)
FEDEX	Federal Express Shipping
PP	Parcel Post
PPD	Post Paid
PM	Priority Mail
S/H, SH	Shipping And Handling
S/H/I, SHI	Shipping, Handling, and Insurance
Snail Mail	U.S. Post Office Delivery
UPS	United Parcel Service
USPS	United States Postal Service
V/M/D	Visa, MasterCard, Discover credit cards

*Table 2-3: **Shipping Acronyms***

BTS	Back To School
HTF	Hard To Find
FAQ	Frequently Asked Questions
IMO/IMHO	In My Opinion/In My Humble Opinion
ITF	Impossible To Find
LMK	Let Me Know
RSVP	Respond As Soon As Possible
TIA	Thanks In Advance
TDF	To Die For
WYSIWYG	What You See Is What You Get

*Table 2-4: **"Chit Chat" Acronyms***

How to...

Chapter 3
Buying Strategies

Your most important weapon in this bidding/buying game is information. Your buying strategies consist of arming yourself with information you need to know—about yourself and your own purchasing tendencies—and whether you are bidding or paying a fixed price. You need to know about the seller and his or her past history and feedback status. The competition you encounter during bidding is certainly a subject of concern, as is how they typically bid on items. Of course, the product and how you judge its worthiness are important areas you want to investigate. First, you want to protect yourself against buying an inappropriate or unsatisfactory product. (Protecting yourself against actual fraud or dishonesty is covered in Chapter 9.)

:: Payment Terms
Payment is due within 7 days after end of auction. I accept paypal, money order or personal check. Please allow 5 business days for personal check to clear. International bidders, I accept paypal, international postal money order and western union money order. Please purchase carefully, because there are no returns unless item is misrespresented.
:: Shipping Terms
I ship USPS first class mail. I only ship insured packages which is the responsiblity of the buyer.

Figure 3-1: Payment and shipping details are important to look at, as well as the description of the item.

QUICK**FACTS**

UNDERSTANDING WHAT YOU'RE PURCHASING

One of the most obvious ways you can protect yourself is to read carefully the description of the item being sold. Do you understand what it is? (For example, is the item the dining room set with the chairs, or just the chairs? Pictures can deceive!) Is the description complete, or is there important information missing? Are the pictures clear, or are they a little blurry in the important areas? What is the seller charging for handling and shipping? Will insurance be available? Do you have PayPal options? Are you restricted to only certain ways of paying for it? Will the seller ship internationally if you don't live in the seller's country? (An example of shipping and payment details is shown in Figure 3-1.) What is the return policy? If you don't like the item, what can you do about it? If it is broken or damaged when you receive it, what can you do?

NOTE

Notice the colors of the feedback. Green indicates positive feedback; gray is neutral; and red indicates negative feedback.

Protect Yourself (Buyer Precautions)

Your first task is to protect yourself by learning all you can about what it is you want to bid on, as well as about the person selling it. A second task is to protect yourself against spending your hard-earned money on something you don't want. You can be buying the wrong item because you don't know it or because you are carried away in the auction momentum, valuing the game more than the thing you are buying. Either way, you'll end up feeling dissatisfied with your purchase.

Review a Seller's Feedback

One of the first things you will do is check out the seller's feedback rating. This tells you how the seller has transacted business in the past and if buyers have been satisfied with the seller's service and products.

1. When you find the item you want to bid on, click the item's title or Gallery picture to see the View Item page.

2. Click the **Read Feedback Comments** link in the Meet The Seller area.

3. You'll see the listings of feedback. Click the tab that is most important for you: **All Feedback** to see all the feedback; **Feedback as a Buyer** to see feedback only from buyers; **Feedback as a Seller** to see feedback of sellers who have sold to the member; **Feedback Left For Others** to see how this member responds to his buyers or sellers.

CAUTION

Sellers have the option of keeping their feedback comments private. Be cautious about dealing with sellers using this practice. They have eliminated one of your most important ways of protecting yourself.

TIP

You can get some understanding of how the seller cooperates and deals with buyers by reading the seller's comments to others. What is the tone of the communication? Are they helpful? Critical? Neutral? Click the **Feedback Left For Others** tab to see the seller's comments for others.

4. Scroll through the feedback ratings, an example of which is shown in Figure 3-2, to find out if they are consistent and positive.
5. Ask yourself these questions:
   - Does the seller deliver the expected item?
   - Is the item delivered on time?
   - Is the item in good shape when it arrives?
   - Is the price as expected?
   - If there are complaints, are they serious defects with the product or delivery, or are they the result of ignorance on the part of the buyer?
   - What is the overall tone of the comments?

Look at a Seller's Other Products

You can see other items available for a seller by clicking the item link to open the View Item page and clicking **View Seller's Other Items** from the list of

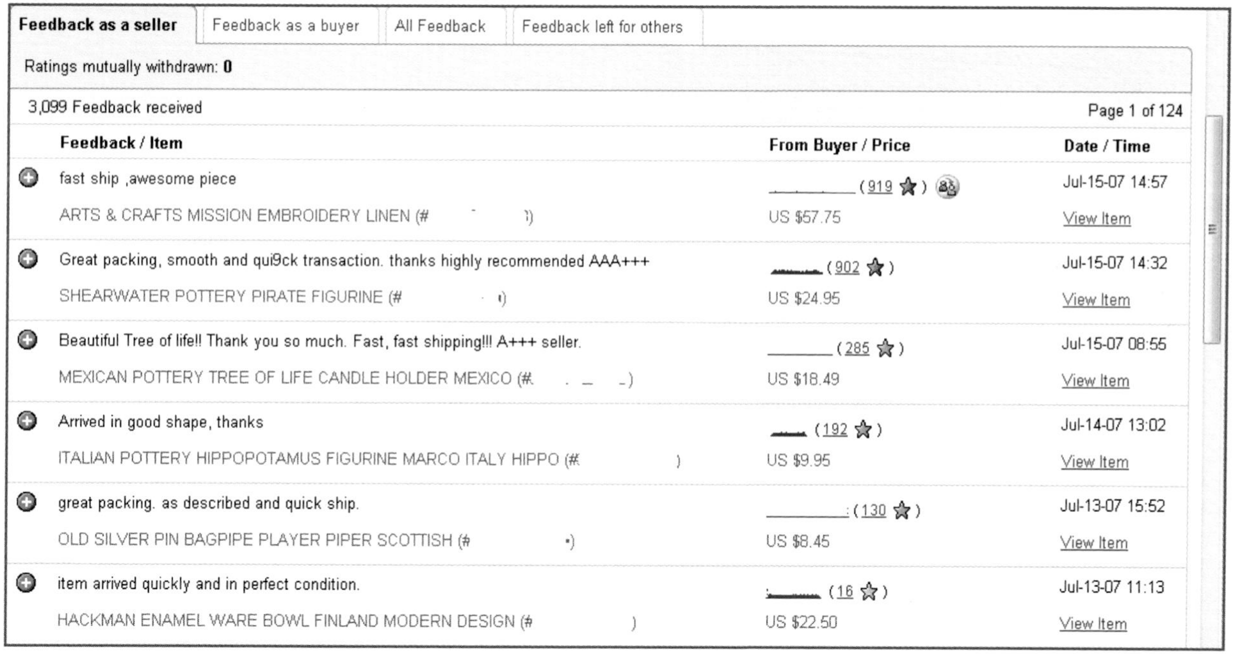

Feedback as a seller | Feedback as a buyer | All Feedback | Feedback left for others

Ratings mutually withdrawn: **0**

3,099 Feedback received — Page 1 of 124

Feedback / Item	From Buyer / Price	Date / Time
fast ship ,awesome piece ARTS & CRAFTS MISSION EMBROIDERY LINEN (#)	(919 ★) US $57.75	Jul-15-07 14:57 View Item
Great packing, smooth and qui9ck transaction. thanks highly recommended AAA+++ SHEARWATER POTTERY PIRATE FIGURINE (#)	(902 ★) US $24.95	Jul-15-07 14:32 View Item
Beautiful Tree of life!! Thank you so much. Fast, fast shipping!!! A+++ seller. MEXICAN POTTERY TREE OF LIFE CANDLE HOLDER MEXICO (#)	(285 ★) US $18.49	Jul-15-07 08:55 View Item
Arrived in good shape, thanks ITALIAN POTTERY HIPPOPOTAMUS FIGURINE MARCO ITALY HIPPO (#)	(192 ★) US $9.95	Jul-14-07 13:02 View Item
great packing. as described and quick ship. OLD SILVER PIN BAGPIPE PLAYER PIPER SCOTTISH (#)	(130 ★) US $8.45	Jul-13-07 15:52 View Item
item arrived quickly and in perfect condition. HACKMAN ENAMEL WARE BOWL FINLAND MODERN DESIGN (#)	(16 ★) US $22.50	Jul-13-07 11:13 View Item

***Figure 3-2:* Feedback comments are an important way to gauge the honesty and reliability of the seller.**

QUICK**FACTS**

UNDERSTANDING FEEDBACK

Feedback comments remain one of the most important tools you have to protect yourself. As an eBay user, you can see three kinds of feedback comments: comments from sellers that have sold to this user, comments from buyers who have purchased an item from this user, and comments the user has given to others. Nevertheless, feedback ratings do have some drawbacks. For instance, new sellers do not have a history, so although you must take care in buying from them, you can also understand their lack of feedback—and they have to start somewhere! You can use other buyer feedback to get a sense of how sellers have handled eBay transactions in the past and how they followed through with the purchases.

A more important drawback to consider is that any buyer can enter misleading or even false and detrimental information about a seller if the transaction is slightly delayed, if the seller has not performed to some hypothetical standard, or if the buyer is just having a bad day. If a seller's feedback ratings are mostly negative, then you can forget about dealing with this seller, but if the feedback comments are overwhelming positive and there are just one or two negative comments, then give the seller a break.

Another shortcoming of feedback ratings is that often a buyer or seller is hesitant to leave negative feedback because the recipient might retaliate and leave negative feedback on the other person's site. Keep the following guidelines in mind when providing feedback:

- Be fair and generous in your expectations of what the other person did. If the item arrived intact and pretty much on time, or if the item is as described, then it probably is not worth a negative comment, even if you are somewhat disappointed.

Continued . . .

Meet The Seller links. A seller might have duplicate items available with fewer bidders, or one of these auctions might be ending sooner than the first one you looked at. You can also access the Seller's Other Items link from the Member Profile page under Items For Sale or from My eBay views, such as Favorite Sellers.

Ask the Seller Questions

Find out all you can about the item you are considering buying before you make a bid. Ask the seller specific questions if the description does not provide the information you need. To ask a seller questions:

1. Browse or search for the item you want. Click the item title or Gallery picture to display the View Item page, such as you might see in Figure 3-3.

2. Click **Ask Seller A Question**.

3. Sign in with your User ID and password, if necessary.

4. The text box for entering your question is shown in Figure 3-4. Type your question and click **Send**. The seller, if he or she is interested in selling the item, will quickly respond to your question.

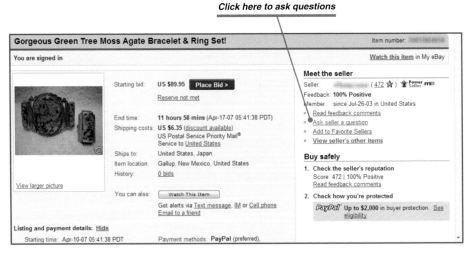

Click here to ask questions

Figure 3-3: **You can find out more about the item you're bidding on from the View Item page.**

UNDERSTANDING FEEDBACK

(Continued)

- If the transaction is not going well, be sure to contact the seller and let him or her know you are dissatisfied. Give the seller a chance to improve the situation.

- If the transaction was clearly and seriously deficient, you can help others by commenting on your experiences. Chances are, yours will not be the only negative comment. (If the transaction is fraudulent, see Chapter 9 for more information.)

- If you get undeserved negative feedback, describe the conditions from your side and go on with life. If you deserve it, describe how you have changed your conditions so that the condition won't recur.

- When giving feedback about a seller, you can give additional detailed seller ratings that allow you to vary the evaluations about the item as described, how the seller communicated, the shipping time, and shipping and handling charges. These are averaged among all the feedback for that seller, and you can see trends more easily (see Chapter 4).

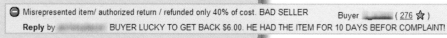

TIP

To respond to feedback that another person has left for you, display the feedback page, and click **Reply To Feedback Received** found beneath the feedback list. Type the User ID or item number and click **Find Feedback**. Click **Reply** and type your comments in the Reply text box. Click **Leave Reply**.

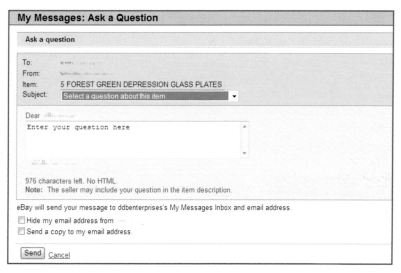

Figure 3-4: *You can send an e-mail to the seller to ask questions or to clarify the condition or terms of the bid.*

Compare Listings

You can compare items in a search listing. This allows you to see items side by side, comparing item descriptions, time left, bids, seller's User ID, price, shipping and handling costs, payment methods, and other variables.

1. On your search listing, click **List View**, if it is not already displayed. The listing display will now show check boxes next to each item.

2. Click the check boxes of those items you wish to compare.

3. Click **Compare** on the top or bottom of the listing display. You have these options:

   - Click **Watch All** to place all selected entries on your Watch list.

   - Click **Remove All** to remove all selected entries from the list.

   - Click **Sort By** to display a menu of sort options.

   - Click **Bid Now** to place a bid on one of the items.

   - Click **Watch This Item** to place this particular item on your Watch list.

If you need to talk to the seller directly, ask when a good time would be to call so that you can continue your conversation about the item. Unless you have placed a bid, you will not have access to the seller's phone number. He or she may give it to you, but may want to know you are a valid buyer first. Some sellers provide Skype buttons in listings and on their About Me page that allow you to contact them for voice or chat communication. See Chapter 5 for more information on Skype.

Look Up the Competition

When buying in eBay auctions, if you seem to be running up against the same bidder—and losing, or if you find that a competitor often bids on items you want, you can get additional information about him or her for that slight edge.

Review Other Bidders

When you are looking at the listing for an item, you also can investigate the other bidders.

1. Find the item for which you are bidding, such as you might find in Figure 3-5, by browsing or searching for an item. Click the title to display the View Item page.

2. Click the **History** link to see a list of bidders. The Bid History page is displayed, as shown in Figure 3-6. If the item is highly priced, the bidder's identity will be hidden. The amount that causes an item's bidders to be hidden is established by eBay, and varies per country.

3. Click the bidder's User ID link to find out additional information.

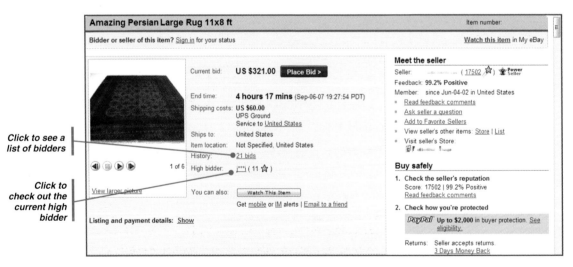

Click to see a list of bidders

Click to check out the current high bidder

Figure 3-5: A listing description contains links to other bidders in the auction.

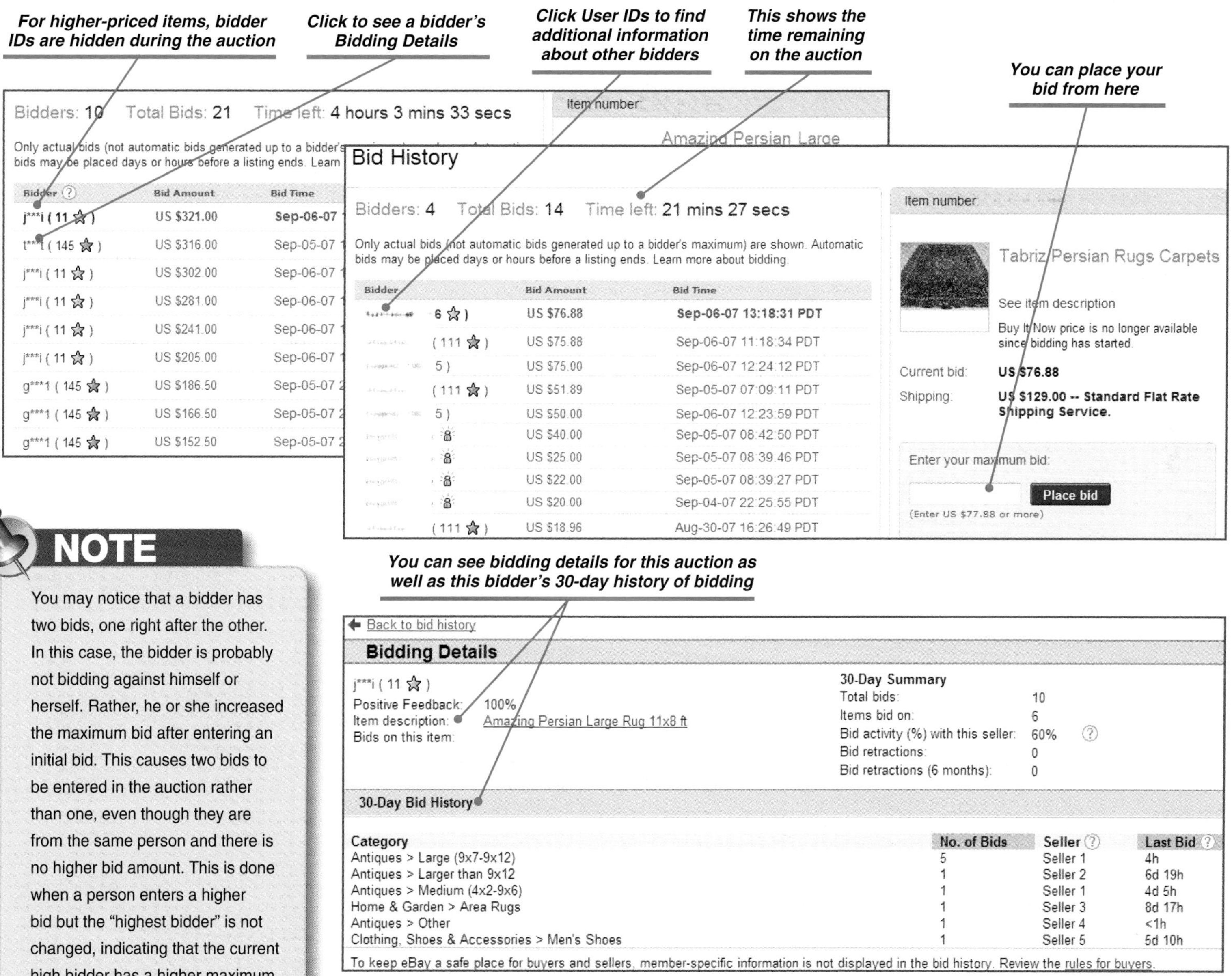

For higher-priced items, bidder IDs are hidden during the auction

Click to see a bidder's Bidding Details

Click User IDs to find additional information about other bidders

This shows the time remaining on the auction

You can place your bid from here

Bidders: 10   Total Bids: 21   Time left: 4 hours 3 mins 33 secs

Item number:

Amazing Persian Large

Only actual bids (not automatic bids generated up to a bidder's maximum) are shown. Automatic bids may be placed days or hours before a listing ends. Learn

Bidder ⑦	Bid Amount	Bid Time
j***i (11 ☆)	US $321.00	Sep-06-07
t***i (145 ☆)	US $316.00	Sep-05-07
j***i (11 ☆)	US $302.00	Sep-06-07
j***i (11 ☆)	US $281.00	Sep-06-07
j***i (11 ☆)	US $241.00	Sep-06-07
j***i (11 ☆)	US $205.00	Sep-06-07
g***1 (145 ☆)	US $186.50	Sep-05-07
g***1 (145 ☆)	US $166.50	Sep-05-07
g***1 (145 ☆)	US $152.50	Sep-05-07

Bid History

Bidders: 4   Total Bids: 14   Time left: 21 mins 27 secs

Only actual bids (not automatic bids generated up to a bidder's maximum) are shown. Automatic bids may be placed days or hours before a listing ends. Learn more about bidding.

Bidder	Bid Amount	Bid Time
6 ☆)	US $76.88	Sep-06-07 13:18:31 PDT
(111 ☆)	US $75.88	Sep-06-07 11:18:34 PDT
5)	US $75.00	Sep-06-07 12:24:12 PDT
(111 ☆)	US $51.89	Sep-05-07 07:09:11 PDT
5)	US $50.00	Sep-06-07 12:23:59 PDT
8	US $40.00	Sep-05-07 08:42:50 PDT
8	US $25.00	Sep-05-07 08:39:46 PDT
8	US $22.00	Sep-05-07 08:39:27 PDT
8	US $20.00	Sep-04-07 22:25:55 PDT
(111 ☆)	US $18.96	Aug-30-07 16:26:49 PDT

Item number:

Tabriz Persian Rugs Carpets

See item description

Buy It Now price is no longer available since bidding has started.

Current bid: **US $76.88**
Shipping: **US $129.00 -- Standard Flat Rate Shipping Service.**

Enter your maximum bid:

[Place bid]

(Enter US $77.88 or more)

You can see bidding details for this auction as well as this bidder's 30-day history of bidding

◀ Back to bid history

Bidding Details

j***i (11 ☆)
Positive Feedback: 100%
Item description: Amazing Persian Large Rug 11x8 ft
Bids on this item:

30-Day Summary
Total bids: 10
Items bid on: 6
Bid activity (%) with this seller: 60%   ⑦
Bid retractions: 0
Bid retractions (6 months):   0

30-Day Bid History

Category	No. of Bids	Seller ⑦	Last Bid ⑦
Antiques > Large (9x7-9x12)	5	Seller 1	4h
Antiques > Larger than 9x12	1	Seller 2	6d 19h
Antiques > Medium (4x2-9x6)	1	Seller 1	4d 5h
Home & Garden > Area Rugs	1	Seller 3	8d 17h
Antiques > Other	1	Seller 4	<1h
Clothing, Shoes & Accessories > Men's Shoes	1	Seller 5	5d 10h

To keep eBay a safe place for buyers and sellers, member-specific information is not displayed in the bid history. Review the rules for buyers.

Figure 3-6: On the Bid History page, you can see who is bidding on an item and how much time is left on the auction.

NOTE

You may notice that a bidder has two bids, one right after the other. In this case, the bidder is probably not bidding against himself or herself. Rather, he or she increased the maximum bid after entering an initial bid. This causes two bids to be entered in the auction rather than one, even though they are from the same person and there is no higher bid amount. This is done when a person enters a higher bid but the "highest bidder" is not changed, indicating that the current high bidder has a higher maximum proxy bid.

CAUTION

Determine how much money you are willing to pay for an item and resolve not to spend more than that. Find out as much as you can about its value, decide what it is worth to you, and then let that be. Remember that the auction (or fixed-price purchase) is a legally binding contract and you legally are required to pay for any item you bid on and win.

NOTE

Chapter 2 describes how to get additional information on other eBay members, such as viewing their ID history, feedback comments, or About Me page.

QUICK**FACTS**

BIDDING IN PREAPPROVED AUCTIONS

You may find that you are not allowed to participate in an auction. In this case, you may see a message informing you that the item being bid on is only available to a restricted list of bidders. If you really want to bid on the item, send a message to the seller asking to be placed on the approved bidder list.

If you are *blocked* from bidding, the seller has specifically placed you on a list of bidders to be excluded or blocked from bidding. In this case, you will not be able to participate in this seller's auctions. This can be for several reasons: you are an international buyer and this seller does not sell internationally; you do not fit the feedback rating profile that is required for this seller; you did not pay for previous winning bids or created other hassles for this seller; and so on. See Chapter 7 for additional information.

Contact Other Bidders

You can contact another bidder, although you are not allowed to try to make a side deal with the bidder or to interfere with the honest give and take of the auction. You can contact a bidder for other reasons, however, especially after the auction is completed.

1. Click the bidder's **User ID** link to open the bidder's eBay My World page.

2. Click the feedback rating (the number next to the star) to display the bidder's Feedback Profile page.

3. On the Feedback Profile page, click the **Contact Member** link.

4. The Contact eBay Member page is displayed, similar to the page previously displayed in Figure 3-4.

5. Type your message and click **Send**. You may need to first enter a group of characters in a text box for security purposes.

Time Your Bid

Sometimes, the way you will be most successful is by timing your bids. In cases where the item is highly desired by others, you may have to vigorously compete. The following sections can help you.

Find the Official eBay Time

The official eBay time is always Pacific Standard Time. To find it, scroll to the bottom of most eBay pages, beneath the links bar in the eBay footer. Click **eBay Official Time**. The page shown in Figure 3-7 is displayed.

SET YOUR TIME DISPLAY FORMAT

You can choose between displaying the time left before a listing ends and displaying the actual ending time. Displaying the time left is the easiest one to track when you are figuring out when to bid.

UNDERSTANDING AUCTION DURATIONS AND RESERVES

You can determine how long your auction lasts and whether or not there will be a reserve that must be met before the auction is valid.

UNDERSTAND AUCTION DURATIONS

Auctions or Buy It Now listings may be held for one, three, five, seven, or ten days. How long depends on the seller and what the item is. Some items, such as tickets or dated objects (such as chocolate Easter bunnies), may be placed for a short period of time, while higher-priced items may be on the market longer so bidders can compare prices and products. If you find an item you want to bid on, you must be aware of the time limitations and how long you have until the auction is over. The listing states the time left and when the end date is. Of course, for Buy It Now auction items, if the first bid is below the Buy It Now amount, the Buy It Now option disappears when the reserve is met, and the auction proceeds as usual until the time limit is reached.

UNDERSTAND AUCTION RESERVE PRICES

Reserve prices are minimum prices that sellers set for their item. The reserve price is not displayed for buyers, so you are bidding blindly as far as the reserve price is concerned. A reserve price assures the seller that he or she will get at least that amount for the item. If the reserve is not met by the end of the auction, the auction completes with no winner. If the reserve is met, then the highest bidder wins the item. In some cases, if the reserve is not met, the seller may notify the highest bidder and accept the bid even though it does not meet the reserve price (although you can't count on that).

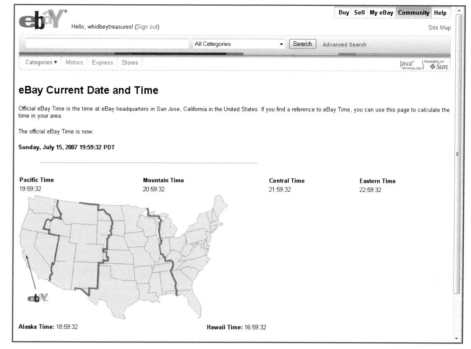

Figure 3-7: *Use the official time and date page to ensure that you are not out of sync in your timing on bidding in an auction.*

To set the time display for time left:

1. Click **My eBay** on the eBay header.

2. On the My eBay sidebar, under My Account, click **Preferences**.

3. Scroll down to General Preferences, and click **Show** for My eBay. The General Preferences options for My eBay will be displayed.

4. To the right of Show Time In My eBay In This Format, click **Time Left**.

5. Click **Apply**. Your time will now be displayed in the Time Left format.

My eBay		
Display this My eBay view first		My Summary ▼
Show time in My eBay in this format		⦿ Time left (5d 02h 26m)
		○ End time/date (Feb-10 07:42:42)

NOTE

In eBay's Buy It Now (BIN) offerings, once you have entered a bid number lower than the BIN price, that fixed price feature disappears and the auction is conducted as a highest-bid-wins-the-item auction. However, at the time of this book writing, that is being reconsidered, and eBay may in the future continue to offer the BIN feature regardless of whether an auction process is occurring or not.

TIP

If you are timing an auction closely, you really need to synchronize your watch with official eBay time, especially if you anticipate vigorous bidding. See Chapter 4 for how to add an item to the Items I'm Watching view or calendar.

QUICK**FACTS**

DELAYING YOUR BID

Many experienced eBay buyers hold their bids until the last minute in order to ensure that they get the lowest price. The idea is that a bidding war will occur when buyers see activity on the bidding front. There is some truth to this, as bidders seem more interested in what others are bidding on; also, every time you enter a bid, someone else must bid higher to get the item. So you might be better off just watching the auction and jumping in at the last minute with your highest proxy bid. Of course, if you really want the item, then saving money may not be the most important object.

FIND THE TIME ON THE LISTING

To find the time for a listing:

1. Open the View Item page for an item by clicking its title or Gallery picture after browsing or searching. The end time is usually displayed under the current bid price.

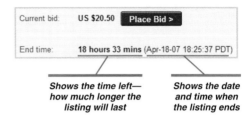

| Current bid: | US $20.50 | **Place Bid >** |

| End time: | **18 hours 33 mins** (Apr-18-07 18:25:37 PDT) |

Shows the time left— how much longer the listing will last   *Shows the date and time when the listing ends*

2. Be sure to note the time left, and track it closely. Add the item to your Items I'm Watching view in My eBay if you want to quickly find it again.

Be a Sniper

You will know you've encountered a sniper when you are the high bidder and someone slips in a higher bid at the last second, squeezing you out of the winning bid. It is allowed by eBay, although it doesn't feel very good to be the victim of a sniper. You can do it, too, however, either doing it yourself or using specialized software.

Bob, the buyer, loves a good sniping opportunity.

USE TWO WINDOWS

To keep an eye on what is going on with the bidding process, and also to prepare your own maximum bid, you need two windows, an example of which is shown in Figure 3-8.

1. Find the item you want. Click the listing title so that the View Item page is displayed.

2. Press **CTRL+N** to split your browser into two windows.

3. Select each window and drag the borders to resize them to fit the screen so that both windows are visible.

4. On one window, click the **History** *n* **Bids** link to see the details of the current bid. Click **Refresh** on your browser to keep the bid current, or press **F5** on your keyboard.

5. On the other window, click **Place Bid** to display the bid entry screen. Type your price and click **Continue**. The Confirm Your Bid page is displayed. (You may have to fill in your User ID and password.) Delay clicking **Confirm Bid** until the time is just right, within the last 30 seconds. (You'll need to test how quickly your bid is processed on your computer and Internet service so you can time it just right.)

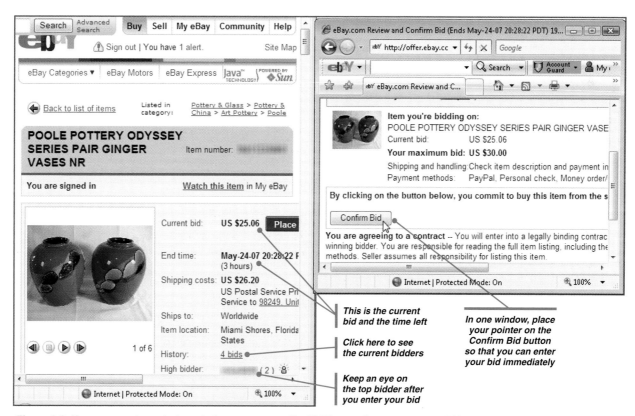

Figure 3-8: *You can use two windows to keep an eye on the bidding, and enter your own bid at the last second of the auction.*

TIP

When sniper bidding, be sure that you are signed in, are on the right window, and have your bidding amounts figured out. (Be sure to notice where the decimal point is!) You don't want to be frantically trying to sign in or calculate the highest bid you can make while the seconds are ticking away.

NOTE

Proxy bidding is not available in multiple-item auctions.

USE SNIPER SOFTWARE

If you do a search on "sniping" in eBay, you will find a variety of sniping software available to buy, as seen in Figure 3-9. These packages automatically watch your auctions, alert you when there is a change, place a time-delayed bid at the last second, and gather and display information for you so you can track your auctions easily and keep on top of them.

Bid Using Several Techniques

Common bidding techniques are proxy bidding and bidding on multiple items.

Bid on Multiple Items

You can bid on multiple items selling in a Dutch auction or on those selling for a fixed price.

BID ON MULTIPLE ITEMS (DUTCH AUCTION)

In a Dutch auction, multiple items are sold at the same price, but with a couple of differences. An example of a multiple-item auction is shown in Figure 3-10. See Chapter 4 for how to bid in a Dutch auction. With a Dutch auction:

Sally, the seller, is preparing to sell her valued collection of dryer lint, collected over many years.

- The seller lists the items, giving a minimum acceptable price.
- Bidders bid on the number of items they want and at what price.

---

60 items found for **sniping** Save this search

List View | Picture Gallery   Sort by: Time: ending soonest ▾   Customize Display

Item Title	PayPal	Bids	Price	Shipping to 98249, USA	Time Left ▲
Featured Items					
SNIPE WITH THE TOP BID SNIPING SOFTWARE: AUCTION SENTRY	ⓟ	≠*Buy It Now*	$9.95	Not specified	17h 47m
GavelSnipe FREE Auction Sniper Software for Sniping	ⓟ	≠*Buy It Now*	$0.99	Digital delivery	1d 05h 46m
GavelSnipe FREE eBay Auction Snipe Software for Sniping	ⓟ	≠*Buy It Now*	$0.99	Digital delivery	1d 06h 19m
SNIPE WITH THE TOP BID SNIPING SOFTWARE: AUCTION SENTRY	ⓟ	≠*Buy It Now*	$9.95	Not specified	2d 17h 56m
eBay's #1 BEST AUCTION BID SNIPER/SNIPING /SNIPE SOFTWARE "Absolutely the best snipe program available on ebay!"	ⓟ	≠*Buy It Now*	$28.79	Free	3d 16h 52m

Figure 3-9: Sniping software is available for optimizing your bid timing and tracking your auctions.

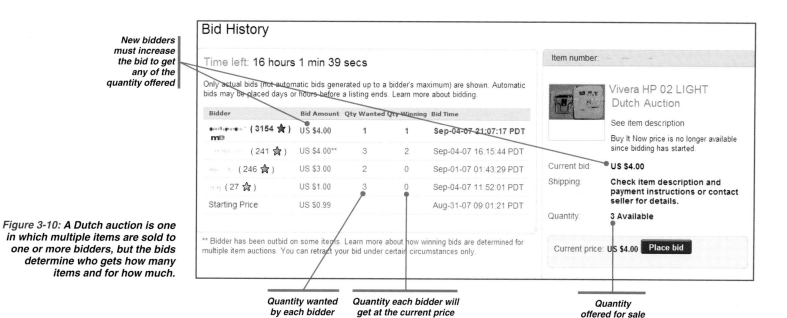

New bidders must increase the bid to get any of the quantity offered

Bid History

Time left: 16 hours 1 min 39 secs

Only actual bids (not automatic bids generated up to a bidder's maximum) are shown. Automatic bids may be placed days or hours before a listing ends. Learn more about bidding.

Bidder	Bid Amount	Qty Wanted	Qty Winning	Bid Time
(3154 ☆) me	US $4.00	1	1	Sep-04-07 21:07:17 PDT
(241 ☆)	US $4.00**	3	2	Sep-04-07 16:15:44 PDT
(246 ☆)	US $3.00	2	0	Sep-01-07 01:43:29 PDT
(27 ☆)	US $1.00	3	0	Sep-04-07 11:52:01 PDT
Starting Price	US $0.99			Aug-31-07 09:01:21 PDT

** Bidder has been outbid on some items. Learn more about how winning bids are determined for multiple item auctions. You can retract your bid under certain circumstances only.

Item number:

Vivera HP 02 LIGHT Dutch Auction

See item description

Buy It Now price is no longer available since bidding has started.

Current bid: **US $4.00**

Shipping: **Check item description and payment instructions or contact seller for details.**

Quantity: **3 Available**

Current price: US $4.00 **Place bid**

Quantity wanted by each bidder

Quantity each bidder will get at the current price

Quantity offered for sale

Figure 3-10: A Dutch auction is one in which multiple items are sold to one or more bidders, but the bids determine who gets how many items and for how much.

NOTE

When a bidder wins a lesser quantity than what he or she bid for, he or she can refuse to buy it, such as in the example of Bidder B with the copper spoons. The bidder doesn't have to pay for partial quantities. In that case, the next bidder in line gets the items, if he or she wants them.

NOTE

Multiple-item auctions are only available if the number of items times the price is less than $100,000.

- The winners pay the lowest acceptable price. That price is the lowest price made by a bidder, who is assured of getting at least one item; that is, his or her bid will zero out the total of the quantities available.

- The highest bidders will win first and get the quantities they want, even if the quantity is oversold.

For example, a seller offers 10 copper spoons at $10 each:

- Bidder A bids $10 for 3 spoons.
- Bidder B bids $10.50 for 5 spoons.
- Bidder C bids $12.00 for 8 spoons.
- Bidders B and C will both pay $10.50 for the spoons.
- Bidder B will only get 2 spoons.
- Bidder C will get all 8 spoons.
- Bidder A will get no spoons since Bidders B and C zeroed out the quantity available.

UNDERSTANDING BID INCREMENTS

When free-bidding on an item, your bid can be anything greater than the current maximum bid (which you may only learn when you enter your own bid amount). You want to use common sense, however, and limit yourself to an amount that is not overly generous. Proxy bidding is different. The automatic increment that eBay uses to increase a bid amount is based on the dollar amount of the bidding in process. Table 3-1 contains the automatic bidding increments that eBay uses. In at least two circumstances, however, you may find that your bid increment is less. For example, if the difference between your maximum bid amount and the next highest bid amount is less than the increment, your winning bid would only be your maximum amount. Or, if your bid won and it was less than the reserve amount, and your maximum bid is more than the reserve amount, your bid would be increased only by the amount needed to meet the reserve amount.

AUTOMATIC INCREMENT	PRICE RANGE OF THE ITEM
$.05	$.01 to $.99
$.25	$1 to $4.99
$.50	$5 to $24.99
$1.00	$25 to $99.99
$2.50	$100 to $249.99
$5.00	$250 to $499.99
$10.00	$500 to $999.99
$25.00	$1000 to $2499.99
$50.00	$2500 to $4999.99
$100.00	$5000 and up

Table 3-1: Automatic Bid Increments

NOTE

Proxy bidding has several advantages. First, you do not have to stand by and closely monitor the auction. eBay makes sure you are the highest bidder until your maximum is reached. Second, you may pay far less than you are willing to pay, since the winning bid may be less than your maximum amount.

BID ON MULTIPLE ITEMS (FIXED-PRICE)

In a fixed-price or Buy It Now format, the seller sells all the items for a fixed price. Bidders enter the number of items they want at the given price. The copper spoons in the previous example would all sell for $10 each to bidders as long as the spoons last. When all the spoons are sold, the listing is over, whether the time has expired or not. You can also buy *lots* of goods, where you buy several of the same items for one price.

Use Proxy Bidding

The most common technique used in eBay is proxy bidding. With proxy bidding, you decide what the maximum amount is that you want to bid on an item (only you know what that amount is). Your bid will be entered at the least amount to be the highest bid at that time. If there are no bidders, your bid becomes the starting bid, even though this starting price may be well under your full bid or maximum amount. eBay will automatically keep you in the auction by bidding in increments until your maximum is reached. If your bid wins before your maximum is reached, you only have to pay the winning bid amount. See Chapter 4 for how to enter a proxy bid.

Use Free Bidding

Another technique, free bidding, is when you bid on an item for the moment. You are not entering the maximum you are willing to pay, but only what will win the current bid. This technique has several shortcomings, however. First, you cannot know what another bidder's maximum bid is, so even though you enter a bid higher than the current amount, it may be less than the maximum specified by another bidder. Second, you must keep reentering your bid rather than relying on eBay to bump up your bid, as it does in proxy bidding, so others will always be able to outbid you quicker than you can respond. You might do this if you only want to bid one amount or if you are unsure how high you want to bid.

Understand Grading and Authentication Services

eBay offers buyers (and sellers) a list of independent companies that help you determine if an item is in good condition and is what the seller says it is. This can increase your confidence that you are not being defrauded. You, as a buyer, pay a small fee to have the item investigated. You may want to have the item *graded* or *authenticated*. You can buy these services for stamps, trading cards, sports autographs and memorabilia, comics, coins, books, Beanie Babies, or jewelry, among other things. eBay, of course, does not guarantee that these services are valid, but they do represent that the companies listed are valid businesses that perform these services.

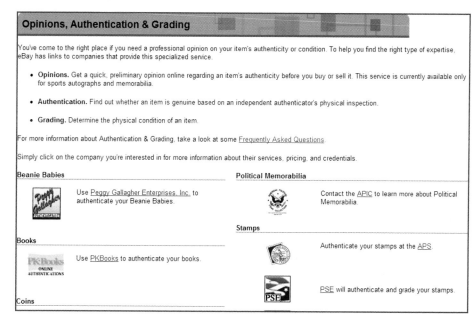

Figure 3-11: *A list of grading and authentication services can be found that will help ensure the validity or quality of an item.*

Find a Grading Service

When you ask someone to *grade* an item, you ask him or her to comment on its condition—what grade is a specific coin, for instance? Is it mint condition? Good? Poor? The grading system depends on what item is being graded, so coins would differ from antique furniture, for example. To find a grading service:

1. Click **My eBay** on the eBay header.

2. Scroll down the My eBay Views sidebar to Related Links. Click **Buying Resources**.

3. Under Services, click **Item Authentication**.

    Services:
    eBay Toolbar
    Item Authentication
    All About Escrow

4. On the Using Authentication And Grading Services, scroll down and click **View A List Of Companies**. A screen is displayed similar to that shown in Figure 3-11.

    View a list of companies that provide these services.

5. Scroll down, look for grading services, and click the company you are interested in.

Use Authentication Services

Authentication services verify that the item is genuine. The seller sends the stones you are interested in buying to a laboratory, such as International Gemological Information (IGI), which grades and appraises the stones, verifying that they are as advertised, and ships them directly to you, the buyer. These services are often already performed by sellers and are advertised in the listing descriptions.

Other services are available to you on-call. For instance, if you are interested in authenticating a book, you can pay a fee for an expert to examine the description of the item, review any photos, ask unanswered questions of the seller, and then issue an opinion to you within a period of time, such as 48 hours.

To find a list of companies that offer these services, follow the steps in "Find a Grading Service," and scroll to the type of service you need.

Use eBay Tools for Bidding Information

eBay offers the eBay Toolbar, which you can use to get information from eBay; eBay Anywhere Wireless, which you can use to receive alerts on your personal digital assistant (PDA) or cell phone; and Microsoft Alerts, which you can use to receive alerts on your computer.

Install eBay's Toolbar

The eBay Toolbar is free and is located on your Internet browser (Microsoft Internet Explorer 5.0, 6.0, or 7.0). The eBay Toolbar provides a quick way for you to search eBay, watch your bids, receive alerts if you are outbid or the bid is

over, and protect your account with the Account Guard feature (see Chapter 9 for more information on Account Guard). To install the eBay Toolbar:

1. Click **My eBay** on the eBay header. Scroll down the My eBay Views sidebar, and under Related Links, click **Download Tools**.

2. On the Download eBay Software page, click **eBay Toolbar**.

3. Click **Download Now**. You'll see a warning dialog box, asking if you want to run or save this file. Click **Run**. The toolbar setup program will execute.

> eBay Toolbar
> The n & improved eBay Toolbar
> Annoucements, the Community h
> features helps protect your eBay a

4. When you are asked if you want to run the software, click **Run**.

5. Read the privacy policy and terms and conditions, and click **I Agree**.

6. A screen is displayed, showing the eBay Toolbar loading. When it is finished, enter your User ID and password and accept or clear the check mark making Yahoo your default search engine. Click **Finish**.

7. Congratulations! Your New Toolbar Is Now Installed page is displayed, with the new eBay Toolbar, as shown in Figure 3-12.

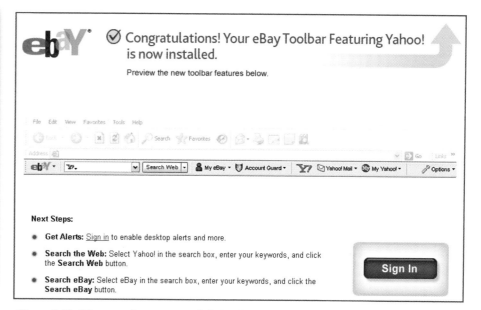

Figure 3-12: When you have successfully loaded the eBay Toolbar and signed in, you are given a quick overview of its features.

Use eBay's Toolbar for Bidding Information

When installed, eBay's Toolbar will be located on your Internet browser, as seen in Figure 3-13.

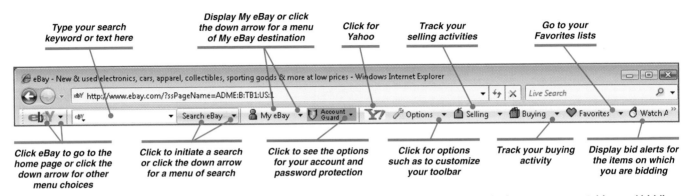

Type your search keyword or text here

Display My eBay or click the down arrow for a menu of My eBay destination

Click for Yahoo

Track your selling activities

Go to your Favorites lists

Click eBay to go to the home page or click the down arrow for other menu choices

Click to initiate a search or click the down arrow for a menu of search

Click to see the options for your account and password protection

Click for options such as to customize your toolbar

Track your buying activity

Display bid alerts for the items on which you are bidding

Figure 3-13: *The eBay Toolbar easily and quickly allows you to search eBay, receive alerts, and see the items you are watching and bidding on.*

NOTE

Your cell phone or PDA (with cell phone capability) must be able to send and receive text messages, which are simple e-mail messages. There may be a charge from your wireless service for this. To get text messages from eBay, you may also have to pay SMS (Simple Message System) charges.

Receive Wireless eBay Alerts

You can receive eBay alerts on a wireless device, such as an Internet-enabled PDA or a cell phone. In other words, you never need to wonder what is happening with your eBay bids (or sale items). You can receive notices:

● When someone outbids you on an active listing.

● When an auction ends and you learn whether you have won or not.

● When a buyer pays for your item.

● Of reminders for listing confirmations, bids made on your item, status reports for auctions you are participating in as buyer or seller, and items you are watching.

TIP

To remove or hide the eBay Toolbar, in Internet Explorer, click **Tools** and then click **Toolbars** on the menu. Click **eBay Toolbar** to deselect it. (In Internet Explorer 5.0 or 6.0, click **View** and then click **Toolbars** to find the toolbar options.)

To instruct eBay to send messages to your wireless device:

1. Click **My eBay** on the eBay header or on the eBay Toolbar.

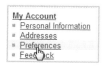

My Account
Personal Information
Addresses
Preferences
Feedback

2. On the My eBay View sidebar, under My Account, click **Preferences**.
3. Click **Show** under Notification Preferences, Notification Delivery.

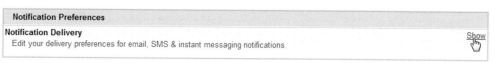

Notification Preferences
Notification Delivery
Edit your delivery preferences for email, SMS & instant messaging notifications.
Show

4. You may need to sign in again to eBay since you are changing personal information.
5. Under Mobile Phone Number For SMS Alerts, click **Add**. The eBay Text Messaging (SMS) Alerts page is displayed, as shown in Figure 3-14.

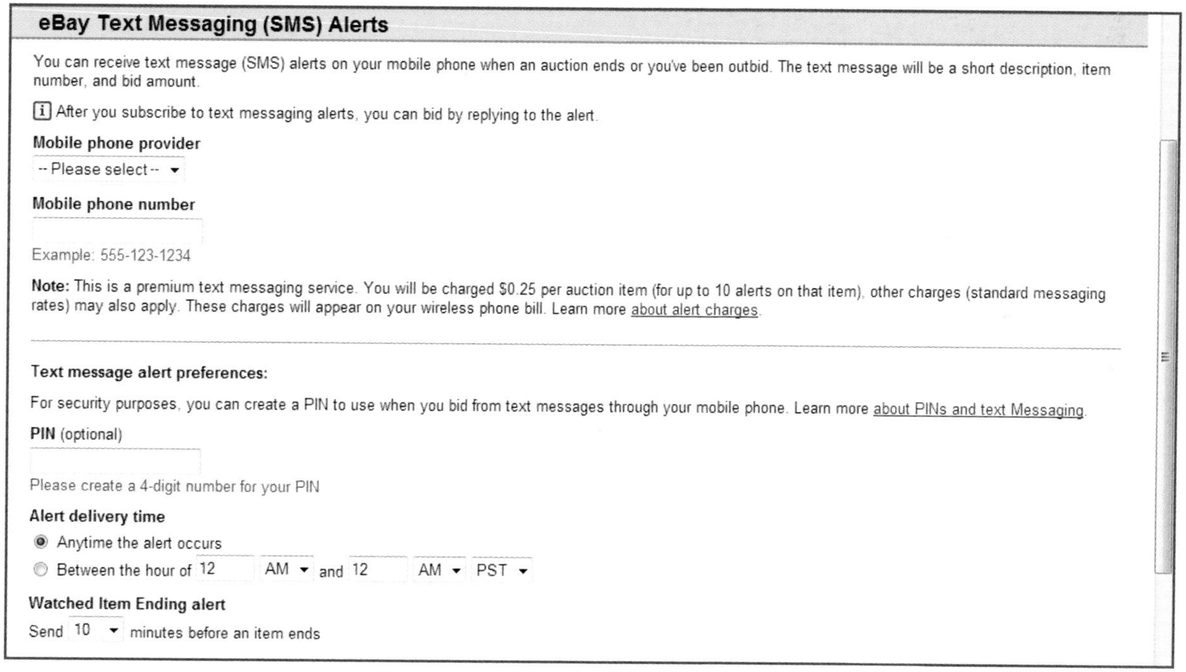

eBay Text Messaging (SMS) Alerts
You can receive text message (SMS) alerts on your mobile phone when an auction ends or you've been outbid. The text message will be a short description, item number, and bid amount.
After you subscribe to text messaging alerts, you can bid by replying to the alert.
Mobile phone provider
-- Please select --
Mobile phone number
Example: 555-123-1234
Note: This is a premium text messaging service. You will be charged $0.25 per auction item (for up to 10 alerts on that item), other charges (standard messaging rates) may also apply. These charges will appear on your wireless phone bill. Learn more about alert charges.
Text message alert preferences:
For security purposes, you can create a PIN to use when you bid from text messages through your mobile phone. Learn more about PINs and text Messaging.
PIN (optional)
Please create a 4-digit number for your PIN
Alert delivery time
Anytime the alert occurs
Between the hour of 12 AM and 12 AM PST
Watched Item Ending alert
Send 10 minutes before an item ends

***Figure 3-14:** You can set eBay text messages to be sent to your Internet-enabled wireless device.*

NOTE

To find all the messaging opportunities available to you, click **Site Map** on the eBay header. Under Buying Resources, click **Wireless**. You will see a page, shown in Figure 3-15, summarizing your choices and sign up buttons to immediately install the options.

QUICKSTEPS

USING INSTANT MESSAGING

You can receive eBay messages on your desktop from AOL, Yahoo!, and Microsoft Messenger services. To sign up for eBay Instant Messaging Alerts:

1. Follow the steps in "Receive Wireless eBay Alerts," and click **Add** next to Instant Message (IM) Alerts instead of Mobile Phone Number For SMS Alerts.

Mobile phone number for SMS alerts	Not subscribed	Add
Instant message (IM) alerts	Not subscribed	Add

2. On the eBay Instant Message (IM) Alerts page, click the **Select IM Messaging Provider** button that applies to you.

   Select Instant Messaging provider:
   - ● Skype
   - ○ AOL
   - ○ Windows Live™
   - ○ Yahoo!

3. Click **Continue**.

4. If you have a messaging account, sign in and click **Sign Up** for the message service. Follow the prompts to send alerts to your e-mail address or to create a new account.

5. When you have finished, your eBay notifications will be changed.

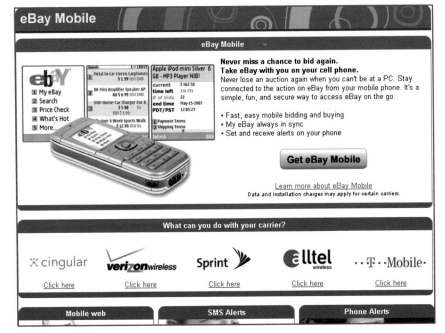

Figure 3-15: *You can sign up for a Mobile Web for eBay on small screens, SMS text messaging alert, and phone alerts.*

6. Click the **Mobile Phone Provider** down arrow. Click a name from the list.

7. Type the mobile phone number.

8. If you want to add additional security to your text messages, type a four-digit pin number in the PIN text box. This is optional.

9. Click the **Alert Delivery Time** buttons that apply to you:
   - Click **Anytime The Alert Occurs** to have a message sent whenever the activity occurs.
   - Click **Between The Hour Of** and fill in the hourly range of when you want to receive the messages.

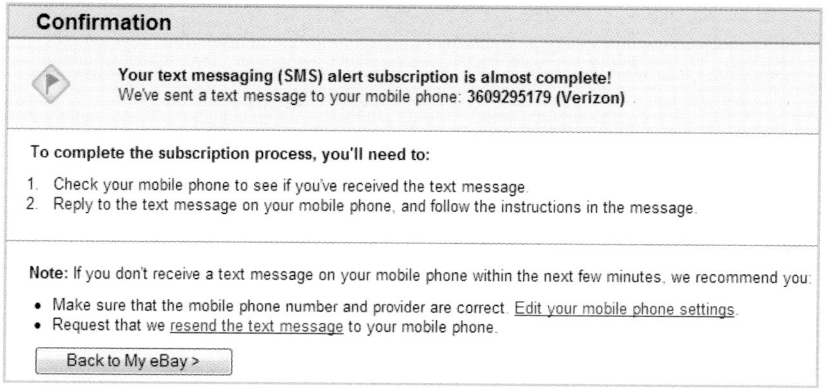

Confirmation

⬦ **Your text messaging (SMS) alert subscription is almost complete!**
We've sent a text message to your mobile phone: 3609295179 (Verizon) .

To complete the subscription process, you'll need to:

1. Check your mobile phone to see if you've received the text message.
2. Reply to the text message on your mobile phone, and follow the instructions in the message.

Note: If you don't receive a text message on your mobile phone within the next few minutes, we recommend you:

- Make sure that the mobile phone number and provider are correct. Edit your mobile phone settings.
- Request that we resend the text message to your mobile phone.

[Back to My eBay >]

10. Under Watched Item Ending Alert, type the number of minutes before an item ends that you want to be alerted.

11. Click **Submit**.

12. On the Confirmation page, you will see that a message has been sent to your mobile phone number. Reply to the text message and follow the instructions in it.

13. Click **Back To My eBay**.

Chapter 4
Making a Purchase

This chapter leads you through the process of actually bidding on an item in eBay, whether it is a fixed-price item, a Buy It Now item, a straightforward auction item, or a live-auction item. You will also see how to track bids, maintaining awareness of them in My eBay until you are ready to bid. You will see how to register for PayPal, or pay for your purchases in a variety of ways. Your transaction is not complete, however, until you receive your package, assess it, and give feedback to the seller. This chapter focuses on those things as well.

Buy or Bid on a Purchase

You have found the item you want to buy, have researched its condition and price, asked the seller questions, and satisfied yourself that you are now ready to bid. You may want to track the item for a while until the time is right to bid, and then you may bid by proxy, on a regular auction item, on a Dutch auction (multiple-item auction), or on a Buy It Now item. First, however, you'll want to double-check that the item is what you want.

Review the Item Listing

When you are preparing to bid, you want to find the item description.

1. Using whatever means fits your search, find the item:
   - You can search through the categories, as explained in Chapter 1.
   - You can use the Search feature, as discussed in Chapter 2.
   - A friend can alert you to the item.
   - You can find it by watching similar items.
   - You might have a passion for collecting the item.

2. In the View Item page scroll to the description, and verify that it is what you want. A sample listing description is shown in Figure 4-1.

3. Examine the price, the shipping and handling information, and the insurance information. Decide how you will pay for it. A sample of shipping and payment details is shown in Figure 4-2.

4. When you are ready to purchase, click **Place Bid** or **Buy It Now**, depending on the listing.

Watch Interesting Items with My eBay and the eBay Toolbar

When you are hot on the trail of an interesting item, you might want to watch it awhile. Or, you might want to monitor items on which you have placed a bid as the auction end grows near. You can track activity using the eBay Toolbar or My eBay. To use the eBay Toolbar, you first need to set your eBay Toolbar options.

Bob the buyer figures out what the shipping and handling charges will be before bidding. He doesn't want any last-minute surprises!

NOTE

You may be able to enter your ZIP code into a Calculate Shipping tool so that you will know exactly how much to pay for shipping.

Figure 4-1: Carefully examine the listing description for as much information about the item as you can get.

Shipping and handling

Ships to
Worldwide

Country: United States ▼	Zip or postal code: 98060	Update

Shipping and Handling	To	Service
US $8.25	98060, United States	US Postal Service Priority Mail® Estimated delivery 2-3 days*

*Sellers are not responsible for service transit time. This information is provided by the carrier and excludes weekends and holidays. Note that transit times may vary, particularly during peak periods.

Shipping insurance
Included (in the shipping and handling cost)

Return policy

Item must be returned within:	3 Days
Refund will be given as:	Money Back
Return policy details:	Since most of our merchandise is on consignment, returns will be determined on an individual basis and are for purchase price only. Shipping, handling and insurance fees are not refundable.

Figure 4-2: Pay careful attention to the shipping and handling information, making sure it is clear and complete.

SET eBAY TOOLBAR OPTIONS

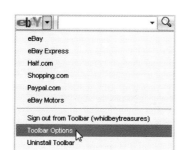

1. On the eBay Toolbar, click the **eBay** down arrow to open the menu. (You have to be signed in first.)

2. Click **Toolbar Options**. The eBay Toolbar Options dialog box is displayed.

3. If not already selected, click the **Display Preferences** tab as shown in Figure 4-3.

   - Set the Search options to search by title, title and description, or item number. Type the number of searches to be included in the Recent Searches list.

   - Select the time format that you want. You can choose between viewing the time the item will end versus the time left before it ends. You can choose **eBay Official Time**, noted in military format, or **My Local Time**, noted in 12-hour blocks.

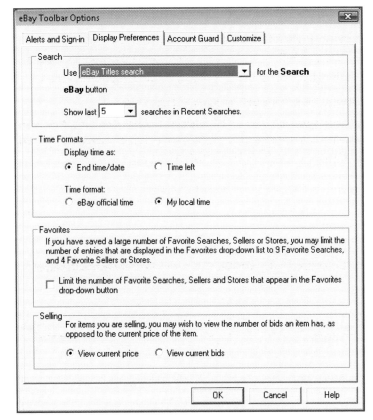

Figure 4-3: The Display Preferences tab of the Toolbar Options page is where you set the timing and mode of buying alerts, selling alerts, and general settings for the timing and display of alerts.

- You can set a Favorites option to limit the number of favorite searches, sellers, or categories that display when you click the Favorites down arrow.
- When viewing items you are selling, you can set the Selling option to display the current price, or you may want to see the current bids.

4. Click **OK** to retain your settings.

USE THE eBAY TOOLBAR TO TRACK ACTIVITY

1. Install the eBay Toolbar, as described in Chapter 3.

2. Sign in by clicking **eBay** and then clicking **Sign In For Advanced Features**. Enter your User ID and password, and click **Sign In Securely**.

3. On the Toolbar, select the following to immediately see your eBay activity:

- Click **My eBay** to display your My eBay page.
- Click **Selling** to display your selling activity (what you have scheduled to sell, what you're selling, what you've sold in the past seven days, and what remains unsold).
- Click **Buying** to see your buying activity (what you are watching, bidding on, have won, and didn't win) and to leave feedback.
- Click **Favorites** to see a list of your favorite searches and sellers.
- Click **Alerts** to see a list of the alerts that are currently active.
- Click **Options** and click the **Customize** tab to change the buttons in the eBay Toolbar.

USE MY eBAY TO TRACK ACTIVITY

1. Click **My eBay** from the eBay Toolbar or from the eBay header.

2. Under the My eBay Views sidebar, click **All Buying** to see a page of all your buying activities: Watching, Bidding, Bid Assistant items, Best Offers, Won, or Didn't Win. You can scroll down the page to see individual views. (See Chapter 1 for information on setting preferences and changing the display in My eBay.) You can also click the links to Watching, Bidding, Best Offers, Won, or Didn't Win to see the individual views.

My eBay Views

My Summary

All Buying
- Watching (29)
- Bidding
- Bid Assistant NEW!
- Best Offers
- Won (7)
- Didn't Win (3)

Make a Proxy Bid

The basic bid type in an auction format is a proxy bid. You tell eBay the maximum amount you are willing to bid for an item, and eBay applies the bid for you in increments against other bidders until your maximum is reached.

1. On the View Item page, click **Place Bid**, as shown in Figure 4-4.

2. On the Place Bid page, type the maximum bid amount, and click **Continue**. Note that eBay tells you what the current bid amount is at and the required increment so you will know what your bid must be in order to be entered into the auction.

3. A summary of your bid is displayed in the Review And Confirm page, as shown in Figure 4-5. If you accept it, click **Confirm Bid**. A confirmation message is displayed that you are now the high bidder.

NOTE

If you submit a bid that is not high enough or that does not meet the reserve price, you will see a message to that effect. You then have an opportunity to increase your maximum bid amount.

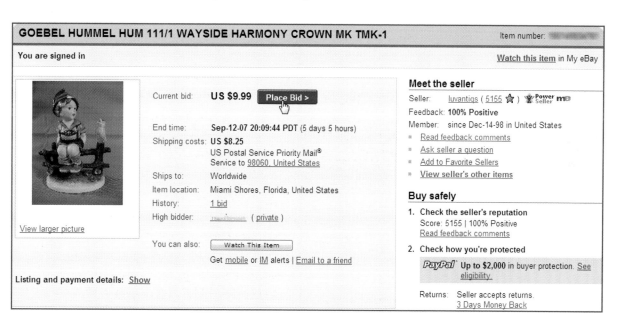

Figure 4-4: The View Item page is where you can bid for the item.

eBay QuickSteps   *Making a Purchase*   **71**

Figure 4-5: When you submit a bid, you review your bid summary before entering your payment options.

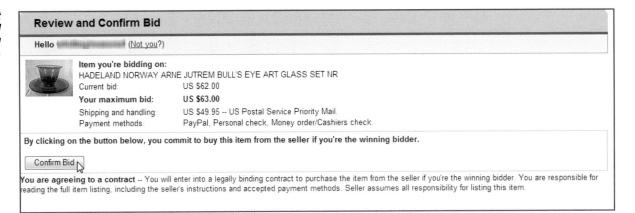

Review and Confirm Bid

Hello ▓▓▓▓▓▓▓▓▓▓ (Not you?)

Item you're bidding on:
HADELAND NORWAY ARNE JUTREM BULL'S EYE ART GLASS SET NR
Current bid: US $62.00
Your maximum bid: **US $63.00**
Shipping and handling: US $49.95 -- US Postal Service Priority Mail.
Payment methods: PayPal, Personal check, Money order/Cashiers check.

By clicking on the button below, you commit to buy this item from the seller if you're the winning bidder.

[Confirm Bid]

You are agreeing to a contract -- You will enter into a legally binding contract to purchase the item from the seller if you're the winning bidder. You are responsible for reading the full item listing, including the seller's instructions and accepted payment methods. Seller assumes all responsibility for listing this item.

TIP

If you are the winning bidder, you will receive an e-mail notifying you of this, providing information about the finances of the transaction and a link to the site.

Bid for Multiple Items

The item shown in Figure 4-6 is an example of a Dutch auction for multiple items. Once you have asked questions and gotten answers to any questions you may have, you can place a bid.

1. Click the **Place Bid** button on the View Item page. The Place Bid page is displayed.

2. Type the maximum price you want to bid and the quantity of items you want, and click **Continue**.

Current bid: US $3.25
Quantity: 3 available

Your maximum bid: US $ [   ] (Enter US $3.25 **or more**)
Your quantity: x 1

[Continue >]

3. A summary of your bid is displayed on the Review And Confirm Bid page. If you are satisfied with the amount, click **Confirm Bid**.

4. Complete payment as directed.

Bid to "Buy It Now"

There are two types of Buy It Now listings: fixed-priced format and auction format.

SILVER Roosevelt Dime coins

You are signed in

View larger picture

Starting bid: US $3.25   [Place Bid >]

End time: **4 hours 48 mins** (May-01-07 00:21:20 PDT)
Shipping costs: Check item description and payment instructions or contact seller for details
Ships to: Worldwide
Item location: United States
Quantity: 3 available
History: Bidders list

You can also: [Watch This Item]
                 Get alerts via Text message, IM or Cell phone
                 Email to a friend

Listing and payment details: Show

Figure 4-6: The multiple-item format allows you to buy a quantity of items for a common bid price.

BUY IT NOW (FIXED-PRICE FORMAT)

With the Buy It Now fixed-price format, an item is sold at a fixed price. The reserve price and the Buy It Now price are the same. There is no auction. This is similar to buying an item in a regular store or its online Web site. The advantage is that you know how much you will pay and you get the item right now.

Beautiful Turquoise Cuff and Ring Set!!!   *Buy It Now* $249.95 $6.35   22d 19h 21m

1. When you find the item you want in the listings, click it to look at the item description.

2. Review the item description, investigate the seller, and do all the other tasks to assure yourself that this is a good deal.

   Buy It Now price: US $249.95   **Buy It Now >**

3. Click the **Buy It Now** button.

4. If the seller has more than one of this item to sell, you may be asked to enter a quantity.

5. On the Review And Commit To Buy page, verify the item purchase price and shipping and handling amounts. If you are satisfied, click **Commit To Buy**, as shown in Figure 4-7.

6. Follow the prompts to complete paying for the item. See "Pay for Your Purchase" later in the chapter.

BUY IT NOW OR BEST OFFER

A Buy It Now or Best Offer allows you to either immediately buy the item now or present a best offer price. The offer must be accepted by the seller within 48 hours or the bid will expire.

1. Click the item link to display the listing. A page similar to that shown in Figure 4-8 is displayed.

Classic Hungarian Cookbook, Culinary Arts Institute, VG   *Buy It Now or Best Offer* $5.00 $2.00   5d 11h 03m

---

NOTE

In order to purchase a Buy It Now item, you must have feedback greater than 0, have a credit/debit card on file, or be ID Verified.

NOTE

With a Buy It Now auction format, there is a beginning Buy It Now amount, and you can buy the item for that amount without going through an auction. There may be a beginning bid amount set by the seller (an amount that is less than the Buy It Now price); however, the option to buy it for that fixed amount goes away when the first bid is placed, unless the bid is less than a reserve amount set by the seller. The item is now sold at the highest bid price, which can be less than or more than the original Buy It Now price. (Note that eBay is reconsidering how the BIN option goes away when a lesser bid is placed.)

PITCHER Criss Cross Crosscross Hazel Atlas depression   *Buy It Now* **$250.00** **$275.00** $15.50   5m

Current bid   ***Buy It Now price***   ***Shipping and handling cost***

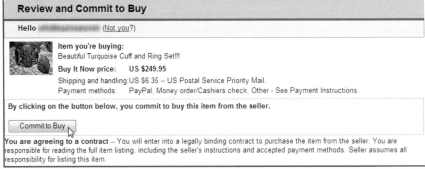

Figure 4-7: You are given an opportunity to review the purchase details before you commit to buy it.

Figure 4-8: You can choose between offering your own best price or paying the Buy It Now price to purchase a Buy It Now or Best Offer format item.

 **NOTE**

Buying in an eBay Store is just like buying on eBay.com. Stores offer auctions, Buy It Now, and combined formats. The advantage of using eBay Stores is that you are dealing with a known and experienced source. To display the eBay Stores page, click **Stores** in the eBay header.

2. Click **Buy It Now** to buy the item immediately, or click **Make Offer** to offer your own price.

3. The steps that follow will depend on your choice. Refer to "Buy It Now (Fixed-Price Format)" to see the steps if you choose Buy It Now. If you click **Make Offer**, you'll see the Best Offer: Submit A Best Offer page.

4. Under Send Your Best Offer Now, type an amount in the Your Offer Price text box, and click **Review Offer**.

5. In the Best Offer: Review And Commit page, look over your offer, and if the price and terms are acceptable, click **Commit Best Offer**.

6. Your best offer will be submitted, as shown in Figure 4-9.

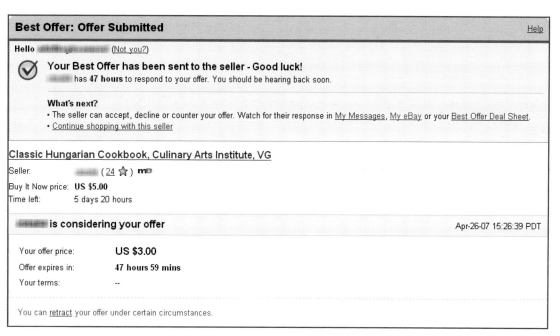

Best Offer: Offer Submitted   Help

Hello ▓▓▓▓▓▓ (Not you?)

✓ **Your Best Offer has been sent to the seller - Good luck!**
▓▓▓ has **47 hours** to respond to your offer. You should be hearing back soon.

What's next?
• The seller can accept, decline or counter your offer. Watch for their response in My Messages, My eBay or your Best Offer Deal Sheet.
• Continue shopping with this seller

Classic Hungarian Cookbook, Culinary Arts Institute, VG

Seller: ▓▓▓▓ (24 ☆) me
Buy It Now price: **US $5.00**
Time left: 5 days 20 hours

▓▓▓▓▓ is considering your offer   Apr-26-07 15:26:39 PDT

Your offer price: **US $3.00**
Offer expires in: **47 hours 59 mins**
Your terms: --

You can retract your offer under certain circumstances.

Figure 4-9: When you submit a Best Offer, the seller can accept, counter, or reject it, or just wait until the offer expires in 48 hours.

Participate in Live Auctions

Selected auction houses are making their live auctions available on eBay. These auctions are scheduled at particular times, and you can join in, either as a spectator or as a bidder, on lots (in a live auction, a *lot* is the same as an item). The following sections explain the steps you go through to bid in a live auction.

FIND LIVE AUCTIONS

1. From the home page, click **Site Map** in the eBay header.

2. Under Categories, click **eBay Live Auctions** to see its home page, as shown in Figure 4-10:

Marketplace Research
eBay Pulse
Giving Works (Charity)
Live Auctions
Revi[ ]s & Guides

● Click **Start Here** to learn how to navigate live auctions.

● Under Categories, click the link to see auctions containing items in the category you want.

welcome
New Users
START HERE

Figure 4-10: With eBay live auctions, you can bid in real-time auctions conducted around the world.

• Under Upcoming Auctions, click a link to see catalogs for these types of auctions.

• On the Live Auction Catalogs page, click **View All Lots (Items) In This Auction**. Browse through the lots until you find one you want to bid on or view.

VIEW A LIVE AUCTION

On the eBay Live Auctions home page:

1. Click **View Live** to the right of the live auction you want to view. A window opens, displaying the auctioned item, as shown in Figure 4-11.

2. If you want to bid, sign in to the auction house by clicking **Click Here To Participate**, as shown in Figure 4-11.

PLACE AN ABSENTEE BID

Before a live auction is opened, you can enter an absentee bid. eBay will gather all the absentee bids, and when the bidding starts, the highest absentee bid will be used like a proxy bid against the live bidders.

1. From the eBay Live Auctions home page, find the catalog containing the lot you want. Click the name of the catalog link.

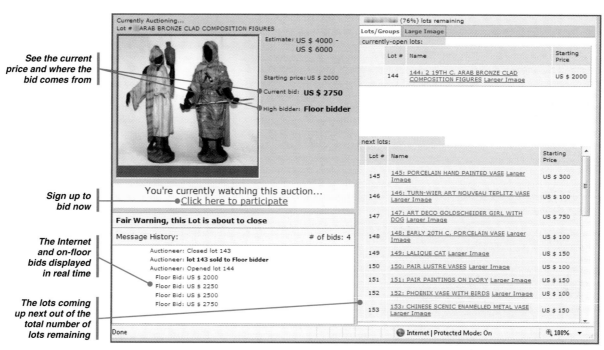

See the current price and where the bid comes from

Sign up to bid now

The Internet and on-floor bids displayed in real time

The lots coming up next out of the total number of lots remaining

Figure 4-11: *The lot being auctioned is displayed, as well as the bid history. You can sign up to bid from this window.*

2. On the catalog pages, find the lots you want to bid on, and click the name of the lots. You may have to first sign in to eBay, accept terms and conditions of the auction, agree to a transfer to third-party authorization, and go through categories or subcategories to find the items.

3. When you find an item, click its name. The description page is displayed, an example of which is shown in Figure 4-12.

4. To place an absentee bid on the item, click **Place Absentee Bid**.

5. In the Place Absentee Bid area, type your maximum amount in the text box. It must be greater than the starting bid above it. Click **Continue**.

6. Follow the instructions as eBay leads you through the process of completing the bid.

LEARNING ABOUT LIVE AUCTIONS

Bidding in a live auction involves learning some new terminology and techniques. You are no longer bidding against other online bidders over a period of days, but are bidding online in a real-time auction, conducted on the floor of an actual auction house:

- Live auctions are organized into *categories*, or themes, of the auctions being held, such as Art, Jewelry & Timepieces, Collectibles & Memorabilia, or Wine, so that you can limit yourself to those live auctions dealing with the items you want.

- Items for a particular auction are listed within a *catalog*, which you can browse during or before the auction is held. Catalogs often follow a theme or category

- Once you have determined your category, you *browse* the catalog looking for interesting items called *lots*. A lot may consist of one or more items that are sold together in a group. Bids are for the whole lot.

- You'll want to learn what the *buyer's premium* is for the auction on which you are planning to bid. The buyer's premium is a percentage of the final price that the auctioneer charges the buyer.

- You can place an *absentee bid* on a lot. An absentee bid allows you to bid before the auction starts. When the auction starts, the highest absentee bid acts like a proxy bid against the live bidders.

Continued . . .

CATEGORIES

- Antiques & Decorative Arts
- Art
- Automotive
- Books & Manuscripts
- Business & Industrial
- Clothing, Shoes & Accessories
- Coins
- Collectibles & Memorabilia
- Dolls & Toys
- Entertainment
- Jewelry & Timepieces

Starts at: US $70.00   **Place Absentee Bid >**

Sign Up before this auction begins.

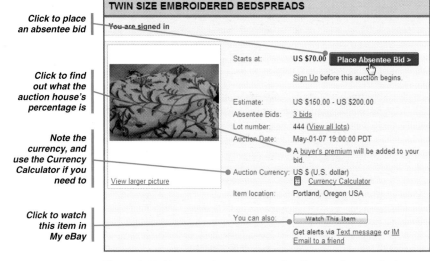

Click to place an absentee bid

Click to find out what the auction house's percentage is

Note the currency, and use the Currency Calculator if you need to

Click to watch this item in My eBay

Figure 4-12: *You can sign up to watch a live auction on the lot description form or cast an absentee bid.*

SIGN UP TO BID IN A LIVE AUCTION

1. From the eBay Live Auctions home page, click **Bid Now**, or, from the Live View window, click **Click Here To Participate**.

   You're currently watching this auction...
   Click here to participate

2. You may be asked to enter your User ID and password.

3. You must review the seller's terms and conditions. Note the premium to be paid and any other charges. Click **I Have Read The Auction House's Terms And Conditions Of Sale And Accept Them**. Click **Continue**.

4. At this point, you may encounter a Seller Authorization Required page, which some sellers require. In this case, you need to fill out a form, review one already presented with your information, or contact the seller for permission to participate in this auction.

5. The Start Bidding Now page is displayed. Click **Continue** to participate in the auction. The active real-time auction will be displayed.

6. To bid, click **Bid Now**.

- During the auction, you can bid or just view the action on the floor.

- Be aware that at least 11 different auction currencies may be used, and not necessarily U.S. dollars, since the auctions are conducted throughout the world. You will be charged the price of the lot; a premium for the auction house (such as 15 to 20 percent); sales tax, when appropriate; customs; shipping and handling; and any other charges determined by the auction house. Check the charges on each lot description.

- Before the auction starts, you can see *corrigenda* (an addendum to printed matter correcting errors), listing lots that have been added or removed from the auction. Click **Urgent Updates** to see these.

TIP

You may see that you are the high bidder and your bid placed in the bid history. If not, it will be because someone else bid first and faster with an equal or larger bid.

NOTE

During an auction, you may see a "Fair Warning" label as a lot approaches its closing. This reminds you that you must bid soon if you want the lot.

BID IN A LIVE AUCTION

You have to be quick in a live auction. The Bid Now button also carries the amount you are bidding. Since in a live auction the amount of the next bid is predetermined, you don't have a choice as to the amount you will bid, only the timing. You'll see your bid in the Message History text pane.

1. After you have signed in to participate in a live auction, look at the Bid Now button and amount of the current bid.

2. When you are ready, click **Bid Now *currency and price***, shown in Figure 4-13, to place a bid against other Internet bidders and those on the auction house floor. Your bid will be immediately placed. You may see your bid pass through the Message History pane along with other Internet and floor bids. You can see that the next bid amount is already calculated as soon you click the Bid Now button.

> Bid Now:
> US $ 220

3. When you are finished with the live auction, click **eBay** on the header to return to eBay.com.

Retract a Bid

Under some conditions, you can retract a bid. There are both timing conditions and reasons why the bid is being retracted that need to be considered (see the "Retracting a Bid" QuickFacts). To retract a bid:

1. On the View Item page, click the **History Bid *n*** link, and scroll down below the Bidder list to You Can Retract Your Bid Under Certain Circumstances Only.

> If you and another bidder placed the same bid amount, the earlier bid takes priority.
> You can retract your bid under certain circumstances only.

2. Click **Retract Your Bid**. (Note that you cannot retract a Buy It Now purchase.)

3. You may have to enter your eBay User ID and password. The Bid Retractions page is displayed. It explains the reasons and seriousness of retracting a bid.

4. Scroll down the Bid Retraction page, and type the amount in the Item Number Of Auction In Question text box.

5. Click the **Your Explanation Of The Retraction** down arrow, and select a reason for the retraction from the menu.

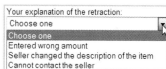

6. Click **Retract Bid**.

Figure 4-13: The Bid Now US $ area tells you how much the next bid will be.

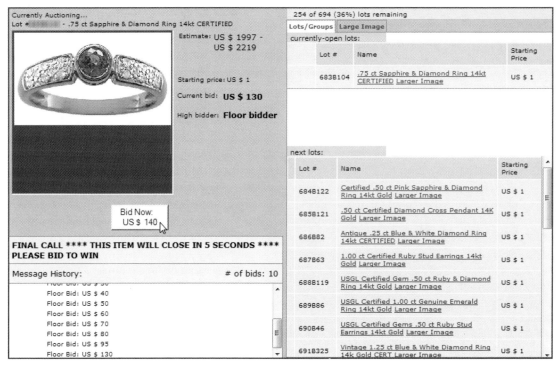

Currently Auctioning...
Lot # ░░░░ - .75 ct Sapphire & Diamond Ring 14kt CERTIFIED

Estimate: US $ 1997 - US $ 2219

Starting price: US $ 1

Current bid: **US $ 130**

High bidder: **Floor bidder**

Bid Now: US $ 140

FINAL CALL ** THIS ITEM WILL CLOSE IN 5 SECONDS ****
PLEASE BID TO WIN**

Message History: # of bids: 10

Floor Bid: US $ 30
Floor Bid: US $ 40
Floor Bid: US $ 50
Floor Bid: US $ 60
Floor Bid: US $ 70
Floor Bid: US $ 80
Floor Bid: US $ 95
Floor Bid: US $ 130

254 of 694 (36%) lots remaining

Lots/Groups | Large Image

currently-open lots:

Lot #	Name	Starting Price
683B104	.75 ct Sapphire & Diamond Ring 14kt CERTIFIED Larger Image	US $ 1

next lots:

Lot #	Name	Starting Price
684B122	Certified .50 ct Pink Sapphire & Diamond Ring 14kt Gold Larger Image	US $ 1
685B121	.50 ct Certified Diamond Cross Pendant 14K Gold Larger Image	US $ 1
686B82	Antique .25 ct Blue & White Diamond Ring 14kt CERTIFIED Larger Image	US $ 1
687B63	1.00 ct Certified Ruby Stud Earrings 14kt Gold Larger Image	US $ 1
688B119	USGL Certified Gem .50 ct Ruby & Diamond Ring 14kt Gold Larger Image	US $ 1
689B86	USGL Certified 1.00 ct Genuine Emerald Ring 14kt Gold Larger Image	US $ 1
690B46	USGL Certified Gems .50 ct Ruby Stud Earrings 14kt Gold Larger Image	US $ 1
691B325	Vintage 1.25 ct Blue & White Diamond Ring 14k Gold CERT Larger Image	US $ 1

NOTE

Bids are accepted from both online bidders and bidders present on the floor. If there are two bids placed for the same amount, the auctioneer recognizes the bid that was placed first. So if you have a bid that is the same as the highest, but you are not the highest bidder, it is because someone else beat you to that bid amount.

QUICK**FACTS**

UNDERSTANDING A BID RETRACTION

Retracting a bid is considered to be an exception. It is generally not permitted.

CONSEQUENCES OF RETRACTING A BID

Retracting bids is a serious matter, and eBay may investigate in some cases where you have several retractions within the last six months, where bids are continuously retracted during the last 24 hours (could be *bid shilling*, which is trying to raise the bid amount), or where a seller has complained. If you are found guilty of

Continued . . .

Talk to the Seller

After you have purchased an item, you may or may not need to talk to the seller. The seller will know you are the winner and will have your address information. If you don't receive your items, or if you have a question about the delivery, however, you may need to contact the seller.

1. On the View Item page (you can find links to the item in your My eBay Items I've Won view, e-mails, and other notifications), click **Ask Seller A Question** in the Meet The Seller area, or click **Contact Member** in the member's Feedback Profile page.

2. The My Messages: Ask A Question page is displayed, similar to that shown in Figure 4-14. Type your question in the text box.

Meet the seller

Seller: ░░░░░ (5155 ☆) ⭐ Power Seller me

Feedback: **100% Positive**

Member: since Dec-14-98 in United States

- Read feedback comments
- Ask seller a question
- Add to Favorite Sellers

Figure 4-14: You can contact the seller during or after a transaction to clarify terms, resolve issues, or discuss other topics related to the transaction.

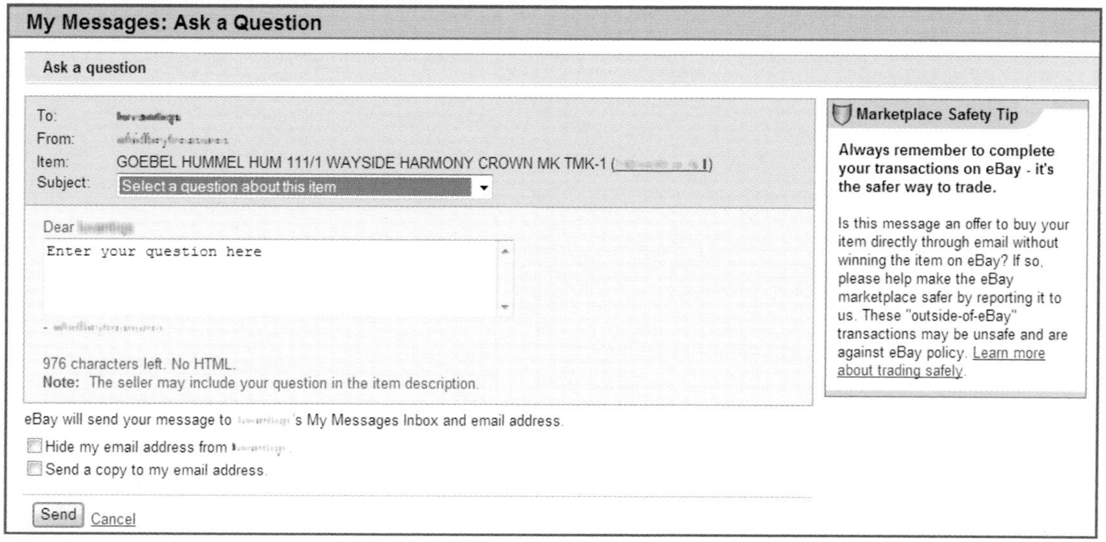

My Messages: Ask a Question

Ask a question

To:
From:
Item: GOEBEL HUMMEL HUM 111/1 WAYSIDE HARMONY CROWN MK TMK-1 ( )
Subject: Select a question about this item

Dear

Enter your question here

976 characters left. No HTML.
Note: The seller may include your question in the item description.

eBay will send your message to   's My Messages Inbox and email address.

☐ Hide my email address from
☐ Send a copy to my email address.

Send Cancel

Marketplace Safety Tip

Always remember to complete your transactions on eBay - it's the safer way to trade.

Is this message an offer to buy your item directly through email without winning the item on eBay? If so, please help make the eBay marketplace safer by reporting it to us. These "outside-of-eBay" transactions may be unsafe and are against eBay policy. Learn more about trading safely.

QUICKFACTS

UNDERSTANDING A BID RETRACTION (Continued)

misusing the retraction feature, your eBay account can be suspended and the number of bid retractions over the past six months will be displayed with your feedback.

TIMING CONSIDERATIONS

- You can retract a bid if there are more than 12 hours until the auction ends. In this case, all of your bids for the listing are retracted.

- You cannot retract a bid if there are fewer than 12 hours left in the auction unless the seller agrees (see Chapter 7 for more information).

- Within the last 12 hours until the auction ends and within one hour of placing your bid, you can retract a bid, and only that bid will be retracted. If you have other bids in the auction, including any during those last 12 hours, they will remain.

Continued . . .

3. Click the **Send A Copy To My E-mail Address** check box if you want a copy too.

4. Click **Send**.

Pay for Your Purchase

When you win a bid, you are sent a congratulatory e-mail/invoice confirming what you have purchased, as shown in Figure 4-15. You must first determine how you will pay for the item. How you pay depends upon what the seller allows. He or she may accept cashier's or personal checks, credit cards, money orders, or PayPal. You will have to arrange your payment according to what he or she accepts and how you want to pay. eBay may help facilitate payment, or you may handle it directly with the seller.

Pay by PayPal

PayPal uses eBay as an intermediary between the buyer and the seller. You provide your bank account or credit card information to eBay, and it pays for your purchases, per your directions, and deposits any refunds into your account. The seller will never know any of your banking or credit account information.

QUICK**FACTS**

UNDERSTANDING A BID RETRACTION *(Continued)*

REASONING CONSIDERATIONS

You can cancel a bid for these reasons:

- The description of the listing has changed so that it is no longer what you want. It must be a substantial change, such as a change in the quality or color perhaps.

- You have entered an incorrect bid amount. In this case, you must first retract the bid, and then reenter the correct bid amount at once.

- You have a question about the item but you cannot contact the seller by e-mail or telephone. This is not about the seller not answering the e-mail or phone, but that the e-mail is returned as undeliverable or the phone number is incorrect.

NOTE

The seller may accept some payments that are not automatically displayed on the eBay-generated form, so be sure to look at the seller's payment description to see if there are payment methods not automatically shown.

NOTE

There are some limitations to the PayPal Buyer Protection program. For instance, the program only covers tangible goods paid for using PayPal within 45 days of paying for the item; it covers items that were not received or that were not the same as the description advertised; and you can only file two claims per year.

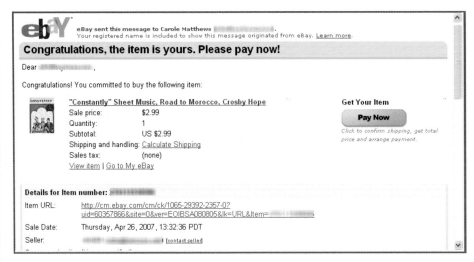

Figure 4-15: A congratulatory e-mail not only reminds you to pay for your new purchase, but also provides you with the options to pay for it.

Using PayPal to pay for your purchases is the recommended way to go: the seller is paid instantaneously, and you will get your item sooner. Also, PayPal offers a Buyer Protection feature that insures your eBay purchases from $200 (the basic) to $2,000 (top tier). This range protection can be for up to $2,000 under certain circumstances, for example if you, the buyer, purchased the item on eBay and paid with PayPal. The seller must be a Verified Premier or Verified Business account holder (see Chapter 6), have feedback of at least 50 of which 98 percent is positive, use PayPal, and be from an accepted country.

1. On the congratulatory e-mail you receive from eBay, click **Pay Now** to link to the payment procedure.

   –Or–

   On the View Item page, click **Pay Now**, as shown in Figure 4-16. You may have to sign in to eBay at this point.

2. The **Review Your Purchase From *sellerID*** page is displayed, confirming where the item should be sent and how much you must pay:

   - First, you will see where the item is to be shipped. If this is incorrect, click **Change Shipping Address**, and make the appropriate adjustments.

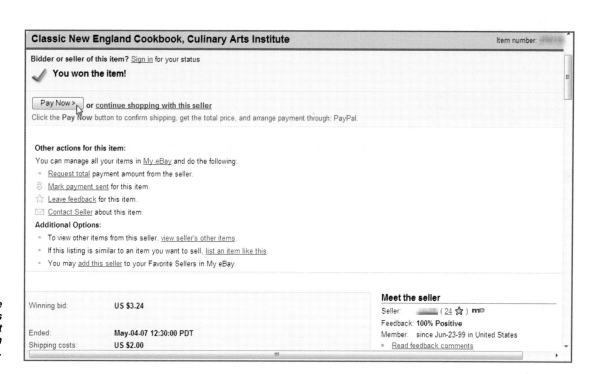

Classic New England Cookbook, Culinary Arts Institute   Item number:

Bidder or seller of this item? <u>Sign in</u> for your status

✓ **You won the item!**

[Pay Now >] or <u>continue shopping with this seller</u>

Click the **Pay Now** button to confirm shipping, get the total price, and arrange payment through: PayPal.

Other actions for this item:

You can manage all your items in <u>My eBay</u> and do the following:

▫ <u>Request total</u> payment amount from the seller.

⑧ <u>Mark payment sent</u> for this item.

☆ <u>Leave feedback</u> for this item.

✉ <u>Contact Seller</u> about this item.

Additional Options:

▫ To view other items from this seller, <u>view seller's other items</u>.

▫ If this listing is similar to an item you want to sell, <u>list an item like this</u>.

▫ You may <u>add this seller</u> to your Favorite Sellers in My eBay.

		Meet the seller
Winning bid:	US $3.24	Seller: (24 ☆) me
		Feedback: **100% Positive**
Ended:	May-04-07 12:30:00 PDT	Member: since Jun-23-99 in United States
Shipping costs:	US $2.00	▫ <u>Read feedback comments</u>

Figure 4-16: When you win a bid, the View Item page recognizes you as the winner and displays the pertinent information. Click Pay Now to begin payment proceedings.

TIP

If you click Request Total From Seller, you will be prompted to send an e-mail to him or her, asking for the appropriate shipping and handling costs. You can type a message to the seller and also direct that a copy of the e-mail be sent to you. The seller, after finding out what the postage is, updates the Review Item description to include that amount and also answers your e-mail with the amount, which you can then enter into the amount to be paid.

● Under Review Payment Details, you will see how your seller accepts payment. Enter the shipping and handling charges if they are not automatically filled in. (Click **Request Total From Seller** if the View Item page does not provide this information.)

Questions about the total? <u>Request total from seller</u>

● You may be given the option of adding insurance (or it may be required). To do so, in the Seller Discounts Or Charges column, click **Add** and then click **Recalculate** to refigure the total amount you owe.

Message to seller:
(optional)

> Please send the total amount to me, including shipping and handling charges.
>
> Thank you,

408 characters left. HTML cannot be displayed.

☑ Send a copy of this email to me.

[Request Total From Seller >]

This will send an email to your seller.

● If you are using an eBay gift certificate or coupon, select the relevant check box.

- Beneath Confirm Payment Method, click **Continue**.
- On the Complete Your Payment page, verify the shipping address and the item details. Scroll down to the Payment Method area, and verify that the default mode of payment that the seller offers is what you want to use. PayPal is usually the default mode of payment. If you want to change the default to another payment method, click **More Funding Options**.

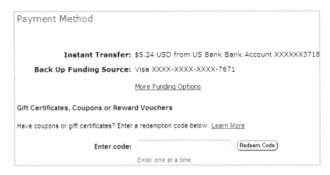

3. Click **Pay** when you are satisfied. At this point, the Payment Complete page should verify that you have successfully made your payment, as seen in Figure 4-17.

4. Click **Return To eBay** to return to your bidding information, or click **View My PayPal Account** to see details regarding your PayPal account.

Sign Up for PayPal

On the Payment Details page, when you are reviewing the amount you owe on the item, you can sign up for PayPal. You will initially be assigned a Personal Account. You can upgrade this to a Premier Account or a Business Account later directly from your PayPal account.

1. On the Review Your Purchase page, you will see the details of the transaction, the send-to address, the payment details, and the Select A Payment Method area. In this last section, you will see the payment methods that the seller accepts. The Pay With Credit Or Debit Card Through PayPal option should be selected. Click **Continue**.

   –Or–

   Go down below My Account in the My eBay Views sidebar, and click **PayPal Account**. Click the link to set up an account. The Sign Up For A PayPal Account page is displayed.

2. Under the New To PayPal area, click **Sign Up**.

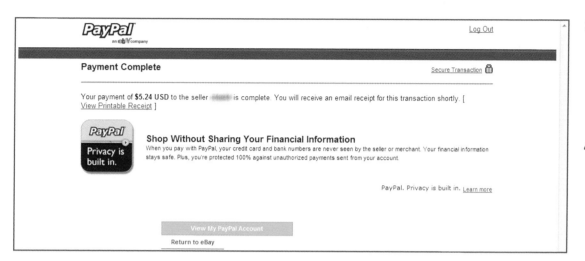

Figure 4-17: *When you have successfully paid your amount through PayPal, you will see a Payment Complete notice verifying this and the amount.*

3. On the Enter Billing Information page, enter the appropriate information: country, credit card number plus expiration date, and that the correct name and address is displayed, as seen in Figure 4-18. Click **Continue**.

4. On the Save Your Information With PayPal page, you first create a password for PayPal that is different from your eBay password (it must contain at least eight characters). In the Security Measure area, type the string of characters in the Enter The Code As Shown text box. Review the PayPal user agreement and privacy policy, and then click **Agree & Continue**.

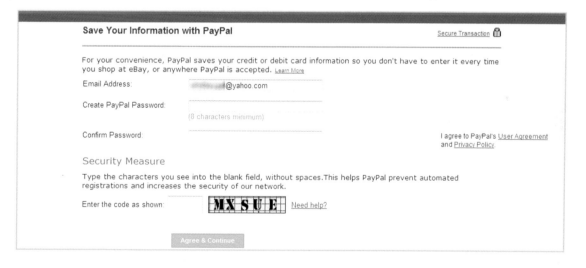

USING OTHER PAYMENT MEANS

PAY BY CHECK OR MONEY ORDER

First, verify that the seller accepts payments by check or money order. (In this case, you pay the seller directly, not eBay.) If the seller accepts such payments, you can select this option when paying and will be given an e-mail form to notify the seller that you intend to pay by check and when. Be aware that your purchase probably will not be mailed to you until your check has been received, deposited, and cleared. Include a copy of the invoice with your payment to the seller to ensure that he or she will credit the appropriate item as being paid. Write the item number on the check. Also, be aware that this method of payment is not protected with eBay's Protection Programs, as with PayPal, eBay Motors, business equipment, etc.

PAY BY CREDIT CARD

Using a credit card, either through eBay's PayPal or through the seller's charge program, is fairly safe, as most credit cards, such as Visa or MasterCard, have programs for protecting buyers from fraudulent use.

USE ESCROW

When you are buying a higher-priced item, say over $500, you can pay for it using www.escrow.com, an escrow service. In this case, the escrow service receives the buyer's money, holding on to it until the buyer receives the item. If everything is acceptable with the buyer, he or she approves distributing the money to the seller. There is a problem, however, with fraudulent escrow services, which is why eBay asks that you use their approved escrow service only, www.escrow.com.

Enter Billing Information

All fields are required unless otherwise noted.

Country: United States

Credit Card Number:

Payment Type: VISA MasterCard DISCOVER AMEX

Expiration Date: / CSC: 475 What's this?

First Name:
As it appears on card

Last Name:
As it appears on card

Billing Address: ███ S. Scurlock
Freeland, ██ █████
United States

Change

Continue

You can review this order before it's final

Figure 4-18: To pay for your purchases, you need to establish a method of paying (PayPal is typically the fastest and most efficient.)

5. On the Complete Your Payment page, verify that the shipping address and amount to be paid are correct. Scroll down to the Payment Method area, and verify that the credit card number is correct. Click **Pay**.

6. You will see the Payment Complete page, verifying that your payment has successfully been made. Click the appropriate link to eBay or your PayPal account.

Sally the seller gives positive feedback to buyers who are quick to pay.

Give Feedback

The final part of the transaction is to give feedback. Giving and receiving feedback is part of the currency you exchange with the seller. In theory, when you pay, the seller leaves feedback for you, and when you receive the item, you

NOTE

Do not pay for purchases with cash or wire transfers. This is risky, since you cannot prove you have paid and you have no protection under PayPal's Buyer Protection Program (insures from $200 to $2,000) or access to eBay's remedies for fraud. (See Chapter 9 for more information.)

give feedback to the seller. In practice, however, it is a bit different. Typically, the seller waits to give feedback until he or she is paid or until he or she receives your feedback (at which point, he or she knows you accept the item). To provide feedback:

1. In My eBay, click **All Buying** on the My eBay Views sidebar.
2. Click **Won**. (From the eBay Toolbar, click **Items I've Won In The Last Week**.) A page similar to that shown in Figure 4-19 is displayed.

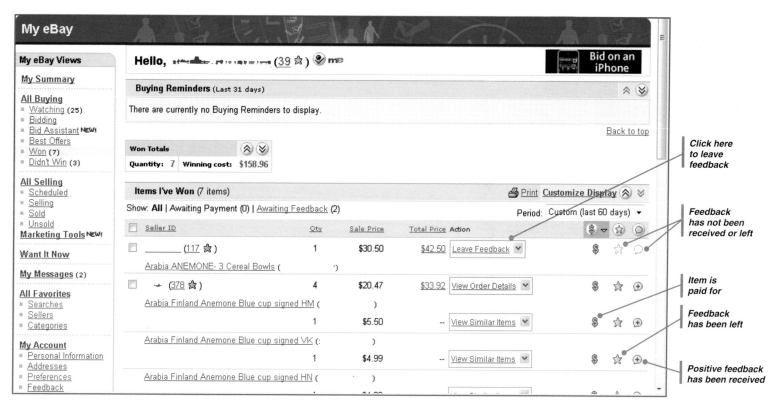

Figure 4-19: Your purchases give you a link to where you can leave feedback and tell you who has given you feedback as well.

TIP

You can hover your pointer over a star to see which description fits the individual rating.

NOTE

Be careful about the content of your feedback. It is a precious thing, and cannot be retracted or cancelled once you click the button. You have the opportunity to leave feedback for 90 days (after 90 days, the listing may be removed from the eBay system).

QUICKSTEPS

USING A BID ASSISTANT

When you want an item, a particular computer game, for example, and there are several available on eBay, but you don't want all of them, and you don't want to spend your time tracking the bids to see which item you might get, you can use the Bid Assistant. With it, you can perform the following actions:

- Select the items you want to bid on. The bids must end more than five minutes apart or Bid Assistant cannot manage bids between them.

- Determine your maximum bid for one of the items.

- Let Bid Assistant do your bidding for you.

The Bid Assistant will bid on the first item that ends first. If that bid exceeds your bid amount, Bid Assistant will bid on the second item and so on, trying to make sure that you win at least one of the items.

Continued . . .

3. Click **Leave Feedback**. The Leave Feedback page is displayed.

4. In the Rate The Overall Transaction area, click the option that is relevant for this seller (see Chapter 3 for an explanation of the various ratings). A text box entitled Please Explain and a section entitled Rate The Seller On The Details Of The Transaction will appear.

5. Type a comment in the Please Explain text box that tells how you feel about the transaction.

6. Click a star to rate the seller in all the details of the transaction, from Very Inaccurate for the item description, to Very Accurate, and so on.

7. Click **Leave Feedback**. You will be congratulated on completing this action.

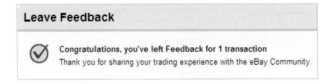

USING A BID ASSISTANT *(Continued)*

1. Using the search feature, find the items you want to bid on. Click the item name and display the View Item page. Click **Watch This Item** for each one.

2. Click **My eBay** on the eBay header and click **Watching** under the All Buying heading on the My eBay Views sidebar.

3. Click the check boxes for the items you want to bid on, and then click **Bid With Bid Assistant**. The Bid Assistant: Place Bid page is displayed, as shown in Figure 4-20.

   - Type a name in the Enter A Name For Your Bid Assistant Group text box to be able to distinguish one from the other.

   - To place separate bids on your items, type the maximum in each item's text box.

   - To place one bid amount for all the items, type the amount in the Enter The Same Maximum Bid To Apply To All Items text box.

4. Click **Continue**. You will see the Bid Assistant: Review Bid page.

5. Click **Confirm Bid** to allow Bid Assistant to do its work of bidding for you up to your maximum bid amount. You are committing to buy any one of the items for up to your maximum bid amount. You will a see Bid Assistant Confirmation page.

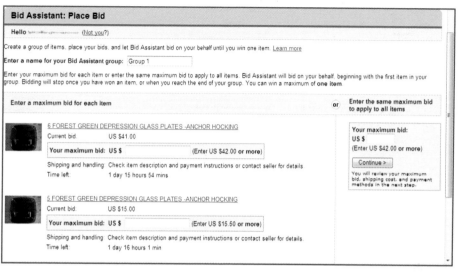

Figure 4-20: Using the Bid Assistant eases your bidding on several items when you want only one.

NOTE

You can also click **Bid with the Bid Assistant** on the View Item page after you have clicked **Watch This Item**.

You are watching this item in My eBay (13 items)
You can also: Bid with Bid Assistant
                Get mobile or IM alerts | Email to a friend

Chapter 5
Learning How to Sell

Selling is to eBay as swimming is to ducks—it's in its DNA. The only missing link in this DNA chain is a buyer for everything that is for sale. eBay does its job by providing visibility to your items to millions of potential customers and a competitive arena in which to conduct the transaction. All you need to do is provide the merchandise a buyer wants, at a completive price (fixed-price listing) or at a market-driven price provided by the bidding process (auction listing), and deliver it as advertised. OK—that seems easy enough, and this and the next three chapters will help you through that process. This chapter provides you information on selling on eBay, from methods you can use to find items for sale, to techniques you can use to help you figure out what to sell and how much it will cost you. In addition, you will learn how to sell on several of eBay's associated sites, such as Half.com.

(Chapter 10 describes how to approach your selling on eBay as a business, including setting up an eBay Store and selling for others.)

Prepare to Sell

In order to sell on eBay, you need basic equipment, such as a computer and a digital camera, services (such as DSL), and items to sell. This section will help you set up the physical items you need to support selling, as well as provide ideas on where to acquire items to sell.

Sell on the Fast Track

Selling on eBay can be as simple or as complex as you want to make it. If you want to just get going and place an item up for bid, you can do that with a minimum of effort and time, or you can formalize your selling and establish a business of selling items on eBay. In any case, the following sections will get you on your way.

SET UP YOUR DESKTOP

You will need equipment and services to connect to and use eBay. Ideally, you should have the following:

- **A newer computer** with the latest operating system and Internet browser (such as Microsoft Vista and Internet Explorer 7.0, which is used in this book). A new desktop computer and monitor can be bought for around $500 without breaking a sweat. Since everything you do on eBay is somehow routed through a computer, you cannot afford to deal with a problematic relic. Your computer doesn't need to run the hottest microprocessor or have gaming-level amounts of memory—it just needs the speed, memory, and storage capacity to handle the level of selling you expect to be doing.

- **Broadband Internet connection** is almost becoming as commonplace as having a cell phone nowadays, and for good reason. Life is too short to wait for listings and pictures to download, not to mention the time you'll save avoiding having to log on to your dial-up service several times throughout the day each time you want to check

TIP

In the last three months of 2006, the total value of all successful closed items on eBay was $14.4 *billion* (source: eBay press release January 24, 2007). By comparison, the gross domestic product (GDP) of Nicaragua is less than $13 billion. Start selling on eBay and get in on this action!

TIP

The latest rage in computer monitors are wide-screen displays similar to that 50-inch plasma TV you just bid on. While widescreens are great for watching movies, they are not ideal for providing the real estate (especially vertical) for viewing several running programs at once, each in their own separate window—for example, your Internet browser, e-mail program, Windows Explorer, an auction management or photo-editing program, and maybe CNN through a TV tuner board.

*Figure 5-1: **Conserve space with all-in-one devices that combine color printing with several other services.***

![NOTE icon]

NOTE

A key element you must obtain to be able to sell on eBay is a seller's account. Unlike the original Sell Your Item form, where you created an account prior to your first listing, the latest Sell Your Item form (in use in late 2006/early 2007) now provides you the opportunity to create the account as you complete your first listing. See Chapter 6 for information on creating listings using the latest Sell Your Item form and setting up your seller's account.

ⓘ Click **Continue** to register as a seller. Once you have registered you can post your listing on eBay and begin selling more.

your listings, messages, and e-mails. Whether you choose cable or digital subscriber line (DSL), fast or really fast, or use less popular services such as wireless broadband is strictly a matter of cost, availability, and convenience.

- **A color inkjet printer** is so inexpensive you can probably get one bundled with your new computer and monitor. Especially helpful are the all-in-one products (see Figure 5-1) that bundle other features, such as faxing, copying, and scanning, in one unit. Flat, horizontal space always seems to be at a premium, and the more you can accomplish in the least amount of space the better.

- **Picture-capturing devices**, such as digital cameras and a standalone scanner (if you don't have the aforementioned all-in-one device) are as important to your eBay selling success as the computer you use to send them to eBay. Quality pictures are an essential component to your listings.

REVIEW THE RULES

There are many items you cannot sell on eBay, and there are pages of rules and practices outlined in the eBay user agreement to which you must abide (the eBay user agreement was presented to you in Chapter 1 when you first registered on eBay, but even if you faithfully read it all, it never hurts to review).

1. On the eBay home page, click **Security Center** on the second links bar.

2. On the Security & Resolution page, under Resources, click **Rules And Polices**.

3. In the Rules & Policies area, click **Your eBay User Agreement** to review several screens of general policies and links to additional information.

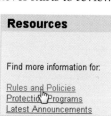

Resources

Find more information for:

Rules and Policies
Protection Programs
Latest Announcements

4. In the Rules For Selling area (shown in Figure 5-2):

- Click **Prohibited And Restricted Items** to see lists of these products.

- Click **Rules For Listings** to read about selling-specific policies, including how you can accept payment and how not to misrepresent items.

- Click **Rules About Intellectual Property** to learn how to avoid running afoul of copyright issues, problems with selling replicas and copies, and how to avoid counterfeits.

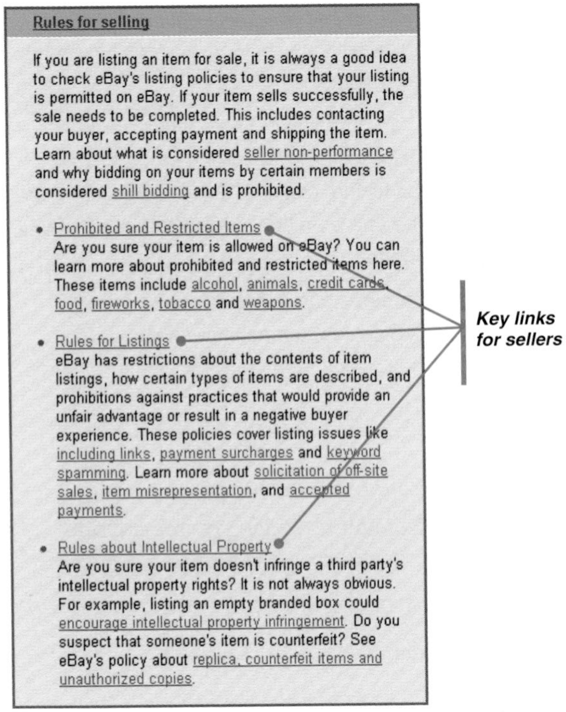

Key links for sellers

Figure 5-2: *Don't jeopardize your eBay career before it gets off the ground—review applicable do's and don'ts.*

NOTE

Be aware that government agencies are not just sitting by idle and watching others reap the profits of their items selling on eBay. In fact, eBay is encouraging them to sell directly on eBay themselves or use trading assistants to sell for them (see Chapter 10 for more information on becoming an eBay authorized trading assistant yourself). Check out what information eBay is providing to government sellers by clicking **Site Map** on the eBay header or, under Sell/Selling Activities, clicking **Government Surplus**.

OBTAIN ACCOUNTS FOR PAYMENT METHODS YOU ACCEPT

The types of payments you will accept for your sales will dictate which accounts you might consider setting up to facilitate processing as well as protect you from unscrupulous buyers. For example, if you want to accept credit and debit card payments (highly recommended), you will need to join a processing service. For most sellers who do not already have a credit card processing service set up for an ongoing business concern, signing up for a PayPal Premier payment service is a good bet (see Chapter 6 for steps to sign up). If you anticipate a high-volume of checks, you might consider signing up with a check guarantee service (for example, www.echo-inc.com) to protect you against fraudulent checks. eBay allows you to accept several forms of payment, but also restricts you from using a few.

You may offer:

- PayPal transfers *PayPal*
- Credit cards *MasterCard* *VISA* *AMEX* *DISCOVER*
- Debit cards
- Bank electronic payments
- Wire (bank-to-bank) transfers
- COD (cash on delivery) or cash in person
- Personal, cashier's, or certified checks and money orders

You may not offer:

- Cash sent through the mail
- Western Union, Moneygram, and other non-bank, point-to-point transfers
- Additional funds added toward your pre-paid credit or debit card
- Any method not specifically authorized by eBay's policies (you can't get creative)

Buy Wholesale on eBay

You've got to love the marketing folks at eBay. Not only do they provide the mechanisms for you to sell your items in an efficient and inexpensive manner to a worldwide market, but they also provide you a channel to buy your items wholesale on eBay "in an efficient and inexpensive manner *from* a worldwide

FINDING ITEMS TO SELL

Unless you are connected to retail channels, you will need to acquire items to sell at the best below-market price you can get. Possible sources include the following:

- **Basements, attics, and closets** provide the most readily available and lowest-cost items (you already own them). Include items of friends and relatives that can be had for nothing or next to it.

- **Thrift stores** contain hidden treasures that can be ferreted out with a sharp, experienced pricing eye and persistent scouring. Go (early) on promotion days to obtain even deeper discounts. (From the PR manager of a national thrift store chain: "You should see this one guy we have who comes in every Monday (.99 cent day) and goes out with two to three cart loads overflowing two feet over the top full of men's suits. Then sells them on eBay—makes a nice little living for himself.")

ValueVillage
the ultimate treasure hunt

- **Garage sales** are typically announced in your local paper and on your nearest telephone pole. Get up early, map out your route, and be done before brunch.

- **Estate sales** liquidate the contents of a household. The quality of merchandise can range from the trappings of the rich and famous to items more commonly found in dumpsters. Depending on how the contents are sold, you can purchase individual items, as in a garage sale; or you can make a bid to purchase the entire lot. Check the auctions section in the classified section of your newspaper for upcoming sales.

Continued . . .

market." To find items to buy in quantity and at a hopefully lower *wholesale* price each:

Click **Categories** on the eBay header. Under the category you want to investigate, click **Wholesale Lots** at the bottom of the list of subcategories. Items available as lots are displayed, as shown in Figure 5-3. You can refine your search by clicking a subcategory on the Narrow Your Results sidebar. (See the "Using Various Selling Techniques" QuickFacts later in the chapter for more information on selling lots.)

Buy Globally on eBay

Many eBay users avoid global transactions because of the extra work and potential pitfalls involved with conducting business outside the borders.

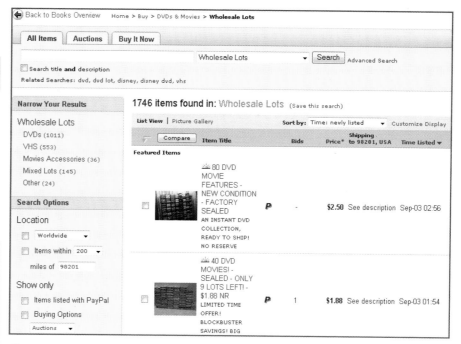

*Figure 5-3: **Buy in bulk lots to get wholesale prices.***

FINDING ITEMS TO SELL *(Continued)*

- **Live auctions** (see Figure 5-4) provide great experience in the world of bidding and overall auction psychology. Check out your Sunday paper for upcoming events. Most cost very little, if anything, to attend and provide invaluable pricing data, networking, and generally entertaining auctioneers. (eBay lets you get in on the action of live auctions from its Live Auctions site. See Chapter 4 for information on bidding in live auctions.)

- **Government surplus** sales and auctions offer equipment for sale from local, state, and federal authorities. Notices are listed in local and national newspapers, and are posted on associated Web sites. The largest generator of surplus material, the Department of Defense, provides sales through its Defense Reutilization Marketing Offices (DRMO) network. See www.drms.dla.mil/html/drmo_sites.html for offices in your area.

- **Tickets** are a hot seller on eBay (over $250 million in tickets alone were sold in 2003). Sell in the Tickets category, and use the Item Specifics feature to provide key information for buyers (selling in categories and the Item Specifics feature is described in Chapter 6). Alternatively, sell on StubHub, an eBay-owned site (see "Sell Tickets on StubHub" later in the chapter).

- **eBay Site Map** provides a More Ways To Find Items area where you can quickly access selling sites and find items by using popular searches.

Figure 5-4: Attend live auctions to network with others and learn about the live auction process.

Their reluctance can be your opportunity to acquire unique items that every other eBay business isn't fighting over. eBay provides searching to its worldwide sites and offers a lot of useful information to help you navigate the labyrinth of currency fluctuations, shipping costs, language problems, and other issues.

1. Click **Site Map** on the eBay header. Under Selling Resources, click **Sell Internationally**.

2. On the Global Trade page, shown in Figure 5-5, click one of the many resource links to learn more about the aspects of selling internationally.

Review global selling pointers

Click a worldwide site to learn about featured items from that country's eBay Web site

Selling global almost doubles your buyer base

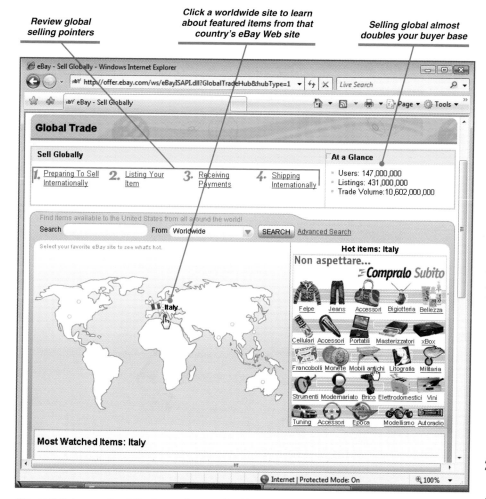

Figure 5-5: *Learn about the ins and outs of selling in the global eBay marketplace.*

Use Drop-Shipping

So you want to become an eBay seller, but you live in a studio apartment without a square foot of space to store items? Not to worry—you can be a successful eBay seller without ever buying, seeing, or touching your items. Using *drop-shipping*, you establish a relationship with a wholesaler, who will package and ship items you sell directly to buyers. As far as the buyer is concerned, the billiard table he or she received came from your studio apartment. You pay the drop-shipper the wholesale cost of the item and shipping and handling costs. To find companies vetted by eBay that drop-ship or that provide lists of companies that do:

1. Click **Site Map** on the eBay header, and under Selling Tools, click **eBay Solutions Directory**.

2. Under Selling Solutions, scroll down and click **Sourcing**.

3. Click the links for any solution providers that indicate they offer drop-shipping services, as shown in Figure 5-6.

CAUTION

The trick to making drop-shipping work is finding a reputable and reliable company with which to partner. Doing a search on Google will produce pages of potential drop-shipping sources, but as with most things on the Internet, it's best to do some homework, such as checking out what others have to say on eBay blogs and groups. Typically, to work with legitimate wholesalers, you will need to have bona fide business credentials (see Chapter 10) and establish a relationship with the company other than just providing them with your credit card number. Be aware that there are plenty of other sellers putting items for sale from the same lists you'll be viewing. Also, be suspicious of recurring subscription fees and other joining-type costs to access their inventory. The cliché, "If it's easy, everyone will be doing it" certainly applies in this case.

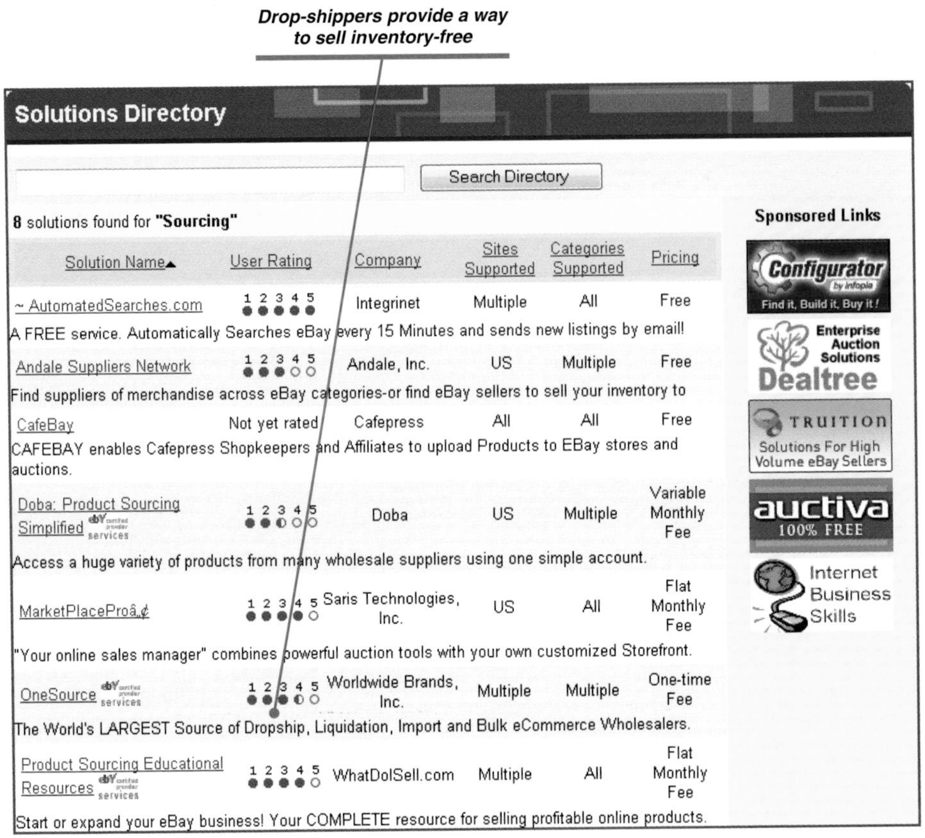

Drop-shippers provide a way to sell inventory-free

Figure 5-6: eBay promotes several sourcing businesses, including those that offer drop-shipping services.

Determine What and How to Sell

You might have gotten a great deal on ice cubes, but if you're selling to Eskimos, you'll probably be disappointed in your sales. While the world marketplace that eBay brings to your listings will insulate you from such a limited audience, it is up to you to offer items for sale that people really want to buy. If you are looking for items to sell, it makes sense to target those that are currently in demand. Besides solving the "what" to sell problem, you also need to consider how much to charge for them. Even if you're letting the competitive bidding process determine the selling price, you'll want to know a product's approximate value to forecast potential profit, set expectations, and establish a reserve price. There are several marketing research techniques you can do on your own, and several fee-based tools are available to get just the level of analysis you need.

See What People Are Buying

It's always best to sell a product that people want (it tends to increase sales!). The following sections can help you determine what to sell.

FIND WHAT'S HOT

Wouldn't it be nice to have a crystal ball and know in advance what people will be buying in the future? Well, in a small sense, eBay offers you that opportunity by posting a calendar of upcoming events that highlight categories featured on its home page. eBay offers this and other tools that provide selling trends and data points on its What's Hot page.

1. Point to **Sell** on the eBay header, and click **Getting Started**.

2. At Seller Central, under Choose A Topic, click **What's Hot**. In the What's Hot section:

   - Click **Merchandising Calendar** to see which/when categories of items will be promoted on the eBay home page and other prominent pages.

   - Click **Hot Items By Category** to see a report (Adobe PDF file) that lists Level 4 categories by the percentage difference between bid and listing growth rates. The greater the percentage spread, the "hotter" the category, as shown in Figure 5-7.

   - Click **eBay Pulse**, which provides a daily look at the ten most popular searches on eBay, the five largest eBay Stores (in terms of active listings), and the most watched items. You can focus the search to specific categories (the default search is across all categories) by clicking the **Category** down arrow and selecting a category. Repeat the procedure to view subcategories within the previously selected category.

<aside>

What's Hot

Selling success often translates into being at the right place, at the right time, with the right product. Check back often to stay on top of the latest promotions and hot items on eBay.

- Merchandising Calendar
  Get advance notice of upcoming seasonal promotions and learn about which items will be spotlighted on the eBay home page.

- Hot Items by Category
  Hot...Very Hot...Super Hot! Discover which categories and products are on fire—where bid to item ratios are high and demand is outpacing supply!

- eBay Pulse
  Track trends, hot picks, and other cool stuff, including: top searches, most watched items, and little known eBay facts.

- eBay Pop
  eBay Pop is a beta site that captures some of the buying buzz, popular trends, and fun things happening on eBay. It's a new way to stay in the know, current with the trends and to impress your family and friends.

</aside>

<aside>

NOTE

A Level 4 category is four levels deep within a main category hierarchy. For example, if you're looking to see how 35-mm black-and-white film is selling, you'll find it under the Cameras & Photo main category in the Film | 35MM subcategories (see Figure 5-7).

</aside>

Category	Antiques ▼
	Antiques
	└ All Categories
	Antiquities (Classical, Amer.)
	Architectural & Garden
	Asian Antiques
	Books, Manuscripts

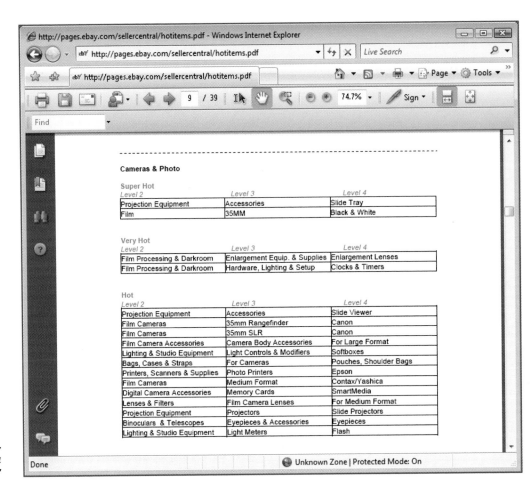

Figure 5-7: eBay provides monthly reports showing which Level 4 categories are "hottest."

- Click **eBay Pop** to see selling statistics and hot sellers, test your costing knowledge by playing "How Much Is It Worth?," (see Figure 5-8) and read articles to get a better sense of the eBay marketplace.

REVIEW WANT IT NOW LISTINGS

Is there a better way to find out what people want to buy than checking their postings for Want It Now items?

1. Type pages.ebay.com/wantitnow in your browser's address box and press ENTER.

2. On the Want It Now page, peruse the Want It Now categories to see if you can spot any trends or to just get a feel for what people are looking to buy. (See "Sell to Want It Now Buyers" later in the chapter for information on making Want It Now sales).

Browse Want It Now

Antiques	Crafts	Real Estate
Art	Dolls & Bears	Specialty Services
Baby	DVDs & Movies	Sporting Goods
Books	Entertainment Memorabilia	Sports Mem, Cards & Fan Shop
Business & Industrial	Gift Certificates	Stamps
Cameras & Photo	Health & Beauty	Tickets
Cell Phones	Home & Garden	Toys & Hobbies
Clothing, Shoes & Accessories	Jewelry & Watches	Travel
Coins	Music	Video Games
Collectibles	Musical Instruments	Everything Else
Computers & Networking	Pottery & Glass	eBay Motors
Consumer Electronics		

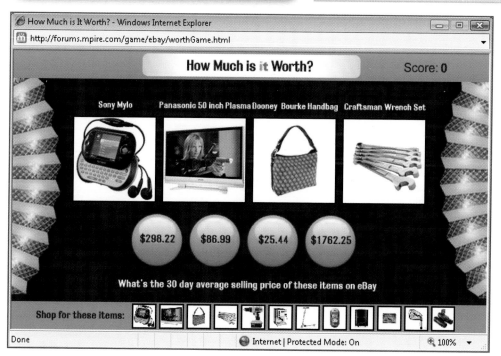

Figure 5-8: *Test your pricing acumen with How Much Is It Worth?*

USE MARKETPLACE RESEARCH

In the vein of "you get what you pay for," eBay provides much greater selling metrics for a fee than it provides in its free offerings. Marketplace Research is a subscription-based service with three levels (see Figure 5-9) that lets you get up to 90 days of past data on several parameters of completed items for auction and fixed-price listings, as well as for eBay Store listings. Current data is also provided for active listings. You can display charts and perform searches to narrow your focus, for example, to specific sellers and eBay Stores.

1. Click **Site Map** on the eBay header. Under Selling Resources, click **eBay Marketplace Research**.

	FAST PASS	BASIC	PRO
Fee	$2.99/2 days Pay-as-you-go. One time usage fee.	$9.99/month Monthly ongoing subscription fee.	$24.99/month Monthly ongoing subscription fee.
Feature Highlights			
Access Levels	2 days access with 60 days of historical data	Access anytime with 60 days of historical data	Access anytime with 90 days of historical data
Historical Completed Items Data	60 days	60 days	90 days
Saved Searches	10 maximum	10 maximum	100 maximum
Top Searches	✔	✔	✔
Top Searches by eBay Site			✔

Figure 5-9: Marketplace Research provides one-time sales metrics, or you can opt for continuous access.

NOTE

Completed listings include fixed-price and eBay Store listings that have sold, as well as auction listings that have reached the end of their duration, regardless if there was a winning bidder. Auction listings that have not received a bid or whose bids did not reach the reserve price are displayed with their prices in red.

HOT 2GB i-Platinum MP4 MP3 FM Pod PMP Player LCD Pink

0    $22.99 $29.99

TIP

If you want to pay to view a more comprehensive list of completed listings, see "Use Marketplace Research" earlier in the chapter.

2. On the Marketplace Research page, under the Choose A Topic sidebar, click each of the links:

- Click **Comparison** to get a side-by-side review of features and costs.
- Click **Frequently Asked Questions** to get answers to common questions.
- Click **Marketplace Research User Guide** to view a PDF document and get details on using the service.

Determine the Price of Items

To help you get a sense of the price you can offer on items for sale or to set your expectation for what an auction listing will bring, you could watch a whole lot of *The Price Is Right* reruns or do a little research on your own.

USE COMPLETED LISTINGS

eBay provides a free viewing of listings that have completed within the last 15 days (see the accompanying Note). You can use these to see the selling price for items similar to what you're considering selling.

1. From the eBay home page, browse categories or use the Search box to locate pages of listings most similar to the items you are selling (see Chapter 2 for more information on locating completed items).

2. On the left sidebar, under Search Options, click the **Completed Listings** check box, along with any other search option you want to apply to focus the search.

3. Click **Show Items** with finished.

REVIEW COMPARISON SITES

Besides eBay and other online auction sites (see Figure 5-10), there are several other price-comparison sites you can use to research product pricing. Three popular sites are:

- www.pricescan.com
- www.pricewatch.com (for computer and electronic parts)
- http://shopping.yahoo.com
- www.google.com/products (a.k.a. Froogle)

Search Options

Location
- ☐ Worldwide ▼
- ☐ Items within 200 ▼
  miles of 98201

Show only
- ☐ Items listed with PayPal
- ☐ Buying Options
  - Auctions ▼
- ☐ More Buying Options
  - Add Store Inventory ▼
- ☐ Free Shipping
- ☐ Get It Fast items
- ☑ Completed listings
- ☐ 🌐 Gift items
- ☐ Items listed as lots

CHOOSING WHAT TO SELL

There is often a difference between what you *need* to sell and what you *want* to sell. *Need* implies getting rid of a collection that is offensive to your spouse to prevent a divorce, while *want* brings to mind visions of success and eBay Businessperson of the Year awards. If your desire is the latter—that is, to become a long-term eBay seller and possibly turn your interest into a business—there are two tenets that will help you succeed where others falter.

SELL WHAT YOU UNDERSTAND

Become knowledgeable about a product line so people come to rely on you as a source of expertise and return to you for repeat sales.

SELL WHAT INTERESTS YOU

The passion for your products will become evident in every facet of your selling experience.

Figure 5-10: *eBay is the biggest dog on the online auction porch, but it isn't the only one.*

A number of calculators that help you determine selling fees are available from third parties. eB Calc (www.ebcalc.com), a maker of eBay-related calculators, offers several calculators for free online use, as shown in Figure 5-11.

Calculate Insertion Fees

A consideration to take into account when deciding what items you want to sell is the selling cost ("A good sale starts with a great buy"). There are several selling costs on eBay:

- **Insertion fee** to list an item on eBay (covered next). The amount you are charged depends on the type of listing (or auction) and your initial pricing. See Chapter 1 for information on the different auction types.

- **Final value fee**, which is determined when a fixed-price sale is made or an auction closes with a winning bidder (see Chapter 6 for more information on calculating and paying final value fees).

- **Optional fees**, such as listing upgrades to make your listings stand out, adding a Buy It Now option to an auction, adding more than one picture to a listing, and fees for using eBay selling-management tools (see Chapters 6 and 7 for descriptions of these fees).

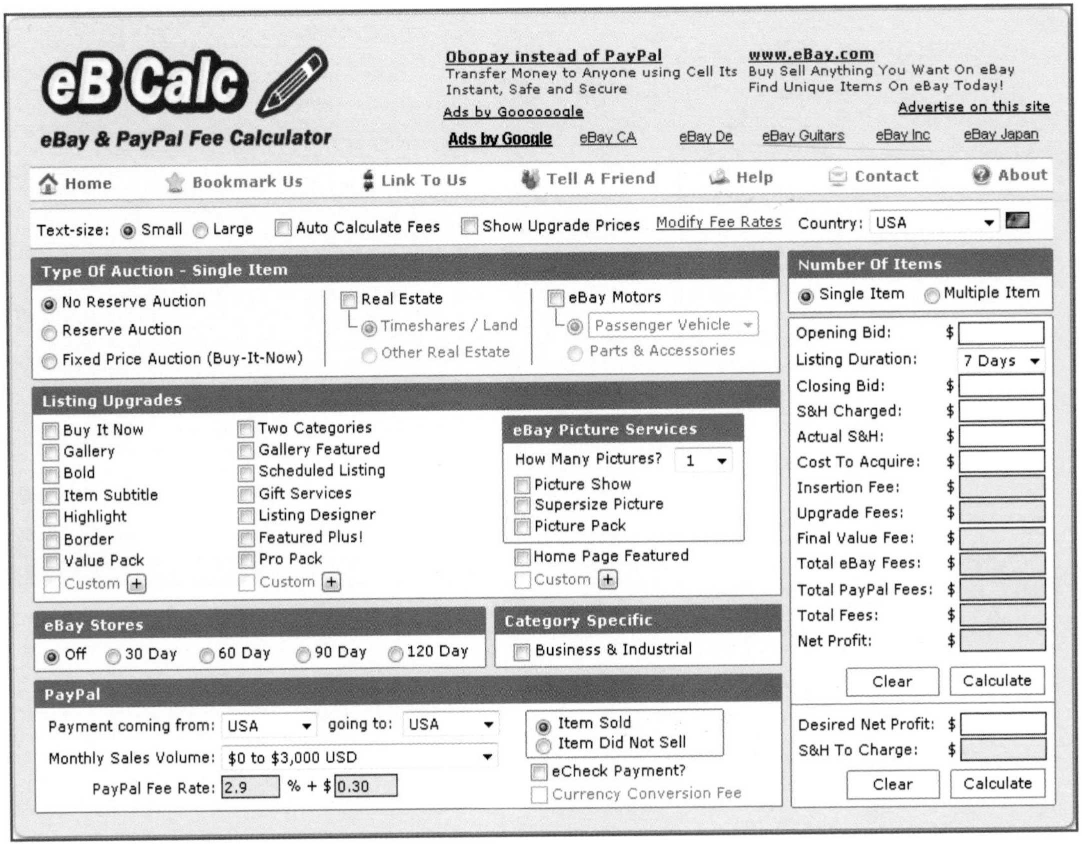

Figure 5-11: **Determine most of your eBay fees before you list an item using free online calculators.**

PRICING OPTIONS	INSERTION FEE BASED ON
Standard (single-quantity item)	Starting price of item
Multiple item (Dutch)	Starting price or fixed price times the number of items (maximum insertion fee is $4.80)
Reserve	Reserve price

Table 5-1: **How Insertion Fees Are Determined**

VIEW INSERTION FEES FOR COMMON AUCTIONS

The insertion fee eBay charges for common listings depends on how you initially price the item in the selling form, as shown in Table 5-1.

Table 5-2 displays the insertion fee amount per category for common listings.

USING VARIOUS SELLING TECHNIQUES

Ask *x* number of eBay sellers what their best techniques are to generate sales and you will get *y* number of answers. If there was a sure bet, every seller would be doing it, and quickly any advantage would be lost. Be aware of the possibilities and see what works for you. (Chapter 6 covers other opportunities for you to maximize sales when you list an item using the Sell Your Item form.)

SELL TO WANT IT NOW BUYERS

Wish you could match items you have for sale or are holding in inventory with a list of items buyers want? Look no further than eBay's Want It Now pages. Not only can you easily find Want It Now posts that you can match, but eBay can monitor new Want It Now posts and let you know when they contain items you have.

SELL LOTS TO OTHER EBAY SELLERS

Lots are packages, groups, or collections of the same or similar items. For example, you could sell 200 scarves in groups of ten. You can choose to sell items at a fixed price, such as $8.99 per lot, or you can list them as auction items. Chapter 6 describes how to list lots.

Continued . . .

STARTING (OR RESERVE) PRICE	INSERTION FEE
$.01 – $.99	$.20
$1.00 – $9.99	$.40
$10.00 – $24.99	$.60
$25.00 – $49.99	$1.20
$50.00 – $199.99	$2.40
$200.00 – $499.99	$3.60
Greater than or equal to $500.00	$4.80

*Table 5-2: **Common Listings Insertion Fees per Category***

VIEW INSERTION FEES FOR OTHER LISTING TYPES

Table 5-3 lists specialty listings and insertion fees.

Use eBay Sites

When most people hear "eBay," they immediately think of the original 1995 business model of selling items by online auction. Main eBay, or, as it is commonly called, "ebay.com," still fundamentally operates with the online auction as its primary focus (which is also the primary focus of this book), but

SPECIALTY LISTINGS	INSERTION FEE
Vehicles (other than motorcycles and powersport vehicles)	$40.00
Motorcycles and powersport vehicles	$30.00 $3.00 for powersport vehicles under 50 cc
Residential, commercial, and miscellaneous real estate	$100 (1-, 3-, 5-, 7-, or 10-day listings) $150 (30-day listing)
Timeshares, Manufactured Homes, and Land	$35 (1-, 3-, 5-, 7-, or 10-day listings) $50 (30-day listing)
Classified Ad (no bidding; interested buyers provide you contact information or call you if you provide a phone number)	$9.95 (30-day listing) $19.90 (60-day listing) $29.85 (90-day listing)

*Table 5-3: **Specialty Listing Insertion Fees***

NOTE

Powersport vehicles include all-terrain vehicles (ATVs), go-carts, jet skis, snowmobiles, and other small-engined vehicles. Fees for eBay Stores are described in Chapter 10.

USING VARIOUS SELLING TECHNIQUES *(Continued)*

ADD BEST OFFER

As an add-on to Buy It Now listings, you can offer buyers to provide you a "best offer" that you can accept or reject. If accepted, the listing is closed and the buyer is obligated to pay you the offered price. Best Offer is a free option you select when listing the item and it appears in item listings ≈Buy It Now or Best Offer. Chapter 6 describes how to add Best Offer to your Sell Your Item form.

GIVE SOMETHING BACK

eBay Giving Works 🎗 allows you to sell and then donate between 10 and 100 percent of the final sales price to a certified nonprofit (eBay maintains an extensive list from which you can choose). Some people only shop at eBay Giving Works events. Chapter 6 describes how to apply eBay Giving Works to your listings.

NOTE

eBay Stores and ProStores are covered in Chapter 10.

TIP

If you don't want your items to appear on eBay Express, you can "opt out" of the default setting. Click **Preferences** on the My eBay Views sidebar, and edit the eBay Express item under Selling Preferences.

eBay Express
Include qualifying items on eBay Express.

---

over time, eBay has developed or bought other venues that you can use to sell items.

To access these eBay sites:

Click the site you want from the eBay header.

–Or–

On the eBay home page, click a site under the Other eBay Companies sidebar.

Other eBay Companies

Half.com	Shopping.com
Kijiji	Skype
PayPal	StubHub
ProStores	StumbleUpon
Rent.com	

SELL ITEMS ON eBAY EXPRESS

For buyers who simply want to buy items immediately with eBay's assurances, conveniences, and reputation standing behind their purchases, eBay Express is the online shopping venue for them (and for you to offer them the items they want). eBay Express offers buyers the opportunity to make multiple purchases from multiple sellers and make one payment for selling and shipping costs. Behind the scenes, PayPal (the only payment option) adjudicates the payment to the respective sellers.

The best part of selling on eBay Express is that you probably don't have to do anything different than you're doing now. Your fixed price, eBay Store inventory, and auction listings with a Buy It Now price will automatically appear on eBay Express, assuming you qualify (you may also be qualified to have your items on another eBay site, Half.com, appear in eBay Express). In order to have your listings appear on eBay Express:

- You must have a feedback rating of at least 100 and have 98 percent or greater positive feedback.
- Your listings must use the Item Specific feature (at least the Condition field) and include a picture and shipping costs (Chapter 6 describes how to create a listing using these requirements).

To see if you qualify to sell on eBay Express:

1. Click **Express** on the eBay header.

2. On the eBay Express home page, click **Sell On eBay Express** on the bottom links bar.

eBay Express Eligibility

We have evaluated your seller profile and the item you want to sell. The results are grouped by seller qualifications and item qualifications. Check the areas where you don't qualify - for some sellers, changing just a few criteria will open the door to selling on eBay Express!

⚠ **We're sorry, you do not qualify to sell on eBay Express.**
You may be able to change some of the criteria listed below to become a qualified seller.

Show All Seller Qualification

Seller Qualifications	Yes	No
Is your feedback score above 100?		•

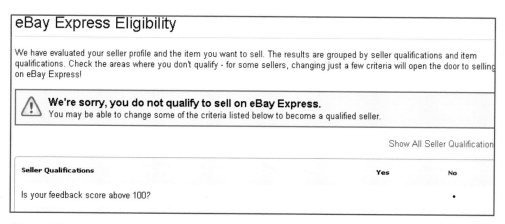

Figure 5-12: eBay only wants experienced sellers' items available on eBay Express.

NOTE

As of spring 2007, eBay Motors is using a variation of the original Sell Your Item form (available for use prior to May 2007) to list vehicles for sale and had not switched over to the revamped Sell Your Item form used for selling other items on eBay.com. Though different in appearance, the two forms include the same essential fields, and you shouldn't have any difficulty in transitioning from one form to the other.

3. Review the qualifications and click the **eBay Express Eligibility** link to see if you qualify, as shown in Figure 5-12.

4. To return to eBay.com, click eBay on the bottom links bar.

SELL CARS AND OTHER VEHICLES ON eBAY MOTORS

You sell vehicles (which includes cars, trucks, motorcycles, trailers, RVs, boats, aircraft, powersport equipment, and parts) using a Sell Your Item form (see Figure 5-13) that is similar to the form used for standard items, except its fields are tailored for the unique properties of vehicles, such as make, model, VIN number, and mileage (see Table 5-3 earlier in the chapter for the insertion fee charged to list a vehicle). To sell a vehicle:

1. Click **Motors** on the eBay header.

2. On the eBay Motors home page header, click **Sell**.

3. On the Sell page, click **Sell Your Item** (or first review the vehicle selling checklist and other tips).

4. Return to the Sell page, select a listing format, and click **Sell Your Item** to start developing your listing. See Chapter 6 for information on listing formats and how to fill out the general aspects of the Sell Your Item form.

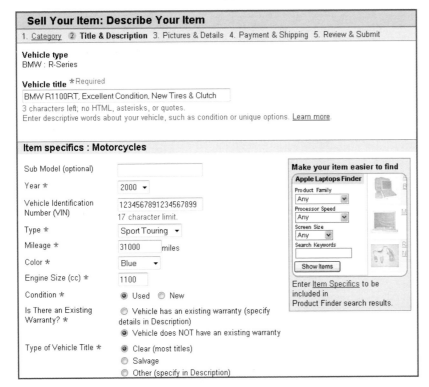

Figure 5-13: *The Sell Your Item form for vehicles provides item-specific fields that make it easier for buyers to locate your item.*

ADD A HALF.COM SELLER ACCOUNT

If you have new or used items you want to sell online at a fixed price, Half.com provides another venue for your items. Though limited to only a small set of categories (books, music, movies, video games, and game systems), Half.com offers buyers several deals on price and shipping (though there is no guarantee that every item is actually half price) and provides sellers with several incentives:

● Streamlined listings, since items are commodity-related (books have ISBN numbers; CDs, DVDs, and other items have UPC numbers). The listing effort of providing pictures and descriptions is already in Half.com's database (similar to the Pre-Filled Item Information feature available in the eBay Sell Your Item form described in Chapter 6). All you need to provide is the condition, optional comments, a price, and offer (or not) an optional expedited shipping service (see Figure 5-14). Half.com reimburses shipping costs to the seller based on the type of shipping service used, type of item sold, and the number of items in the packaging.

Figure 5-14: *A simple two-step listing form makes selling items on Half.com a snap.*

TIP

If you don't already have an eBay seller's account, creating a Half.com seller's account allows you to list items on both Half.com and eBay.com.

● No insertion fee, as costs are calculated only when your items sell.

● Links to your eBay listings.

● Qualified sellers have their Half.com listings also appear on eBay Express (use the eBay Eligibility tool described in "Sell Items on eBay Express" to see if you are a qualified seller).

● Capabilities to easily list multiple items.

To sell on Half.com, you have to create a seller's account similar to your eBay seller's account (see Chapter 6 for information on setting up an eBay seller's account). To create a Half.com seller's account, you will need to provide credit card and telephone numbers for identification purposes and checking account data for direct deposit of payments.

1. On the eBay home page, click **Half.com** under the Other eBay Companies sidebar.

2. On the Half.com header, click **My Account** to create the seller's account.

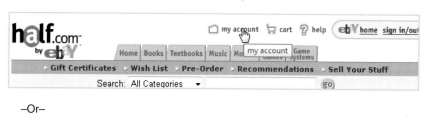

–Or–

Click **Sell Your Stuff** on the Half.com header to start listing your first item (see Figure 5-14) and set up your seller's account in the same process.

LIST YOUR PROPERTY ON RENT.COM

If you have an apartment, condo, townhouse, or house for rent, Rent.com provides a one-fee way for you to reach millions of potential renters. All you need to do is register with your e-mail address and password, fill out an easy three-page listing form, and provide a credit card for billing purposes. When you sign a lease from a Rent.com member, you'll pay Rent.com a $375 fee charged to your credit card. To get started:

1. On the eBay home page, click **Rent.com** under the Other eBay Companies sidebar.

2. Click **List A Property On Rent.com** on the Rent.com header, and then click **Get Started Now** on the Managers tab. Sign in by entering your e-mail address and password.

3. Create your listing by providing contact and property information.

SELL TICKETS ON STUBHUB

Have extra season or single tickets for sporting events, concerts, or Broadway shows? Sell your tickets through StubHub, and when notified by StubHub of a sale and to whom, you can mail the tickets to buyers with a pre-paid, FedEx shipping label you print out. Or you can also send your qualifying tickets to StubHub in advance and allow buyers to purchase them right up to the date of the show. There is no listing fee, and you can change the ticket price as the market determines its value. After a sale, StubHub pays you by check or by

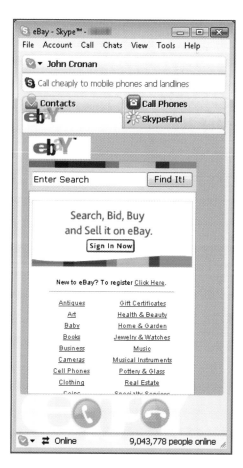

PayPal an amount equal to the selling price less their 15 percent commission. To start selling (or buying), you will need to create, yes, another account.

1. On the eBay home page, click **StubHub** under the Other eBay Companies sidebar.

2. Click **Register** on the StubHub header, and fill out the registration form.

3. After registering or signing in, click **Sell** on the StubHub header. On the Sell Tickets page, click the respective **Get Started** button to sell your tickets by mailing them directly to the buyer or by sending them to StubHub for last-minute delivery potential, as shown in Figure 5-16.

*Figure 5-15: **Use Skype instead of a browser to find and sell items on eBay, as well as to communicate with buyers.***

QUICKSTEPS

ADDING SKYPE TO YOUR LISTINGS

So what does a free (or at any rate, cheap) Voice-over Internet Protocol (VoIP) Internet phone service have to do with selling on eBay? Well, when you use the eBay version of Skype (see Figure 5-15), there are features that provide several reasons for you to consider using it. While using your computer to place free calls to anyone else in the world who is also in front of their computer using Skype is certainly neat, eBay ups the ante by adding buying- and selling-related features. To add the Skype button to your listings to let buyers know they can cheaply contact you by phone or chat:

1. Create an eBay Skype account if you don't already have one (on the eBay home page, click **Skype** under the Other eBay Companies sidebar, and download the free software).

Get Started
Skype is free and easy to download, instal use. Click the button to start downloading

2. Click **My eBay** on the eBay header, and click **Preferences** under the My Account sidebar.

3. Scroll down to the Member-To-Member Communication Preferences section, click **Show**, and then click **Add**.

4. On the Skype Preferences page, click **Link A Skype Name** to show your Skype status on your listings and let buyers contact you.

Continued . . .

UICKSTEPS

ADDING SKYPE TO YOUR LISTINGS
(Continued)

5. Log on to Skype, and on the menu bar, click **Tools**. Click **Options** on the drop-down menu, and then click **Privacy** on the Options page sidebar. Verify that the **Allow Anyone To Contact Me** option is selected.

6. Click the **Show Advanced Options** button, and select the **Allow My Status To Be Shown On The Web** check box. Click **Save** when finished. (You might have to go back to your Skype Preferences page in My eBay and add your Skype name to your eBay account.)

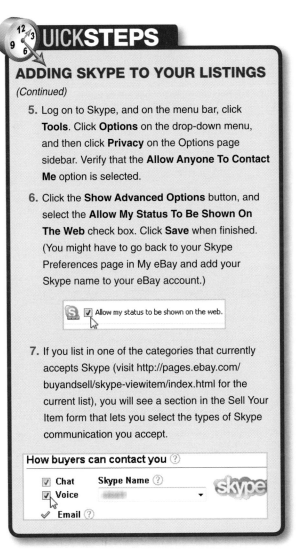

7. If you list in one of the categories that currently accepts Skype (visit http://pages.ebay.com/buyandsell/skype-viewitem/index.html for the current list), you will see a section in the Sell Your Item form that lets you select the types of Skype communication you accept.

Figure 5-16: *Start listing your tickets for sale by choosing whether you want to mail your tickets to buyers upon sale or to StubHub to allow for last-minute sales.*

How to...

- *Creating a Good Title*
- *Take Quality Pictures*
- *Describing Your Item*
- *Create a Custom Item Description*
- *Understanding the Sell Your Item Form*
- *Search for a Category Using Keywords*
- *Using Pre-Filled Information*
- *Browse for a Category*
- *Select a Recently Used Category*
- *Enter the Item Titles*
- *Customizing the Options Used in the Selling Form*
- *Use eBay Picture Services*
- *Adding Pictures and Videos*
- *Self-Host Your Pictures*
- *Describe Your Item*
- *Add a Theme and Layout*
- *Using a Counter*
- *Price the Item*
- *Understanding Quantity*
- *Schedule a Listing*
- *Add Payment Information*
- *Calculate Shipping Costs*
- *Establish Miscellaneous Policies*
- *Use Visibility Upgrades*
- *Correct Errors and Omissions*
- *Finalize Your Listing*
- *Obtain a Seller's Account*
- *Signing Up for a PayPal Premier Account*

Chapter 6
Listing an Item to Sell

In this chapter you will learn how to list an item for sale on eBay. The eBay *Sell Your Item* form is divided into several sections that walk you through the process, from choosing a category where your item will be cataloged, to creating a title and a description of the item, to adding pictures, providing payment and shipping details, and then ending with an opportunity to review your finished listing and make any last-minute changes (and if you are a first-time seller, an opportunity to obtain a seller's account).

The sections in this chapter walk you through the Sell Your Item form and dissect the actions involved. Details on using the form to stimulate sales are covered throughout this chapter, as well as in Chapter 5. Selling on eBay as a business is covered in Chapter 10.

CREATING A GOOD TITLE

Quickly, in 55 characters or less, tell The Donald (Trump) why he should hire you for a $250,000-a-year position. Keeping that metaphor in mind will help you craft titles for your items that will bring buyers to them and entice buyers to take the subsequent steps of viewing your pictures, reading your description, and submitting a bid. Buyers will be scanning lists looking for interesting titles. You will only have a few seconds of a buyer's time to entice him or her to look at your item in more detail.

Good item titles follow generally accepted protocols that have stood the test of (eBay) time:

● Clearly describe your item, using keywords that a bidder might typically use to find the item.

● Place the more important keywords toward the beginning of the title.

● Search for items that are similar to yours and see what other sellers are using to describe their items. For example, look at completed auctions and sales to view the titles used by successful sellers.

● If your item has associated branding, model names, or other unique descriptors, be sure to include them. "KitchenAid 5-qt Artisan 325-watt Mixer, Black" provides a whole lot more information and potential keyword hits than just "Mixer." This is also a good example of using both specific (KitchenAid, Artisan, 325-watt) and general (Mixer, Black) keywords for searchers who know exactly what they want and those who only kind of know what they are looking for.

Continued . . .

Prepare to Create a Listing

In order to place an item for bid in an eBay auction, create a Buy It Now listing, or add items for sale to an eBay Store (see Chapter 10), you will use the Sell Your Item form to create a listing that your potential customers will use to learn about your item. All you need to get started is to be registered on eBay (see Chapter 1 for information on how to do this). At the end of your first listing, eBay will require you to obtain a seller's account (see "Obtain a Seller's Account" later in this chapter).

Listing an item on eBay is best performed if you accomplish a few preliminary tasks prior to sitting down with the Sell Your Item form on the computer in front of you:

● Formulate a title that accurately describes your item, entices buyers, and allows them to easily find it when searching (see the "Creating a Good Title" QuickFacts).

● Obtain digital-format pictures of the item (see "Take Quality Pictures").

● Have notes formulated in your mind or, better yet, write out an accurate description of the item (see the "Describing Your Item" QuickFacts and "Create a Custom Item Description").

● Research comparable items to have a selling price in mind (Chapters 2 and 5 describe techniques you can use to find comparable values).

● Weigh the item (including packing material) so you have that information available when selecting shipping services (see "Calculate Shipping Costs" later in the chapter).

Take Quality Pictures

The fastest, cheapest, safest, and easiest way to obtain pictures for use on a selling form is to use a digital camera (unless the items are flat and can be placed on a flatbed scanner). For images that are designed to be displayed online, even a low-cost digital camera will be adequate (and thousands are for sale on eBay!).

You don't need to be a professional photographer or own a studio to produce quality pictures that capture a bidder's interest. There are several basic photographic pointers, however, that you can use to separate your listings from the pack.

CREATING A GOOD TITLE *(Continued)*

- Don't waste valuable characters by including buzzwords that no one would use in a search. You might consider your item a "fantastic" item, but unless your item is associated with the Fantastic Four, forget it.

- Don't assume the category name will carry over and support finding your item by a bidder. For example, if you are selling Classics Illustrated Juniors comic books and place them in the Books | Children's | Classics category, make sure you repeat "Classics" in your title.

THINK COMPOSITION

Photographic composition defines the detail, orientation, and symmetry of the picture. In eBay parlance, this boils down to taking pictures that focus on the item you are selling. If you are selling a silver place-setting, concentrate on the silverware itself, not on how well you can set a dining room table. Close-up pictures show details a buyer will be interested in; save the panoramas for your next trip to the Grand Canyon!

THINK SIZE

That new gazillion-megapixel camera takes great pictures, as evidenced by the striking print that comes off your inkjet printer. Most bidders and buyers, however, don't want to wait the two and a half hours it would take to download that picture. Use a *resolution* that is suitable for viewing online (anything over 100 pixels is unnecessary). Also, *size* relates to composition—a small picture makes it hard to see detail. eBay recommends a 1024×768 (pixels) size.

UTILIZE GOOD LIGHTING

Dark, backlit, and shadowed pictures show you are either an amateur photographer or haven't taken the time to create a quality picture—neither of which adds to your selling potential. Use a flash, unless you have added auxiliary lighting or have good natural lighting. There is no additional cost to take several shots with a digital camera until you have one that provides your item in its "best light."

CREATE A MINI-STUDIO

Even if you are a casual seller, it is worth your time to set up an area that provides a pleasing environment for your pictures. For example, if selling furniture, you might have a kit of backdrop sheets, clamps, floodlighting, and a dolly available. When selling small items, such as glassware, you might line an open box with fabric to create an instant setting or purchase a commercial light box, such as the Cloud Dome (www.clouddome.com).

DESCRIBING YOUR ITEM

An item description serves several basic purposes.

- It captures a buyer's attention using fonts, color, pictures, and other design elements.

- It clearly describes the item you are selling in terms of what it has to offer and the condition it is in.

- It acts as a placeholder for photos and graphics that support the text.

- It informs the bidder of transaction details, such as payment and shipping/handling (payment and shipping are addressed separately later in the Sell Your Item form, though many sellers prefer to explain their policies in their descriptions).

- It helps you avoid potential headaches (or legal action) by accurately describing the item so that the buyer cannot claim that the item is not as described.

ENHANCE YOUR PICTURES

Despite your best efforts, sometimes you are just unsatisfied with the results of your picture taking. Fortunately, most digital cameras come with at least rudimentary picture-editing software, and if they don't, you can purchase programs designed for the novice photographer, the professional photographer, and everyone in between. Editing programs such as Adobe's Photoshop and Photoshop Elements allow you to change resolution, sharpen images, adjust color, and otherwise change several other image attributes (see *Photoshop QuickSteps* or *Photoshop Elements 3 QuickSteps*, published by McGraw-Hill/ Osborne, for more information on editing pictures).

Create a Custom Item Description

eBay gives the seller a lot of latitude in creating an item description that is outside the boundaries of the tools and features on the Sell Your Item form. With only minimal knowledge, you can put together what is essentially your own Web page using Hypertext Markup Language (HTML) editors or adding the HTML code yourself. You can create eye-catching listings that include backgrounds, multiple pictures, a logo, and links to other Web pages that support the item, you as the seller, and your other eBay activities, as shown in Figure 6-1.

USE A WYSIWYG HTML EDITOR

The easiest way to create a Web page that you can use as your item description is to purchase a WYSIWYG (What You See Is What You Get) HTML editor, such as Microsoft FrontPage, that lets you use word processor-type controls to format text, add pictures, and create links.

USE HTML TO FORMAT TEXT

HTML employs a series of tags that identify the elements in a Web page. Tags consist of a tag name enclosed in angle brackets, and normally come in pairs. Tags are placed at the beginning and end of an element, usually text that you want to identify, with the ending tag name preceded by a slash. For example,

UNDERSTANDING THE SELL YOUR ITEM FORM

eBay divides the Sell Your Item form into three pages, with each page containing one or more sections that subdivide the page into areas of tasks needed.

THE SELL PAGE

The Sell page is an introductory page where you find information on selling and select a place to catalog your item within an eBay *category*. Categories, such as Nonfiction Books, help organize the millions of listings on eBay into similar grouping so that they can be found more easily by buyers.

THE CREATE YOUR LISTING PAGE

The main work in the Sell Your Item form takes place in five sections on the Create Your Listing page:

1. **What You're Selling** is where the category(ies) you selected on the Sell page are shown and where you can go back and change them if you choose.

2. **Describe Your Item** is where you catch the bidder's attention with words (title, subtitle, and a detailed description), pictures (photos, scanned images, and graphics), and other visual enhancements.

3. **How You're Selling** is where you select the selling format (auction, fixed price, or eBay Store) provide pricing, auction duration, and quantity details.

4. **Payment Method You Accept** is where you indicate to buyers the types of payments you accept.

5. **Shipping** is where you indicate to buyers how you want to handle shipping costs and options, and inform them where the item is physically located.

Continued . . .

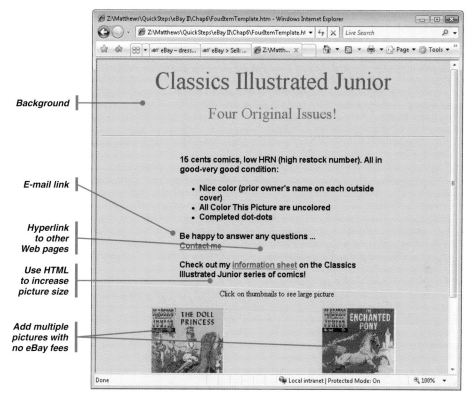

Figure 6-1: *Create listings that showcase your item with formatting, custom layouts, additional pictures, and hyperlinks.*

"Buy Now!" uses the bold tag to identify the word "Now." The phrase would display as Buy **Now**!

You can type your own tags in the HTML tab of the item description, or you can use a text editor, such as Notepad.

ADD PICTURES USING HTML

Pictures in the eBay selling form (and in Web pages in general) are not actually an integral part of the page; they are hosted, or linked, to the Web page from the Web server where they are located. All you have to do is add some HTML to your item description that points to the stored location.

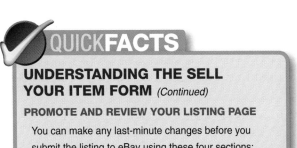

UNDERSTANDING THE SELL YOUR ITEM FORM *(Continued)*

PROMOTE AND REVIEW YOUR LISTING PAGE

You can make any last-minute changes before you submit the listing to eBay using these four sections:

1. **Make Your Listing Stand Out** lets you add listing upgrades.

2. **Recommendations For Your Listing** lets you review recommendations from eBay to better your chances of having a successful sale.

3. **Preview Your Listing** is where you see your listing as it will look to bidders.

4. **Fees** is where you review listing fees.

You can link to as many pictures of your item as you want.

1. In the selling form's Description area HTML tab, or in a text editor, use the IMG tag and SRC attribute (see *HTML QuickSteps*, published by McGraw-Hill/Osborne, to learn about using HTML and for descriptions of HTML terms, such as tag and attribute), and type *<IMG SRC="URL to picture">*. For example, if your picture, ParlorLight.jpg, is hosted on www.acmehosting.com in a folder named Jones, you would type *<IMG SRC="http://www.acmehosting.com/Jones/ParlorLight.jpg">*.

2. Preview your description and make any desired changes, such as combining an alignment tag to shift the picture on the page (for example, adding <CENTER> before the IMG tag will center the picture horizontally on the page).

Select a Category

All items on eBay are cataloged into categories, which provide a hierarchical listing of general-to-specific organization of the millions of items listed in auctions. As there are around 35,000 categories to choose from, you want to ensure that your item is cataloged in a logical place where buyers would most intuitively look for it.

To start the process of selling on eBay:

1. Click **Sell** on the eBay header.

   –Or–

   Point to **Sell** on the eBay header, and click **Sell An Item**.

In either case, the first page of the Sell Your Item form, the Sell page, displays as shown in Figure 6-2.

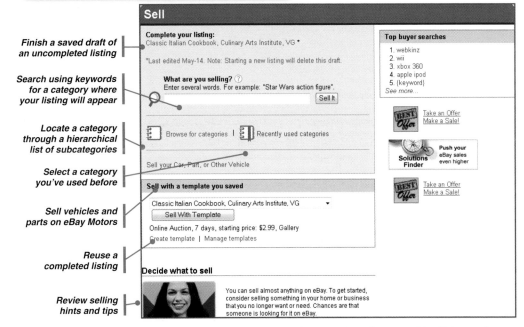

Finish a saved draft of an uncompleted listing

Search using keywords for a category where your listing will appear

Locate a category through a hierarchical list of subcategories

Select a category you've used before

Sell vehicles and parts on eBay Motors

Reuse a completed listing

Review selling hints and tips

*Figure 6-2: **The first page of the Sell Your Item form provides links to place your item within a category, sell on eBay Motors, or use forms you've used previously.***

NOTE

Not all items for sale on eBay use the standard Sell Your Item form. Specialty sites, such as eBay Express, eBay Motors, and Half.com, use their own selling forms to list items (see Chapters 5 and 10 for more information on selling in eBay specialty sites).

2. Browse the Sell page, and check out any of the links eBay provides to review selling hints (see Chapter 5 for ways to find items for sale and other selling-related techniques and strategies).

3. eBay provides several paths you can use to select a category. Type keywords (words that relate to your item) in the What Are You Selling? search box, and click **Sell It**. eBay will display a list of categories of similar items that you can choose from (see "search for a Category Using Keywords").

–Or–

Click **Browse For Categories** to start from a top-level category and work your way down into more specific subcategories, ultimately choosing your listing category (see "Browse for a Category").

–Or–

Click **Recently Used Categories** to choose from recent categories you used in other listings. The first time you use the Sell Your Item form, you might not see this option since you have no category history (see "Select a Recently Used Category").

(Alternatively, you can use the Sell page to list vehicle-related items on eBay Motors and use selling forms you've worked on previously, shown in Figure 6-2.)

Search for a Category Using Keywords

You can find a category to list your item in by providing keywords that relate to your item and having eBay search its listings inventory and seeing where other sellers are listing like items.

1. On the Sell page, type one or more keywords in the What Are You Selling? text box (see Figure 6-2).

2. Click **Sell It**. The Sell: Select A Category page displays one or more category hierarchies, listed in order by an estimate of the percentage of items found in each, as shown in Figure 6-3.

CAUTION

Choosing a second category will double your insertion fee as well as certain upgrade fees, such as those incurred when you make your listing title bold. The final value fee, however, will not be increased, nor will the fees increase for Scheduled Listings and Home Page Featured (including eBay Motors Featured) upgrades. Also, you cannot include a second category for adult items (you can only list in two subcategories within the Mature Audiences category), Dutch auctions (see Chapter 1 for a description of Dutch auctions), real estate, and for capital equipment (Business & Industrial category). You can list eBay Motors parts and accessories in both eBay Motors and eBay.com, but you cannot list a vehicle outside of eBay Motors (Chapter 10 describes selling on eBay Motors).

QUICKSTEPS

USING PRE-FILLED INFORMATION

There are several categories that are tied to product identifiers, which provide pre-filled item information and pictures for you. For example, if you choose a book category, you are given the opportunity to enter an ISBN number, title, or author's name; for a music CD, you can enter a UPC code, title, or artist. You can use the information provided (see Figure 6-4) or create your own item description (see the "Describing Your Item" QuickFacts earlier in the chapter).

Continued . . .

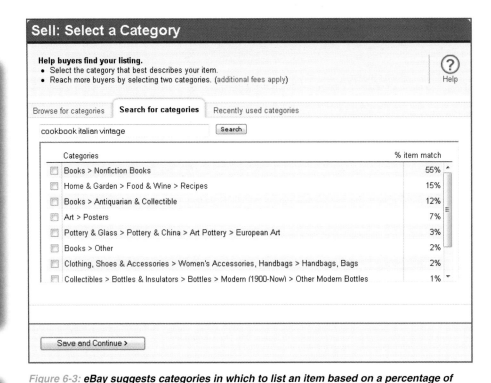

Figure 6-3: *eBay suggests categories in which to list an item based on a percentage of found keywords.*

3. Click the check box next to the main category that you want to use. When you select the check box, you'll see Categories You Have Selected below the category list. Click **See Sample Listings** to review the type of listings your item will be among. (To make your item more accessible to buyers, you can have the item listed in an optional second category, increasing your exposure and potentially increasing the final price by as much as 17 percent, according to eBay).

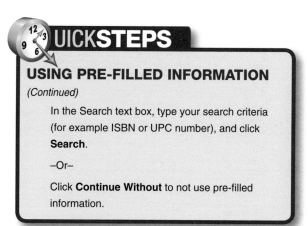
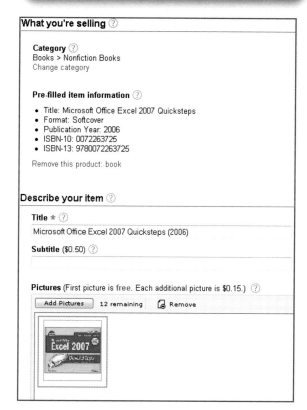

What you're selling ⑦

Category ⑦
Books > Nonfiction Books
Change category

Pre-filled item information ⑦
- Title: Microsoft Office Excel 2007 Quicksteps
- Format: Softcover
- Publication Year: 2006
- ISBN-10: 0072263725
- ISBN-13: 9780072263725

Remove this product: book

Describe your item ⑦

Title ✱ ⑦
Microsoft Office Excel 2007 Quicksteps (2006)

Subtitle ($0.50) ⑦

Pictures (First picture is free. Each additional picture is $0.15.) ⑦

Add Pictures   12 remaining   🗑 Remove

*Figure 6-4: **Pre-filled information describes your commodity item and adds a picture when available.***

The first category you select will be your main category; the second category selected will be your for-fee second category.

Categories you have selected
- Books > Nonfiction Books | See sample listings | Remove

–Or–

Change categories by clearing the check box next to your selected category or by clicking **Remove**.

–Or–

Reenter a keyword in the search text box, and click **Search** to try again using different keywords.

–Or–

Click one of the two other tabs to find categories using alternate methods (described next).

4. Click **Save And Continue**. If you didn't select a second category in step 3, you might see a window where you can add a second category (some categories you select won't generate this window). Accept the default No Second Category, or select one of the recommended second categories if that's what you want. Click **Continue**.

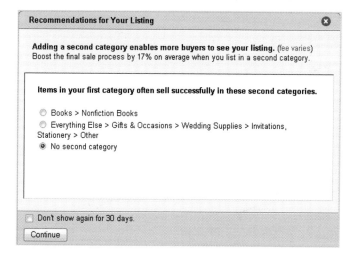

Recommendations for Your Listing   ⊗

Adding a second category enables more buyers to see your listing. (fee varies)
Boost the final sale process by 17% on average when you list in a second category.

Items in your first category often sell successfully in these second categories.

○ Books > Nonfiction Books
○ Everything Else > Gifts & Occasions > Wedding Supplies > Invitations, Stationery > Other
◉ No second category

☐ Don't show again for 30 days.

Continue

–Or–

If you sell commodity-type items, such as books or DVDs, you will see a window where you can use pre-filled item information (see the "Using Pre-Filled Information" QuickSteps).

In either case, the second page of the selling form, Sell: Create Your Listing, will display.

Browse for a Category

You can manually move through the category hierarchy to find a category for your item by using a category selector.

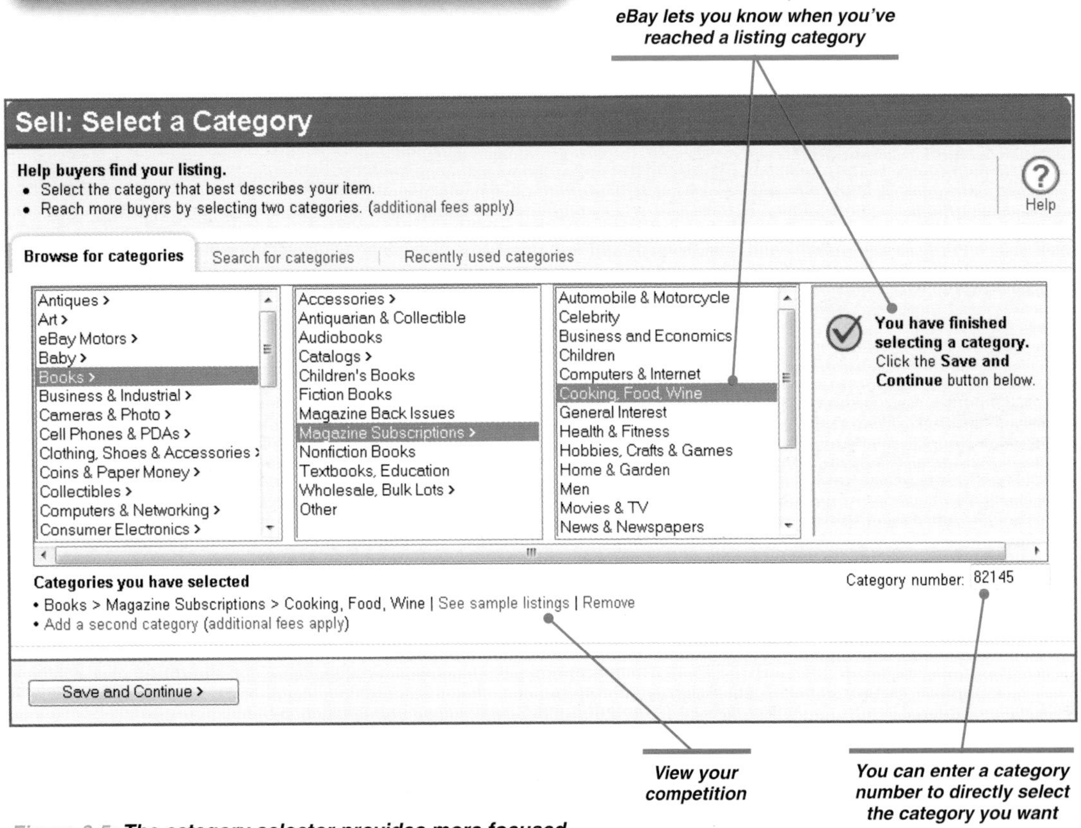

TIP

If you know the category number of the category you want, type the number in the Category Number text box under the category selector, and press **ENTER**.

eBay lets you know when you've reached a listing category

Sell: Select a Category

Help buyers find your listing.
- Select the category that best describes your item.
- Reach more buyers by selecting two categories. (additional fees apply)

(?) Help

Browse for categories | Search for categories | Recently used categories

Antiques >	Accessories >	Automobile & Motorcycle
Art >	Antiquarian & Collectible	Celebrity
eBay Motors >	Audiobooks	Business and Economics
Baby >	Catalogs >	Children
Books >	Children's Books	Computers & Internet
Business & Industrial >	Fiction Books	Cooking, Food, Wine
Cameras & Photo >	Magazine Back Issues	General Interest
Cell Phones & PDAs >	Magazine Subscriptions >	Health & Fitness
Clothing, Shoes & Accessories >	Nonfiction Books	Hobbies, Crafts & Games
Coins & Paper Money >	Textbooks, Education	Home & Garden
Collectibles >	Wholesale, Bulk Lots >	Men
Computers & Networking >	Other	Movies & TV
Consumer Electronics >		News & Newspapers

(✓) **You have finished selecting a category.** Click the **Save and Continue** button below.

Categories you have selected
- Books > Magazine Subscriptions > Cooking, Food, Wine | See sample listings | Remove
- Add a second category (additional fees apply)

Category number: 82145

[Save and Continue >]

*Figure 6-5: **The category selector provides more focused subcategories after you choose a higher-level category.***

View your competition

You can enter a category number to directly select the category you want

1. On the Sell page, click **Browse For Categories**. On the Sell: Select A Category page, click the category in the list box to the left. The next level of subcategories is displayed in the box to the right, as shown in Figure 6-5.

Browse for categories

2. Select the subcategory you think best applies, and either a new list of more focused subcategories is displayed in a list box to the right, or you will see a message letting you know there are no more subcategories below the one you have chosen. You also know you have reached a final category when the Category # indicator contains a number (see Figure 6-5).

3. When finished, click **Save And Continue**. Depending on the category you selected you might be given the opportunity to select a second category or be presented with a window to use pre-filled information (see the "Using Pre-Filled Information" QuickSteps).

This will be the title of your listing. Fill it with words about your item that buyers would enter in a search. ⊗

More help | Show/Hide Options

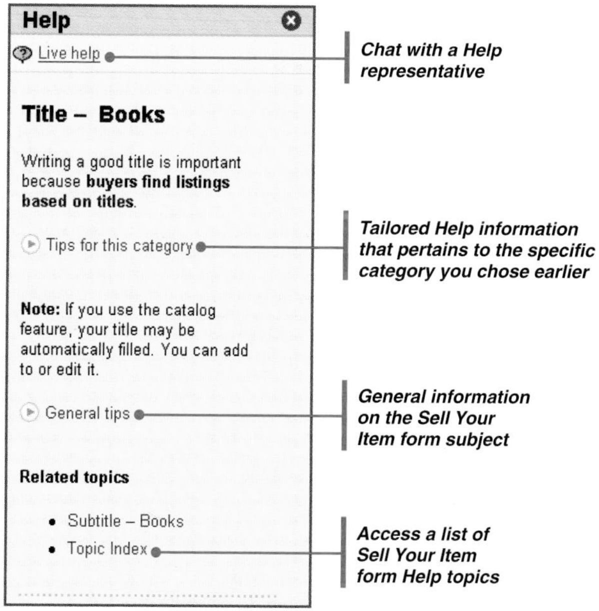

Help ⊗

⊙ Live help ●——————— **Chat with a Help representative**

Title – Books

Writing a good title is important because **buyers find listings based on titles.**

▶ Tips for this category ●——————— **Tailored Help information that pertains to the specific category you chose earlier**

Note: If you use the catalog feature, your title may be automatically filled. You can add to or edit it.

▶ General tips ●——————— **General information on the Sell Your Item form subject**

Related topics

• Subtitle – Books
• Topic Index ●——————— **Access a list of Sell Your Item form Help topics**

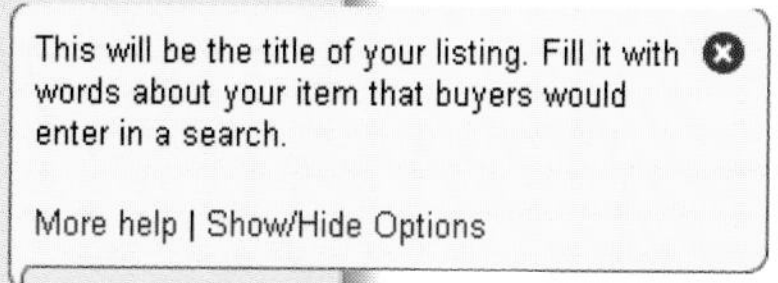

Figure 6-6: The Help pane provides links to topics that assist you in filling out the Sell Your Item form and access to chat with Help personnel.

Select a Recently Used Category

If you are listing an item that you've already listed, you can quickly select it from a list of recently used categories.

1. On the Sell page, click **Recently Used Categories** (the first time you use the Sell page, you might not see a Recently Used Categories link, since you have no category history).

–Or–

On the Sell: Select A Category page, click the **Recently Used Categories** tab.

2. In either case, click the check box next to the category you want to use, similar to that shown in Figure 6-3.

3. Click **Save And Continue** when finished. Depending on the category you selected, you might be given the opportunity to select a second category or be presented with a window to use pre-filled information (see the "Using Pre-Filled Information QuickSteps).

Create Your Listing

The second page of the Sell form, Sell: Create Your Listing, is the "meat and potatoes" part of the listing process. Here you will perform the actions that will advertise your item in words, pictures, and design. Also, you will determine pricing, payment methods, and shipping considerations. As with most aspects of eBay, there is a default set of features as well as options and upgrades.

Enter the Item Titles

Your title can make or break a sale. Spend a few extra minutes ensuring it describes your item accurately and with keywords buyers will likely be using (see the "Creating a Good Title" QuickFacts earlier in the chapter).

CUSTOMIZING THE OPTIONS USED IN THE SELLING FORM

By default, not all possible options that are available for use on the Sell Your Item form are displayed. You can customize the selling form so that only the options you typically use are shown and streamline your listing process. (To follow along in this book, you might want to initially select all of them). To view the available options and make changes:

1. At the top of the Sell: Create Your Listing page, click **Show/ Hide Options**.

   Show/Hide Options

   –Or–

   Click the small **Help** icon ⑦ in the area of the form where you want to add or hide an option, and click **Show Hide/Options** in the Help balloon.

2. In the left pane of the Customize Form window (see Figure 6-7), click the category of options you want to see (if you clicked Show/Hide Options from the Help balloon, the applicable category will be selected for you).

3. In the right pane, select or clear the options you want see or hide.

4. Click **Save** when finished.

TIP

The green asterisk next to an option on the Sell Your Item form denotes a mandatory entry. **Description** ＊ ⑦

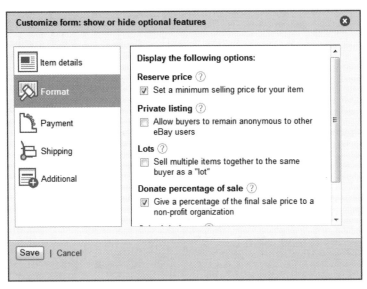

Figure 6-7: **You can customize the Sell Your Item form to show or hide several options.**

ADD THE ITEM TITLE

There are few rules you must follow when adding a title. You cannot use HTML to enhance your 55-character (including spaces) title, nor can you use asterisks or quotation marks. You can **bold** your title to make it stand out. See "Use Visibility Upgrades" later in the chapter.

In the Describe Your Item section, type your title in the Title text box.

ADD A SUBTITLE

Subtitles, for a fee ($0.50), allow you to double the 55-character limit imposed by the Item Title box. Subtitles are used to add amplifying information and

differentiate your item from a list of similar items, allowing you to load the title with keywords the buyer will be using to find the item. Subtitles are governed by the same limitations as titles.

In the Subtitle box, type your amplifying information, adhering to the 55-character limit. (If you go over the limit, eBay might do some "editing" for you.)

Use eBay Picture Services

eBay Picture Services provides one free hosted picture and includes several free and for-fee features. For most new (and many experienced) sellers, eBay Picture Services provides an easy and reasonably valued way to include pictures in listings.

ADD PICTURES

1. Under Describe Your Item | Pictures, click **Add Pictures** [Add Pictures]. A three-tab page displays with the Enhanced tab selected. If you haven't already used Enhanced eBay Picture Services (which is recommended), eBay will need to install a small add-on program to your browser. (You do not have to install the file to use the *Basic* eBay Picture Services—just click **Cancel**, click the **Basic** tab, and follow similar steps to the following, though you will not be able to use convenient editing tools.) Your browser's security setting typically prevents the installation without your permission. Click the security bar,

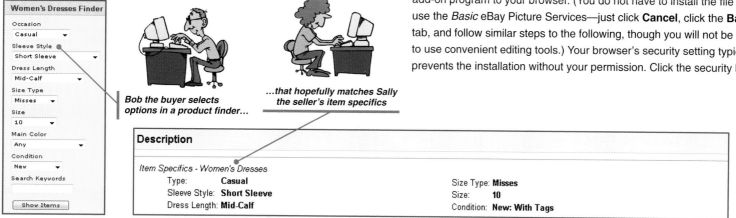

Figure 6-8: *Item specifics let you provide information that buyers can use to search for just the item they want.*

ADDING PICTURES AND VIDEOS

As the saying goes, a picture is worth a thousand words. Pictures (which include photos, scans, and graphics) and videos can go a long way in supplementing the descriptive text of your item. Your picture and video options depend on how you host, or store, your material. Pictures and videos are not physically added or copied to the selling form—you type a link to where the material is hosted.

ADD PICTURES

Hosting options include:

- eBay Picture Services, using basic or enhanced features (see "Use eBay Picture Services").
- Self-hosting, using your own hosting site or a third-party service (see "Self-Host Your Pictures").

To use pictures in your listing:

1. Create the JPG, PNG, or GIF file using a digital camera, scanner, or drawing program (see "Take Quality Pictures" earlier in the chapter).

2. Link the picture to the Sell Your Item form through eBay Picture Services (where you first upload the picture from your computer to eBay) or a hosting Web server.

ADD VIDEOS

You can link to videos you own (see Chapter 5 for information on eBay's intellectual property rights policies).

1. Upload the video to one of eBay's approved video hosting sites: AOL, Google, Microsoft, MySpace, or YouTube.

2. Add a link to the video in your item description.

click **Install ActiveX Control** from the menu, and accept any subsequent messages to install the add-on.

2. Click **Add Pictures** in the 1. (Free) box. In the Open dialog box, browse to locate the picture you want to appear in the listing. Double-click the picture, and a thumbnail appears in the box. A larger view of the selected picture displays in the preview area to the right of the thumbnails, as shown in Figure 6-9.

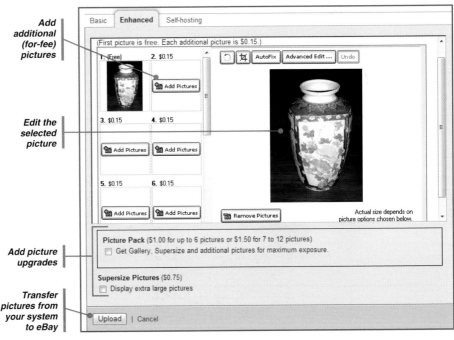

Figure 6-9: **Adding pictures to eBay Picture Services is a simple process of locating the files on your local system.**

–Or–

If using Basic eBay Picture Services, click **Browse**. The path to your picture is shown without either a thumbnail or larger preview of the image.

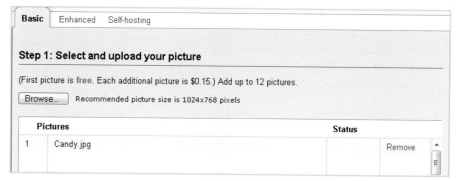

3. Add additional pictures, or select options from the preview area (see "Edit Your Pictures," next).

4. Click **Upload** at the bottom of the page. The picture(s) will be uploaded to eBay through your Internet connection and will appear in the Sell Your Item form. To remove a picture, select it and click **Remove**.

EDIT YOUR PICTURES

You can perform several actions from the preview area on pictures you host using Enhanced eBay Picture Services (these actions are not available to pictures you choose using the Basic Picture Services tool).

Click the thumbnail you want to change:

- Click the **Rotate** button to rotate a picture. Each time you click the button, the picture in the preview area rotates counterclockwise 90 degrees.

- Click the **Crop** button to trim a picture. Sizing handles appear on the picture in the preview area. Drag the preview picture's border or corner to the rectangular area you want to display. You can move the crop rectangle by placing your mouse pointer over the area and dragging the four-sided pointer. The shaded area outside the new border will not display in the listing. When you click another image, the cropping will be done.

- Click **AutoFix** to automatically apply brightness and contrast changes to the picture.

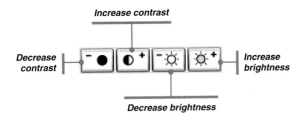

Increase contrast

Decrease contrast

Increase brightness

Decrease brightness

- Click **Advanced Edit** to gain access to contrast and brightness buttons that allow you to manually increase or decrease those settings. Click **Save** in the Advanced Edit window to keep the changes.

- Click **Undo** to reverse a change.

- Click the **Remove Pictures** button to remove a picture.

UPGRADE YOUR PICTURES

eBay provides several ways you can increase the effectiveness of your pictures (see Figure 6-9):

- **Add additional pictures** ($0.15 each), up to a maximum of 12.

- **Picture Pack** is a package deal of features—up to six pictures, supersizing, and Gallery Picture listing ($1.00, or increase from seven to 12 pictures for $1.50).

- **Supersizing** a picture that, when selected by the bidder, displays an enlargement up to 11×8 inches in size ($0.75).

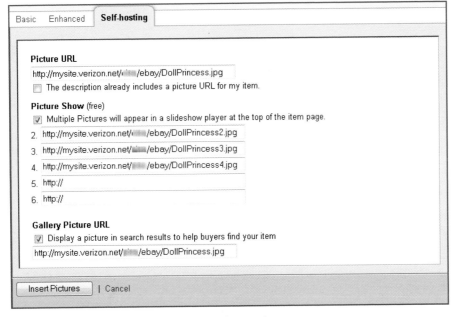

Figure 6-10: **You can link the pictures that show up in your listing to their Web server storage locations, or URLs.**

Self-Host Your Pictures

The Self-Hosting tab (see Figure 6-10) provides a way to link the Sell Your Item form to pictures that are stored on a Web site, for example, from your own Web server or from a site hosted by your Internet service provider (ISP). There really isn't a benefit to self-hosting your picture over eBay Picture Services if you use this method, but it is sometimes necessary if you use a third-party hosting service. You still only get one free picture, and the tool is less user-friendly than Picture Services, especially the Enhanced tool. To self-host your pictures:

1. Under Describe Your Item | Picture, click **Add Pictures** and click the **Self-Hosting** tab.

2. In the Picture URL text box, type the URL for the picture after http://, for example, http://www.mysite.com/comicbooks/superman1.jpg. If applicable (see the accompanying Tip), click **The Description Already Includes A Picture URL For My Item** check box.

TIP

A better way to use self-hosting is to include the picture's location (URL—Uniform Resource Locator) directly in the item's description, avoiding having to manually add each picture's URL in the Sell Your Item form. This way, you can add as many pictures as you want at no cost. See "Create a Custom Item Description" earlier in the chapter for more information on creating descriptions that include pictures.

NOTE

eBay takes a special interest in sellers of items that are downloaded to buyers in a digital format, such as .mp3 or .pdf files. To offer these items, you must only accept PayPal for payment, have a PayPal (Verified) Premier or Business account, and provide a Web address or other means for delivery. Also, you will be asked to confirm that you are authorized by the legal rights owner to sell the item or are yourself the legal rights owner. If you are selling digitally delivered items, click **List As A Digital File Or Information** between the Pictures and Description areas of the Sell Your Item form.

Digital Items ⓘ

ⓘ Use this option if your item is a digital file or information that will be made available to the buyer online or delivered electronically
List as a digital file or information

3. If you want to add more pictures (limit of six) that will be included in a picture show where buyers can cycle through them, click the **Multiple Pictures Will Appear** check box. Five more text boxes will appear where you can add more URLs.

4. To include a Gallery picture ($0.35) that appears in pages of listings next to your title, click the **Display A Picture In search Results To Help Buyers Find Your Item** check box. Type the URL in the text box that appears, or accept the URL for the picture that is displayed by default. (You can change the Gallery picture at the bottom of the Picture area.)

5. Click **Insert Pictures** when finished. The picture(s) you selected will appear in the Sell Your Item form.

6. Click **Preview** at the bottom of the Picture area to see how your picture(s) will appear in the listing. If you chose the Picture Show option, you can cycle through the pictures you are hosting (you might have to temporaly allow pop-up windows in your browser for the Preview Your Listing window to open). Click **Close** at the bottom of the window to return to the listing.

1 of 4

View larger picture

Describe Your Item

eBay provides two text palettes you can use to enter text that will appear to buyers as the item description. In the Standard tab, you can enter plain text and enhance it with word processing-like styles to spice up the formatting, or in the HTML tab, format it using HTML tags you apply. In addition, you can paste text (with or without HTML tags) from another program (for example, Microsoft Word) or paste text/HTML from a template you've created to use over and over for similar items (see the "Describing Your Item" QuickFacts and "Create a Custom Item Description" earlier in the chapter for more information on writing and structuring descriptions).

1. In the Describe Your Item | Description area, click the **Standard** tab, and start typing your description. Select text by dragging over it, and use the formatting toolbar to apply formatting styles, as shown in Figure 6-11. Press **ENTER** to create new paragraphs.

TIP

When creating your description, periodically click **Save Draft** at the bottom of the description entry window. A copy of your description, as well as your other Sell Your Item form selections and entries, is saved. The last thing you want to have happen is a computer or Internet "oops" that deletes a lot of your effort and time. If a problem occurs in your listing, return to the Sell page and click your listing title to continue filling out the form.

Sell

List using the original Sell Your Item form.
Complete your listing:
Classics Illustrated Junior *

*Last edited Apr-18. Note: Starting a new listing will delete this draft.

–Or–

Click the **HTML** tab, and type your description. Format the text by typing the applicable HTML tags.

Standard **HTML**

Check spelling   Inserts

\<FONT face=Arial size=2>\<FONT size=2>
\<P align=center>\<FONT color=#fb0034 size=5>\<STRONG>Crosby, Hope &
\<P>\<STRONG>Crosby\</STRONG>, Hope and Lamour are featured on the
Produced by Paramount Music Corporation, copyrighted 1942. Include refrains

–Or–

Paste formatted text or HTML-tagged text from another program, such as Microsoft Word or an HTML editor (see "Create a Custom Item Description" earlier in the chapter for more information on setting up your item description outside of the Sell Your Item form).

2. Click the **Check Spelling** button to spell check your title, subtitle, and description. Bidders are not typically interested in whether you have an English degree, although a poorly constructed listing will raise some eyebrows. In the Check Spelling window, shown in Figure 6-12, errors are highlighted in red in the titles or description, and the Change To box contains the first recommended suggestion from the Suggestions box. Accept or select a suggestion, or type a different word. Click **Change**

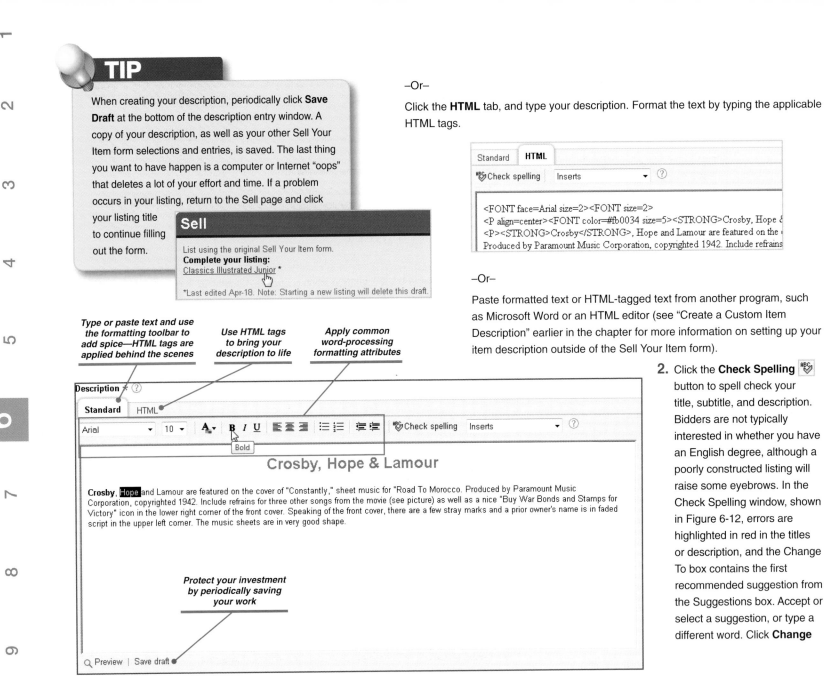

Type or paste text and use the formatting toolbar to add spice—HTML tags are applied behind the scenes

Use HTML tags to bring your description to life

Apply common word-processing formatting attributes

Description *

Standard   HTML

Arial   10   A   **B** *I* U   Check spelling   Inserts

Bold

Crosby, Hope & Lamour

Crosby, Hope and Lamour are featured on the cover of "Constantly," sheet music for "Road To Morocco. Produced by Paramount Music Corporation, copyrighted 1942. Include refrains for three other songs from the movie (see picture) as well as a nice "Buy War Bonds and Stamps for Victory" icon in the lower right corner of the front cover. Speaking of the front cover, there are a few stray marks and a prior owner's name is in faded script in the upper left corner. The music sheets are in very good shape.

Protect your investment by periodically saving your work

Q Preview | Save draft

Figure 6-11: **You can type or paste text in the Description tabs, and apply word-processing formatting and HTML tags.**

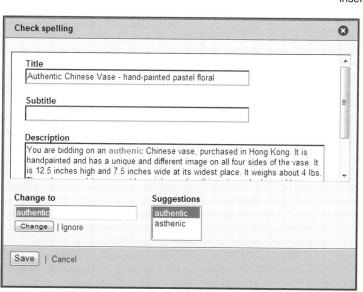

Create an Insert

Create and store for future listings up to five personalized Inserts. Entries will appear in the Inserts drop-down list.

Name your Insert

20 Characters maximum

Enter your text or HTML

4000 Characters maximum (HTML or text)

[Save] Cancel

to replace the red-highlighted word or click **Ignore** to skip it. In either case, the next misspelled word is highlighted in red. Click **Save** when finished.

3. Click the **Inserts** down arrow, and click **Create An Insert** to name and type (or paste) the text for the insert (if you don't see this option, see the "Customizing the Options Used in the Selling Form" QuickSteps earlier in the chapter). Inserts allow you to create and save text segments for use in item descriptions (or to insert the entire item description and use it as a template) in future listings. You can have up to five inserts of 4,000 characters or less each.

–Or–

Click the insert you want, either a previous insert you created or an eBay-provided insert. For example, the Seller's Other Items insert adds a link to your other items for sale, and the Add To Favorites List insert lets buyers add you to their Favorite list. (Ensure that you place your insertion point in the item description where you want the insert to be placed.)

4. When finished, click **Preview** at the bottom of the Description window to see how your description will appear in the listing buyers will see.

Add a Theme and Layout

In the Listing Designer section of the selling form ($0.10 fee), you can easily add some flair and choose how your description and pictures are arranged. *Themes* provide a template of color and graphics that support a design, a topic of interest, or an eBay category. *Layouts* let you choose how to locate pictures of your item in relationship to your listing description.

1. In the Listing Designer area, click the **Enhance Description With A Theme And Picture Layout** check box.

Listing designer ($0.10) ?
☑ Enhance description with a theme and picture layout

*Figure 6-12: **Catch potentially embarrassing typos by checking the spelling in your title, subtitle, and description.***

2. Click the **Select A Theme** down arrow, and select a category of available themes. After the Web page refreshes, the themes within the selected category are displayed in the associated Select Design list box.

3. Select one or more designs. A miniature representation (or *thumbnail*) of each design appears in the sample area.

4. Click the **Picture Layout** down arrow, and select how you want to arrange your description and pictures. A sample of each choice is displayed in the sample area as you click it.

5. Click **Preview** to see how your theme and layout choices will look together in your listing, as shown in Figure 6-13.

Price the Item

Pricing is an art as old as the history of the first buy-sell transaction, balancing what a seller thinks he or she can obtain for an item against what a buyer thinks it is worth in monetary terms. eBay pricing can be even more interesting as you

QUICKSTEPS

USING A COUNTER

A counter keeps track of the number of times a page has been viewed, providing a measure of how many bidders and buyers have viewed your listing. You can choose to display the count or keep the count hidden from everyone but yourself (in either case, the counter appears at the top of the listing).

Click the **Visitor Counter** down arrow, and click **Basic Style** 01234 or **Retro-Computer Style** 01234.

–Or–

Click **Hidden** to keep the counter private.

–Or–

Click the default blank option to omit a counter.

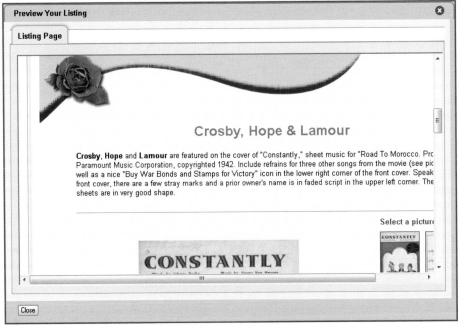

Figure 6-13: *Enhance your item description using theme and layout features.*

add the complexity of bidding to the mix (see Chapter 5 for pricing techniques). There are three pricing formats you can choose from:

● The standard online auction starting price (required) and possible reserve price.

● A fixed-price format (Buy It Now price).

● A blend of online and fixed-price formats.

(If you have an eBay Store, you will be provided an additional option for adding Store inventory; Chapter 10 describes eBay Stores.)

SET ONLINE AUCTION PRICING

You need to establish the price where bidding will begin for your item. This is also the lowest price you will accept for your item—unless you decide to use a *reserve* price, which is a price unknown to the bidders until the bidding action has reached that pricing threshold.

You can also blend a bidding-style and fixed-price listing by starting with an auction format and then adding a Buy It Now price (if you're qualified to be a fixed-price seller). The Buy It Now price is only available until the first bid is made. At the point of the first bid, the icon will no longer appear on your live auction page and the auction will continue on a bidding basis only.

In the How You're Selling section, under Selling Format:

Chapter 5 describes the fees for inserting the various selling formats.

1. Click the **Online Auction** tab. In the Starting Price text box, type the price where you want the bidding to start (for multiple items or Dutch auctions, the minimum starting price is $0.99).

2. If you elect to establish a reserve price, click **Change** (if you don't see this option, see the "Customizing the Options Used in the Selling Form" QuickSteps earlier in the chapter). In the Set Reserve Price window, shown in Figure 6-14, type the price in the Reserve Price text box, and click **Save**.

3. If you want to include a starting auction price and a Buy It Now option, set your starting price, add a reserve price if you want one, and in the Buy It Now Price text box, type your price.

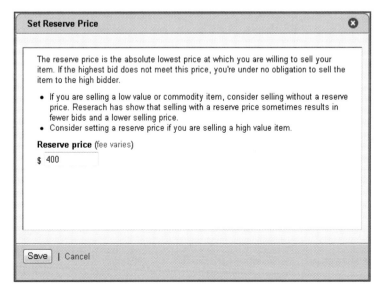

Figure 6-14: **A reserve price protects you from getting "burned" on an item, but it may deter buyers.**

UNDERSTANDING QUANTITY

For most sellers, you will use the default (1) in the Quantity text box, but if you sell more than one of the same or similar item, you need to understand how multiple items and lots are handled.

SELL MULTIPLE ITEMS

Multiple-item bidding is handled differently, depending on the auction format: online auction or fixed price (Buy It Now):

- Multiple-item listings for online auctions (or Dutch auctions) require bidders to specify a quantity and bid amount, resulting in a final bid amount by multiplying the two values. All bidders pay the same amount, that of the lowest successful bidder (determined when the quantity has been bid to zero).

- Fixed-price listings handle multiple-item purchases by simply multiplying the quantity the buyer wants by the price of the item.

On the Online Auction tab, type the quantity in the Quantities text box if you are selling multiple items. To sell multiple items, you must have a minimum feedback rating of 30 or be ID Verified (if you have a PayPal account and offer PayPal payments, you can cut the feedback requirement to 15).

SELL LOTS

Lots are packages, groups, or collections of the same or similar item. To sell lots, you first need to display the Lot text boxes instead of the default Quantity text box (see the "Customizing the Options Used in the Selling Form" QuickSteps earlier in the chapter).

Lots (?)
☑ Sell multiple items together to the same buyer as a "lot"

Fill out the **Number Of Lots** and **Items Per Lot** text boxes with your applicable number of lots and items for sale.

SET FIXED-PRICE LISTING PRICING AND INCLUDE BEST OFFER

If you qualify—that is, you have a feedback rating of 10 or greater, or you have proved your identity by using ID Verify; offer PayPal as a payment and you only need a feedback rating of five—you can establish a fixed *Buy It Now* (or in eBay shorthand: BIN) price that lets a buyer purchase the item at that price. Also, you can optionally let buyers offer you a price they are willing to pay—their best offer.

1. In the Selling Format area, click the **Fixed Price** tab.

2. Type the sales price in the Buy It Now Price text box.

3. Click the **Allow Buyers To Send You Their Best Offer For Your Consideration** check box if you want to offer this option. Select how you want to respond to offers.

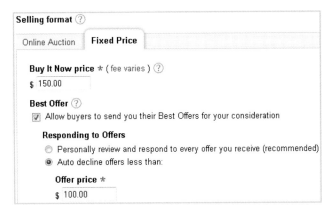

Schedule a Listing

You can schedule your listing to last for one of several different durations and determine when to start the sale.

1. In the Selling Format area, click the **Duration** down arrow, and select the number of days you want your listing to last. (To be able to use a one-day listing, you must have either a feedback rating of 10 or a feedback rating of 5 and accept PayPal as a payment method.)

NOTE

A private auction cannot be used if you are selling multiple items. Private auctions are typically used to sell adult products, items of high value, and those items that might otherwise embarrass bidders if others knew they bid on them.

NOTE

There is a lot of debate over the optimal duration to sell an item. Unless you have a specific reason to use the one-day option (such as the time-sensitive expiration date of an event ticket, or if you have a large inventory of the same item that you just want to turn over quickly), you're probably better off gaining more exposure for your item with a longer duration. On the other hand, will a ten-day auction deter bidders who want their purchase sooner rather than later? A seven-day auction gives potential bidders a week to find your auction and doesn't cost you any extra—our vote!

NOTE

In order to use the Start Time feature to schedule a start time other than when the listing is submitted, you must have a credit card on file with eBay.

2. By default, a sale will start when you submit the listing and end the number of days later you chose as the duration. For example, if you submit a seven-day listing at 8:35 P.M. on Sunday, October 7, 2007, the listing will be scheduled to end at 8:35 P.M. on Sunday, October 14, 2007. If you want to start a sale up to three weeks in advance (in 15-minute increments), you create a scheduled listing. Click **Schedule Start Time** ($0.10 fee), click the **Date** and **Time** down arrows, and choose the day and time you want the listing to start (if you don't see this option, see the "Customizing the Options Used in the Selling Form" QuickSteps earlier in the chapter).

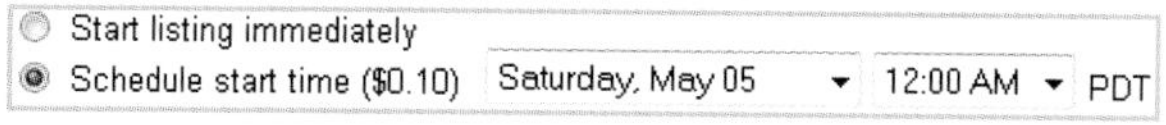

○ Start listing immediately
◉ Schedule start time ($0.10)   Saturday, May 05   ▼   12:00 AM ▼ PDT

3. If you don't want the User IDs of buyers displayed in a listing, you can designate the listing as private (if you don't see this option, see the "Customizing the Options Used in the Selling Form" QuickSteps). Click the **Allow Buyers To Remain Anonymous To Other eBay Users** check box.

Private listing ⑦
☑ Allow buyers to remain anonymous to other eBay users

Add Payment Information

You have several choices in how you inform successful bidders how to pay you (see Chapter 5 for information on acceptable forms of payment you can offer). The options you choose will appear in the Payment Details section in the listing the bidder or buyer sees, as shown in Figure 6-15.

Payment details

Payment method	Preferred/Accepted	Buyer protection on eBay
PayPal (MasterCard, VISA, AMEX, DISCOVER, eCHECK)	Seller Preferred	**PayPal** Up to $2,000 in buyer protection. See eligibility
Money order/Cashiers check	Accepted	Not Available
Personal check	Accepted	Not Available
Other - See Payment Instructions for payment methods accepted	Accepted	Not Available

Figure 6-15: **The payment methods you accept on the Sell Your Item form appear in the Payment Details section of the listing your customers see.**

Additional payment methods ⓘ

☐ Money order / Cashier's check	Merchant credit card
☐ Personal check	☐ Visa / MasterCard
☐ Other / See item description	☐ Discover
	☐ American Express

CHOOSE PAYPAL

The first option to appear in the Payment Methods You Accept area is for PayPal, eBay's own online payment service. Unless you accept credit card payments through a merchant account, you will need to accept PayPal for that purpose. Accepting PayPal is highly recommended as a convenient and safe way for buyers to make payments. There is no cost to the buyer, and if you offer PayPal solely, you can take advantage of PayPal's Buy Now feature that provides immediate payment from the buyer's PayPal account to yours. See the "Signing Up for a PayPal Premier Account" QuickSteps later in the chapter.

1. Click the **PayPal** check box (if you see a blue check mark next to PayPal, you have set a preference to have PayPal offered on all your listings).

2. Ensure that the e-mail address in the Email Address For Receiving Payment text box is the correct address for your PayPal account (if you don't have an account, type the e-mail address you will use, and create the account later in the listing process).

3. Click the **Require Immediate Payment When Buyer Uses Buy It Now** check box if you only offer PayPal (any additional payment methods you have selected will be cleared) and you are offering a Buy It Now price. This check box will only be available if you have a Premier or Business PayPal account.

ACCEPT ADDITIONAL FORMS OF PAYMENT

The Sell Your Item form can display four other payment methods in addition to PayPal, though by default, only two are shown in the form: Money Order/Cashier's Check and Personal Check. To accept credit cards through a merchant account (you can accept Visa, MasterCard, Discover, and American Express) or to steer the buyer to your item description for payment instructions:

1. Click the **Help** icon next to Additional Payment Methods in the Sell Your Item form.

2. In the pop-up message, click **Hide/Show Options**.

3. In the Customize Form window, click **Payment** and then click the applicable payment methods you want to appear in the form. Click **Save** when finished.

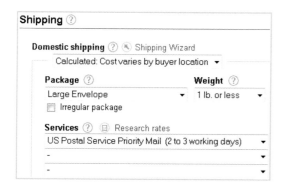

DESCRIBE PAYMENT INSTRUCTIONS

The Sell Your Item form provides a limited selection of payment methods to display in the Payment Details area of the listing (see Figure 6-15), but you can dictate other terms by including payment instructions in the item description or in the Additional Checkout Instructions area, described later in the Sell Your Item form

Calculate Shipping Costs

You have several methods of telling your bidders and buyers how much (if any) shipping charges will be. eBay's tools calculate the cost based on the shipping parameters provided by United States Postal Service (USPS) and United Parcel Service (UPS) for standard packages and www.freightquote.com for freight items over 150 pounds. If you would rather not use calculated costs, you can specify a flat cost, no cost, or a cost to be determined after communicating with the buyer.

LET EBAY AND THE BUYER CALCULATE SHIPPING

eBay can calculate shipping for most packages using USPS and UPS services. All you have to do is provide basic shipping information, and eBay will fill in the Sell Your Item form for you, displaying the cost to the buyer at the top of your listing based on their ZIP code and allowing the buyer to change the ZIP code to see costs for other locales. You can either provide the information in the fields on the form or let a wizard fill it in for you.

1. In the Shipping area, under Domestic Shipping, click the Shipping Options down arrow, and click **Calculated: Cost Varies By Buyer Location**. Select the applicable Package, Weight, and Services options. (If you don't see this option, see the "Customizing the Options Using in the Selling Form" QuickSteps.) Select either the **3 Domestic** or **3 Domestic And 3 International Services** options).

   —Or—

   Next to the Domestic Shipping title, click **Shipping Wizard**. The Shipping Wizard window opens and shows that the wizard is divided into three sections: Item Information, Services, and Insurance. Click **Next**.

Shipping Wizard		
1. Item information	2. Services	3. Insurance

   Welcome to the Shipping Wizard!

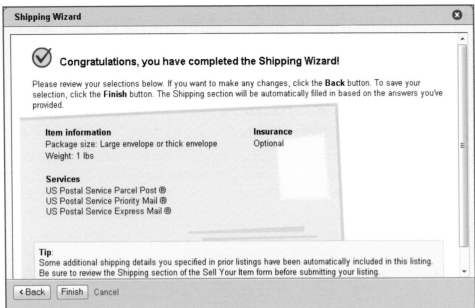

Figure 6-16: *The Shipping Wizard walks you through the details needed to offer services from USPS and UPS that match your package's size and weight, including insurance.*

2. In the next several screens, select the following information, clicking **Next** between screens:

- **Package size** (letter, small package, large package).

- **Package weight** (in pounds and ounces).

- **Irregular packaging criteria.**

- **Seller ZIP code** (establishes where package will be sent from), **Shipping Service** (USPS or UPS), and **Level Of Service** (Priority Mail, Ground, 2nd Day Mail).

- **Shipping Insurance** (not offered, optional, or required; free insurance up to a $100 package value for UPS and USPS Express Mail).

3. When done, review your choices, as shown in Figure 6-16, and click **Finish**.

SPECIFY FLAT-RATE SHIPPING

You can establish one cost for each level of shipping service you offer.

1. In the Shipping area, under Domestic Shipping, click the Shipping Options down arrow, and click **Flat: Same Cost To All Buyers**. (If you want to offer free shipping, click the **Free Shipping** check box and skip to the next section.)

2. Click the first **Services** down arrow, and select the service you want to offer.

3. In the Cost column, type the amount you will charge. (Don't know what to charge? Click **Research Rates** to run a shipping calculator.)

4. Repeat steps 3 and 4 to offer up to three services and charges.

OFFER SHIPPING OPTIONS

You can offer additional shipping incentives and options to provide better value for your buyers. (If you don't see these options, see the "Customizing the Options Used in the Selling Form" QuickSteps.) In the Customizing Form window Shipping pane, select the **Apply Shipping Discount When Buyer Purchases Multiple Items From Me** check box to see the Combined Shipping Discount option, and in the Shipping drop-down list, select one of the domestic or international services options.)

1. Under Combined Shipping Discounts, click the check box that describes the rule applicable to your shipping method (calculated or flat rate). Combined shipping discounts let buyers combine multiple items they buy from you into one shipping order, saving shipping costs. Click **Edit Rules** to establish your discounts.

2. Under Domestic Options, click **Change** to open a window where you can perform the following actions:

   - Select insurance options you will offer. (UPS offers free insurance for items valued up to $100.)

   - State a handling time (how many business days it will take you to get the item packaged and to the shipper).

   - Establish a handling fee for your time and materials to package the item and get it to a shipper. This fee is added to the shipping cost, but is not identified to the buyer.

   - Offer Get It Fast, a program that promotes you as getting items to buyers quickly. To provide Get It Fast, you need to select an expedited shipping service and select a handling time of one business day.

DISPLAY YOUR ITEM'S LOCALITY

When you register on eBay, you provide an address that is assumed to be the location for the item you're selling. If your item is not in the vicinity displayed in the Sell Your Item form, you can easily change it.

1. In the Item Location area, click **Change Location**. If selling within the United States, type the ZIP code of the item location, and click **Apply**. The associated city and state will fill in for you, as shown in Figure 6-17.

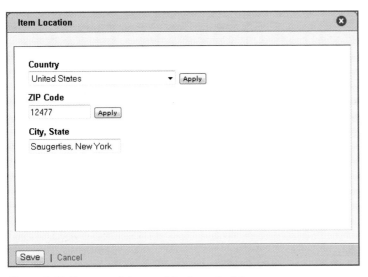

Item Location

Country
United States ▾ [Apply]

ZIP Code
12477 [Apply]

City, State
Saugerties, New York

[Save] | Cancel

Figure 6-17: **To accurately use shipping calculators, you need to make sure eBay is aware of the item's shipping location.**

–Or–

If the item is located in a different country, click the **Country** down arrow, select the applicable country, and click **Apply**. If the country uses postal codes similar to a ZIP code, type it in the ZIP Code text box, and click **Apply**. Otherwise, type the city and region where it's located.

2. Click **Save** when finished.

Establish Miscellaneous Policies

The last section on the Sell: Create Your Listing Page lets you limit which buyers you'll sell to, apply sales tax, create a return policy, and provide a catch-all area where you can provide any remaining details for the listing you want to convey to the buyer.

If any of these features are not shown on your Sell Your Item form, click the **Help** icon next to Additional Information, click **Show/Hide Options**, and in the Customize Form window, select the options that are unchecked, and click **Save**.

SET BUYER'S REQUIREMENTS

The Buyer Requirements area lists any class of buyers you want to prevent from buying or bidding on your items.

1. After selecting this option and saving it from the Show/Hide window, change the list or adjust several of the settings by clicking **Add Buyer Requirements**.

Additional information ⑦

Buyer requirements ⑦
Block buyers who:
- Are registered in countries to which I don't ship
- Have a feedback score equal to or lower than -1
- Have received 2 Unpaid Item strikes in the last 30 days
- Have bid on or bought my items in the last 10 days and have met my limit of 25 who have a feedback score of 5 or lower ⑦
Change buyer requirements

2. In the Buyer Requirements window, select the limitations you want, and click **Save** when done.

ADD SALES TAX

See Chapter 5 for reasons why you will probably want to charge sales tax. (Can you say IRS?)

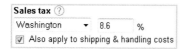

1. Click the **Sales Tax** down arrow, and click the state where you pay taxes.

2. Type the percentage your state charges for your locale. If your state requires tax on both shipping and handling costs, click the **Also Apply To Shipping And Handling Costs** check box.

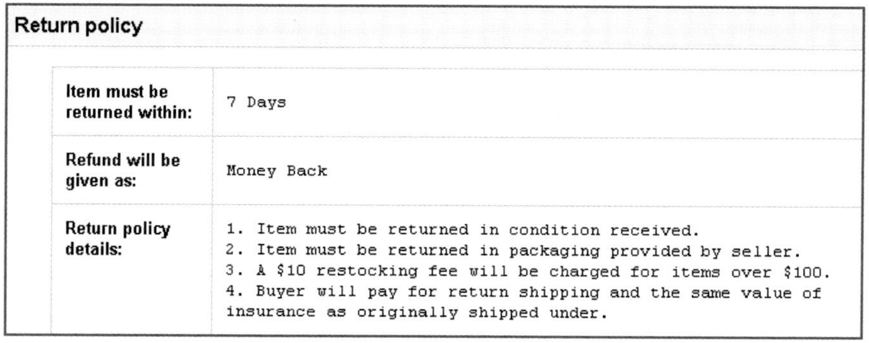

CREATE A RETURN POLICY

A clearly stated return policy (see Figure 6-18) in the listing may save you money and hours writing e-mails to a disgruntled buyer and avoid more severe actions (see Chapter 9 for information on handling problem transactions).

1. In the Return Policy area, click the **Returns Accepted** check box.

2. Click the **Item Must Be Returned Within** down arrow, and click the number of days you will allow as a grace period.

3. Click the **Refund Will Be Given As** down arrow, and click the refund method you will use.

4. In the Refund Policy Details text box, consider covering the following:

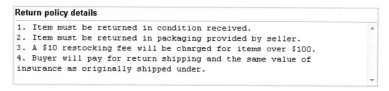

- **Who will pay** for shipping the item back to you

- **Degree of package opening/use of the item** you will accept

- **Returned checks** if not written to proper "Pay To The Order Of"

- **Restocking fee** a merchant charges to return the item to inventory

Return policy

Item must be returned within:	7 Days
Refund will be given as:	Money Back
Return policy details:	1. Item must be returned in condition received. 2. Item must be returned in packaging provided by seller. 3. A $10 restocking fee will be charged for items over $100. 4. Buyer will pay for return shipping and the same value of insurance as originally shipped under.

*Figure 6-18: **Better to state your policies up front in your listing than argue with a disgruntled buyer via e-mail.***

ADD CHECKOUT INSTRUCTIONS

The Additional Checkout Instructions text box provides a free text area where you can clarify any aspects of the transaction with your buyer that need further explanation. For example, you could convey to buyers that you'll be on vacation for a few days and won't be able to respond to e-mails.

1. Now is a good time to make sure that anything you have stated in your item description and the Additional Checkout Instructions text box doesn't conflict with any settings you selected in the form.

2. Click **Save And Continue** at the bottom of the Sell: Create Your Listing page. If you missed any required entries on the page, eBay will "gently" point that out to you and prevent you from continuing until you correct the flagged omissions. When all is in order, you will continue to the final page of the Sell Your Item form.

Sell: Create Your Listing

⚠ Please provide the correct information in the highlighted fields.

Promote and Review Your Listing

The last page in the Sell Your Item form provides you with the opportunity to add visibility upgrades; see your listing as a bidder or buyer will see it, both in search results and when they select it; review eBay recommendations; review your listing fees; and make any changes before you submit your listing to eBay.

Sell: Promote and Review Your Listing

Make your listing compelling
Review how your listing will appear to buyers and add features to help you sell successfully.

ℹ Click Edit Listing to go back to the previous page rather than using your browser **Back** button.

Edit Listing   Help

Use Visibility Upgrades

You can employ several options to attract attention to your listing. Whether their cost justifies their advertising potential to bring more buyers to your listing is one of those great philosophical questions for the ages, although eBay is quick to provide statistics that support they do.

TIP

Look to eBay to offer savings by combining several upgrades into a package deal.

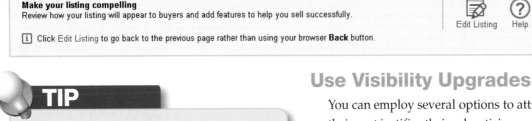

value pack
Get the Essentials - For Less!
Gallery • Subtitle • Listing Designer
$0.65 (Save $0.30)*   Add Now

pro pack
Big Upgrades, Big Savings
Bold • Border • Highlight • Featured Plus! • Gallery Featured
$29.95 (Save $18.95)*   Add Now

Bold
Draws additional attention to a listing by bolding the text when the listing is part of search results. Bold listings are shown to increase final price by an average of 25%.*

FEATURE	COST	DESCRIPTION
Bold	$1.00	Accentuates your item title with boldface type.
Border	$3.00	Adds a purple frame around the listing.
Featured Plus!	$19.95	Adds your listing to the Featured Items (beginning) area of its category list and in the list generated by a search.
Gallery Featured	$19.95	Supersizes the basic Gallery features by adding your listing to the Featured Item section in Gallery pages (as well as in the standard Gallery list) and increasing your picture size.
Gallery Picture	$0.35	Provides a thumbnail picture you choose of your item next to your auction listing and lists your item and picture in Gallery View.
Gallery Plus	$0.75	Enlarges pictures that appear in searches. Includes Gallery picture.
Gift Items 🎁	$0.25	Adds a Gifts And Services icon next to your item title, lists your item in Gifts View, and attracts bidders and buyers to your gift services, such as gift wrapping and direct shipping to the gift's recipient.
Highlight	$5.00	Surrounds your auction details with a colored background in auction listings.
Home Page Featured	$39.95	Provides a randomly selected exposure to your listing under the Featured Items list on the eBay home page (listings are rotated, and there is no guarantee) as well as on the Featured Items list on other pages (with the exception of mature audience listings, auction-related software, and items in questionable taste).
Subtitle	$0.50	Provides a second 55-character line to describe your item in search results.

Table 6-1: **Listing Upgrades**

Recommendations for your listing

You can increase your chances of success by taking the following steps:

Offer to ship to Canada
Items available to Canada will appear on eBay.ca and are 6% more likely to sell on average.

Edit Listing

In the Make Your Listing Stand Out area, click the check boxes next to the upgrades that you want for your item, as shown in Table 6-1. Several upgrades, when selected, reflect their changes on your listing sample shown below the list upgrades.

Correct Errors and Omissions

"It ain't over 'til it's over" certainly applies to making changes to your listing. eBay makes it quite easy for you to see how your listing will appear to buyers and make any changes.

1. Click **Preview Your Listing** at the bottom of the Make Your Listing Stand Out section. You will a Listing Page tab, and next to it, a Listing In search Results link. Review your work in the Listing Page tab to see how your View Item page will display, and then click the link to see how your listing stacks up with similar listings that appear to buyers when searching (see Figure 6-19). The pertinent upgrades are available in the Listing In search Results tab so you can see how they enhance your listing. Click **Close** when finished to return to the Sell: Promote And Review Your Listing page.

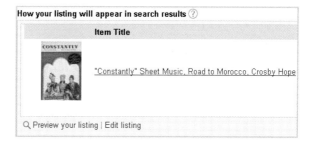

2. Evaluate eBay's suggestions in the Recommendations For Your Listing area. Give more credence to the recommendations that don't incur additional fees!

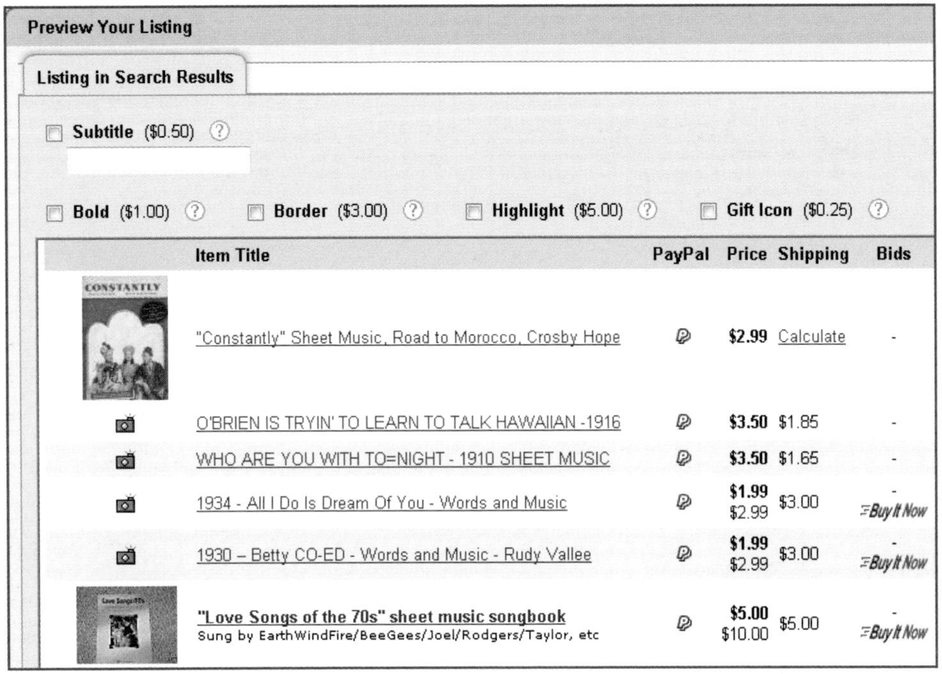

Preview Your Listing

Listing in Search Results

☐ Subtitle ($0.50) ⑦

☐ Bold ($1.00) ⑦   ☐ Border ($3.00) ⑦   ☐ Highlight ($5.00) ⑦   ☐ Gift Icon ($0.25) ⑦

Item Title	PayPal	Price	Shipping	Bids
"Constantly" Sheet Music, Road to Morocco, Crosby Hope	📧	$2.99	Calculate	-
O'BRIEN IS TRYIN' TO LEARN TO TALK HAWAIIAN -1916	📧	$3.50	$1.85	-
WHO ARE YOU WITH TO=NIGHT - 1910 SHEET MUSIC	📧	$3.50	$1.65	-
1934 - All I Do Is Dream Of You - Words and Music	📧	$1.99 $2.99	$3.00	- ⁼Buy It Now
1930 – Betty CO-ED - Words and Music - Rudy Vallee	📧	$1.99 $2.99	$3.00	- ⁼Buy It Now
"Love Songs of the 70s" sheet music songbook Sung by EarthWindFire/BeeGees/Joel/Rodgers/Taylor, etc	📧	$5.00 $10.00	$5.00	- ⁼Buy It Now

Figure 6-19: **See how your listing will compare to your competition's listings when buyers search for items.**

⬤ CAUTION

Resist the habit of using your browser's Back button or pressing **BACKSPACE** on your keyboard to return to the Sell: Create Your Listing page to make changes. Instead, click any of the **Edit Listing** links, or risk getting undesired results.

3. In the Fees area, review your listing fees and evaluate whether the cost is commensurate with the expected value of your sale.

Fees ⑦

Fees	
Insertion fee:	$0.40
Additional pictures:	$0.30
Picture Show:	Free
Gallery:	$0.35
Listing Designer:	$0.10
Total:	**$1.15**

4. View your account balance and verify the details of your account by clicking **Account Balance**. (See "Obtain a Seller's Account" in this chapter for information on eBay payment options.)

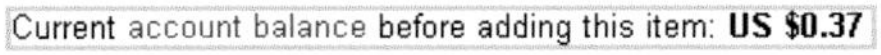

Current account balance before adding this item: **US $0.37**

5. Click **Preview Your Listing** at the bottom of the page to see how your listing will look in its entirety when selected by potential buyers, as shown in Figure 6-20. Click **Close** when finished to return to the Sell: Promote And Review Your Listing page.

Sally the seller views and closes the listing preview before submitting the listing…

…that Bob the buyer will see after searching for the item

Finalize Your Listing

The last steps to finish your listing are as simple as clicking a button or two (if you've sold anything on eBay previously). If you are posting your first sale, you will be guided to set up a seller's account.

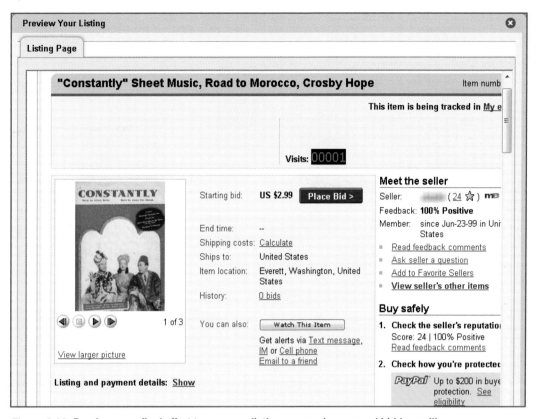

Figure 6-20: *Preview your final effort to see your listing as your buyers and bidders will.*

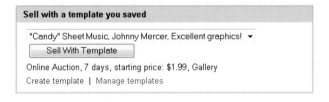

1. At the bottom of the Sell: Promote and Review Your Listing page, click the **Save This Listing As A Template** check box if you plan on selling similar items in the future (first-time sellers will have the opportunity to do this later). You will be able to retrieve a copy of your Sell: Create Your Listing page, saving you from having to duplicate a lot of work. (You can save subsequent updates to the template using the Save check box.)

2. Click **List Your Item** when you are ready to place the listing. There will be no opportunity to back up after you click this button. As shown in Figure 6-21, eBay will congratulate you (as it should!) and will send you an e-mail confirming the listing.

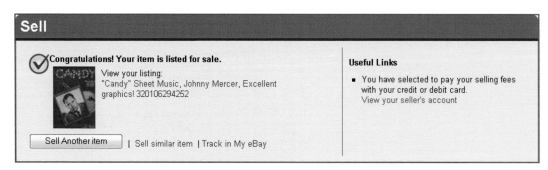

Figure 6-21: *Pat yourself on the back for a job well done!*

–Or–

Click **Continue** if you are a first-time seller (see "Obtain a Seller's Account," next).

Obtain a Seller's Account

In addition to *registering* on eBay (see Chapter 1), to sell on eBay, you have to obtain a separate seller's account that:

● Verifies your registration information.

● Identifies who you are through one of your financial accounts.

● Determines how you will pay eBay for the various selling fees you will incur.

Before you start the online process, gather the credit or debit card and checking account numbers you want to associate with your seller's account. (If you don't have or don't want to use these accounts with eBay, you can use ID Verify. See Chapter 1 for more information on ID Verify.)

1. After completing your first listing, sign in with your eBay User ID and password.

2. On the Place Credit Or Debit Card On File page, shown in Figure 6-22, provide credit or debit card and other information to ascertain your identity.

3. In the Select Your Payment Option area, click **Automatically Charge Fees To Credit Or Debit Card** if you want to pay your selling fees on your selected card.

Place Credit or Debit Card on File

Enter your credit or debit card information as it appears on your monthly statement. Your card will not be charged unless you authorize us to do so to pay selling fees.

Live help

Credit or debit card number

MasterCard VISA DISCOVER AMEX

Information is protected on eBay's secure servers.

Expiration date
–Month– ▼   –Year– ▼

Card identification number

3-digit number on the back of the card. For American Express, use the 4-digit number on the front. Learn more.

Cardholder name
John Cronan

Address on your monthly statement
1302 Grand Ave

City
Everett

State   **ZIP code**
WA ▼   98201

Select your payment option:
◉ Automatically charge fees to credit or debit card
○ Use bank account to pay fees. Credit card will only be used to verify identity

Continue >

*Figure 6-22: **Credit and debit cards can be used for charging selling fees and to identify who you are.***

UICKSTEPS

SIGNING UP FOR A PAYPAL PREMIER ACCOUNT

PayPal—eBay's embedded payment service that can be used for paying just about anything eBay has to offer in terms of fees and sales—provides a cheap and easy way for new sellers to accept credit card payments directly from buyers (the preferred method of payment for most buyers). You can accept payments from your PayPal Personal account (you might have one, but it's limited to five transactions every 12 months), a Premier account (recommended for new sellers), or a Business account (when you are seriously selling on eBay).

Continued . . .

–Or–

Click **Use Bank Account To Pay Fees** to allow eBay to withdraw selling fees from a checking account. Your credit card information is retained by eBay only for identity purposes.

Click **Continue**. (If you selected to use your bank account, you will be given the opportunity to provide that information. Click **Continue** when finished.)

4. The Sell: Complete Your Listing page displays a condensed form of the Sell: Promote And Review Your Listing page, described earlier in the chapter. Click **List Your Item** to complete the listing and receive eBay's congratulatory message, similar to that shown in Figure 6-21.

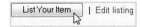

List Your Item | Edit listing

QUICKSTEPS

SIGNING UP FOR A PAYPAL PREMIER ACCOUNT *(Continued)*

Figure 6-23 outlines the benefits of each account. You can upgrade a Personal account, add a Premier account in addition to your Personal account (limited to one each), and create a new Premier account.

1. Click one of the omnipresent links on eBay to go to PayPal, or visit www.paypal.com from your Web browser.

2. From the PayPal home page, click **Sign Up** in the PayPal header.

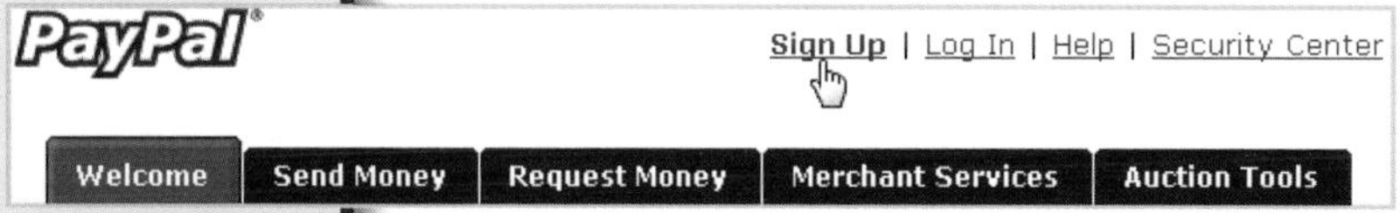

3. On the Choose Account Type page (see Figure 6-23), review the features and benefits of the three account types. To set up a Premier account, if you have a PayPal Personal account, click **Upgrade** in the Already Have A PayPal account area.

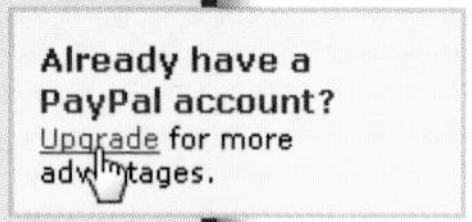

   –Or–

   If you are creating your first PayPal account, under Premier Account, click **Start Now.**

   In either case, provide the information requested in the respective forms to obtain a Premier account.

Account Benefits	Personal	Premier	Business
Send money	✔	✔	✔
24-hour fraud surveillance	✔	✔	✔
Customer Service availability	✔	✔	✔
eBay Tools	Limited	✔	✔
Merchant Services	Limited	✔	✔
Accept credit or debit cards	Limited	✔	✔
PayPal ATM/Debit Card		✔	✔
Multi-user access			✔

Figure 6-23: **PayPal accounts are directed toward eBay sellers at all selling levels (source: PayPal Web site).**

How to...

Chapter 7
Managing Your Sale

In this chapter you will learn what to do after you click the List Your Item button on the Sell Your Item form until the listing closes. The real work of selling on eBay starts when you submit that selling form. There are several actions you can take to monitor active sales while the listings are live, including communicating with bidders; changing a listing; adding to the item's description; or canceling a bid, a scheduled listing, or even the entire sale. Also, you might want to learn as much as you can about your prospective buyers.

Fortunately, eBay provides Selling views in My eBay, a great tool to help you manage and keep track of the most common things that are required during the auction or sale. (See Chapter 8 for information on what to do after the listing closes.)

NOTE

The management activities described in this chapter are designed for the new or casual eBay seller. If you have dozens of items for bid or sale at a time, see Chapter 10 for techniques and tools that are geared toward selling on eBay on a volume or business basis.

TIP

You can customize how most of the Selling views appear and change the order in which they appear on the All Selling page. See Chapters 1 and 2 for information on working with My eBay controls and customization features.

NOTE

Listings don't always stay put. Items that initially appear in the Items I'm Selling view will move to the Items I've Sold or Unsold Items view after the auction or sale is completed. Also, scheduled auctions that first are displayed in the Scheduled Items view will appear in the Items I'm Selling view after the auction or sale starts.

Organize My eBay Selling Views

You can customize a great deal in the My eBay views that is associated with selling items, making your management of multiple listings that much easier. See Chapters 1 and 2 for additional information on using My eBay.

View Selling Activities

There is no better place to start managing sales than from the My eBay All Selling page, shown in Figure 7-1. Selling activities are divided into *views*.

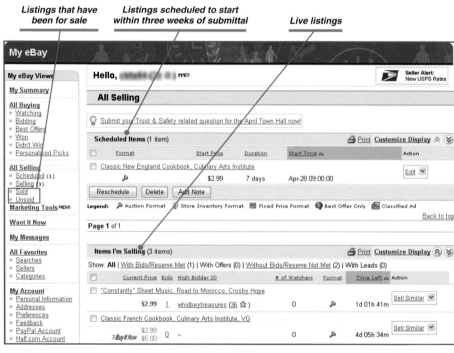

Figure 7-1: *The All Selling page in My eBay is a great central location to view any items that are for sale, will go on sale, or that have been for sale recently.*

Items for sale on your My eBay page that are in "play"—that is, have bids against them—will sell when the auction closes, and are displayed in bold green text. Items that are waiting for that first bid are shown in red. Fixed-price (and eBay Store) items are displayed in black (see Figure 7-2).

Open the All Selling page by clicking **My eBay** on the eBay header and then clicking **All Selling** on the My eBay Views sidebar. (Your views may be in a different order from what is shown here.)

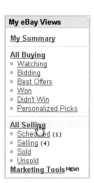

Selling activities views include:

- **Scheduled Items** lists items that are scheduled to start at a future time (up to three weeks from the time you submit each selling form).

- **Items I'm Selling** displays those items that are currently for sale or bid.

- **Selling Totals** provides a snapshot of items for sale, classified ads submitted, and the number of amount of sold items for the last 60 days.

	Current Price	Bids	High Bidder ID
☐ "Constantly" Sheet Music, Road to Morocco, Crosby Hope			
	$2.99	1	whidbeytreasures (36 ☆)
☐ Classic French Cookbook, Culinary Arts Institute, VG			
Buy It Now	$2.99 $5.00	0	--
☐ Classic Italian Cookbook, Culinary Arts Institute, VG			
Buy It Now	$2.99 $5.00	0	--
☐ Classic Hungarian Cookbook, Culinary Arts Institute, VG			
Buy It Now or Best Offer	$5.00	--	--

Figure 7-2: **You can quickly distinguish among the status of your listings by learning the color-coding scheme.**

- **Selling Reminders** act as constant "nags" to ensure that you don't forget key selling points, such as listings that will be closing soon, feedback yet to be provided to buyers, and items to be shipped.

You can choose how far back to display listings (the maximum is 60 days) that appear in the Items I've Sold and Unsold Items views. Click the **Period** down arrow below the view's title bar, and select the length of time from the drop-down list. You can also remove listings from the views. If you want data that goes back farther than 60 days, you will need to use an auction management tool such as eBay's Blackthorne. Chapter 10 describes selling tools.

- **Items I've Sold** displays listings and activities (such as filtering and sorting listings), and provides actions you can perform for completed sales with a winning bidder or buyer (such as leaving feedback and checking on payment and shipping status).

- **Unsold Items** displays listings and provides actions for completed sales that closed without a winning bidder or buyer.

Make a Selling View Your Home Page

You can access several of the selling views each time you open Internet Explorer or by clicking your browser's home page button.

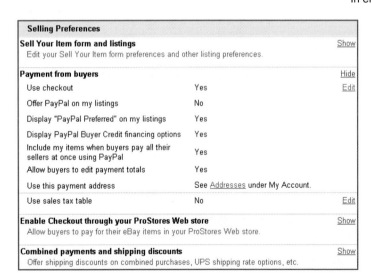

1. Click **My eBay** on the eBay header, and then click the selling view you want as your home page from the My eBay Views sidebar.

2. On the Internet Explorer toolbar, click the **Home Page** down arrow, and click **Add Or Change Home Page**.

3. In the Add Or Change Home Page dialog box, click **Use This Webpage As Your Only Home Page** if you want the All Selling page as a single home page for your browser.

   –Or–

   Click **Add This Webpage To Your Home Page Tabs** if you want to display the All Selling page as a tab next to your home page. In either case, click **Yes** when finished.

4. To quickly display the All Selling page, click the **Home Page** icon on the Internet Explorer toolbar or press **ALT+M** to display the Home Page menu, and click the page.

Change Selling Form Preferences

The options you chose the first time you used the Sell Your Item form to create a listing are retained and appear as default preferences when you use the selling form again. You can change these options so they are displayed the next time you sell an item.

1. On the My eBay sidebar, under My Account, click **Preferences**.

2. In the Selling Preferences section, click **Show** next to the preferences you want to change, as shown in Figure 7-3, to display the available options and current settings.

Figure 7-3: *You can change the default settings that appear in the Sell Your Item form.*

Preferences   Show all

✓ **Your changes have been saved.**
   Note: It may take a few minutes for your changes to be shown below.

3. Click **Edit** to be directed to another page to make your preference changes (see Figure 7-4), and click **Submit**. Ensure that you get a confirmation statement that your changes were accepted.

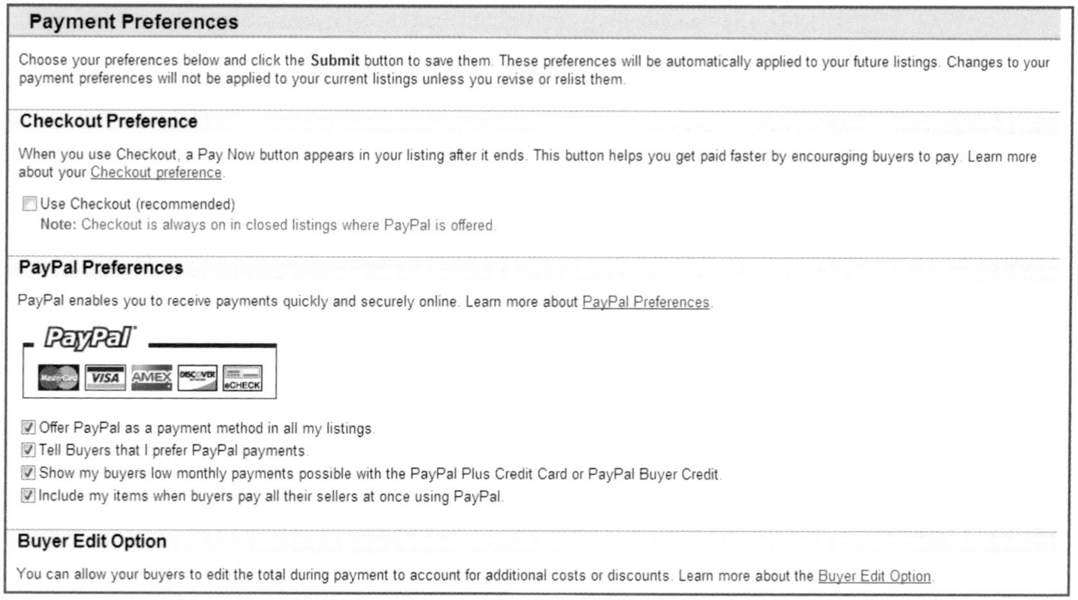

Payment Preferences

Choose your preferences below and click the **Submit** button to save them. These preferences will be automatically applied to your future listings. Changes to your payment preferences will not be applied to your current listings unless you revise or relist them.

Checkout Preference

When you use Checkout, a Pay Now button appears in your listing after it ends. This button helps you get paid faster by encouraging buyers to pay. Learn more about your Checkout preference.

☐ Use Checkout (recommended)
  Note: Checkout is always on in closed listings where PayPal is offered.

PayPal Preferences

PayPal enables you to receive payments quickly and securely online. Learn more about PayPal Preferences.

PayPal
MasterCard VISA AMEX DISCOVER eCHECK

☑ Offer PayPal as a payment method in all my listings.
☑ Tell Buyers that I prefer PayPal payments.
☑ Show my buyers low monthly payments possible with the PayPal Plus Credit Card or PayPal Buyer Credit.
☑ Include my items when buyers pay all their sellers at once using PayPal.

Buyer Edit Option

You can allow your buyers to edit the total during payment to account for additional costs or discounts. Learn more about the Buyer Edit Option.

*Figure 7-4: **Select preferences and options that will help customize the Sell Your Item form.***

Manage Current Selling Activities

While completing the Sell Your Item form, you are in total control of the process, but once the sale goes live, bidders and buyers pretty much run the sale. So would this be a good time for that seven-day vacation to Maui? Not unless you have wireless Internet access from your beach cabana. It's still your listing, and a number of things can crop up that might require timely attention.

Reschedule a Scheduled Listing

You can reschedule a listing up until the time it starts.

1. Click **My eBay** on the eBay header. Click **All Selling** on the My eBay Views sidebar, and scroll down the All Selling page to the Scheduled Items view.

–Or–

Under All Selling on the My eBay Views sidebar, click **Scheduled**.

2. Click the check box to the left of the listing title you want to reschedule, and click **Reschedule**.

3. On the Reschedule Items page, shown in Figure 7-5, click the **Reschedule To Start On** down arrows, and select a new date and time for the listing to start.

4. Click **Reschedule**.

TIP

Use the My Note feature in My eBay to annotate your selling listings and provide reminders or comments that only you will see. For example, you could identify your "secret" bottom line you would be willing to sell Best Offer listings. Chapter 1 describes how to create and display My Notes.

☐ Classic Hungarian Cookbook, Culinary Arts Institute, VG
Buy It Now or Best Offer $5.00 -- --
My Note: Accept Best Offer of at least $3.00

Reschedule Items

Please set the new start time below and click the **Reschedule** button.

Title	Format	Duration	Start Time △
Classic New England Cookbook, Culinary Arts Institute	🔧	7 days	Apr-28 09:00:00

Legend: 🔧 Auction Format | 📋 Store Inventory Format | ▦ Fixed Price Format | $ Best Offer Only | 🖼 Classified Ad

Page 1 of 1

Reschedule to start on Thursday, Apr 26, 2007 ▼ 08:30:00 ▼

[Reschedule] [Cancel]

About eBay | Announcements | Security Center | Policies | Site Map | Help

Copyright © 1995-2007 eBay Inc. All Rights Reserved. Designated trademarks and brands are the property of their respective owners. Use of this Web site constitutes acceptance of the eBay User Agreement and Privacy Policy.

*Figure 7-5: **Scheduled listings can be rescheduled as long as the listing has not started.***

Find Your Listings Outside of My eBay

You can use several methods to find and view your current listings outside of My eBay.

FIND WHERE YOUR AUCTIONS AND SALES ARE LISTED

You can find out where a listing is located, including which page it is on within a category.

1. From My eBay, copy the item number of the item you want or have keywords in mind.

2. Click **Site Map** on the eBay header. In the Sell | Selling Activities area, click **Where Is My Item**?.

3. In the search: By Item Number page, type (or paste) the item number of the listing you want to locate (or type keywords used in the item title), select **Find Location Of Item**, and click **search**.

Enter item number
270111938506   [Search]
○ Find item listing
● Find location of item

4. Click the item title to open the listing, or click any of the levels in the category hierarchy, as shown in Figure 7-6.

Sally the seller says the item number can be retrieved from your listing confirmation e-mail, one of the views in My eBay, or an individual View Item page for a listing

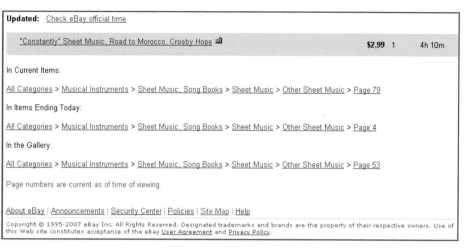

Figure 7-6: *Quickly find out where your listing is located, and open it or any of its subcategories.*

BOOKMARK A LISTING

You can easily display any of your listings anytime you have your browser open by creating a *Favorite* link to the listing page.

1. Open the eBay listing View Item page that you want to be able to view quickly.
2. In Internet Explorer, click **Add To Favorites** to the left of the pages tabs, and click **Add To Favorites** from the drop-down menu.

   –Or–

   Press **CTRL+D**.

3. In the Add A Favorite dialog box, accept the name to locate the link in the main Favorites folder.

   –Or–

   Click **Create In** to select an existing folder.

   –Or–

   Click **New Folder** to create one.

   In all cases, click **Add** to close the Add A Favorite dialog box.

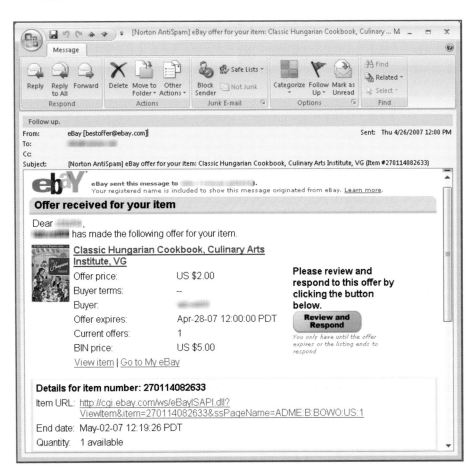

TIP

To quickly see listings that have offers in your Items I'm Selling view, click **With Offers** on the Show a bar.

> **Items I'm Selling** (3 items)
> Show: **All** | With Bids/Reserve Met (0) | With Offers (1)
> ☐ Current Price Bids High Bidder ID

4. To view your listing, click the **Favorites Center** ☆ button to the left of the page tabs (or press **ALT+C**), and locate your link in the Favorites list. Click the link to open the page in your active Internet Explorer tab.

–Or–

Point to the link, and click the **Open In New Tab** arrow ➡ to the right.

Respond to Best Offers

If you list Buy It Now items (not in conjunction with an auction), you have the option of letting buyers send you an offer that is less than your selling price. If you receive a best offer, you will be notified by e-mail (see Figure 7-7) and will also receive a selling reminder. In addition, you can always review your best offers by clicking the **Respond To Offers**

 link in the Items I'm Selling Action column.

> **Selling Reminders** (Last 31 days)
> 🐷 I have 1 item with offers from buyers.
> 📦 I need to ship 1 item. Purchase and print shipping label through PayPal.
> ☆ I need to leave feedback for 1 item.

1. Click one of the links to view the best offer. In each case, the Best Offer: Offer Received page (also known as the Best Offer Deal Sheet) displays, as shown in Figure 7-8.

2. There are several actions you can take from your Manage Best Offers page (see Figure 7-8) once you list an item with a Best Offer feature. Click **Accept Offer** to accept the offer as provided by the buyer and close the listing. The buyer is obligated to pay the offer price and shipping costs.

–Or–

*Figure 7-7: **The Review And Respond button in the e-mail notification provides a link to where you can manage your best offers.***

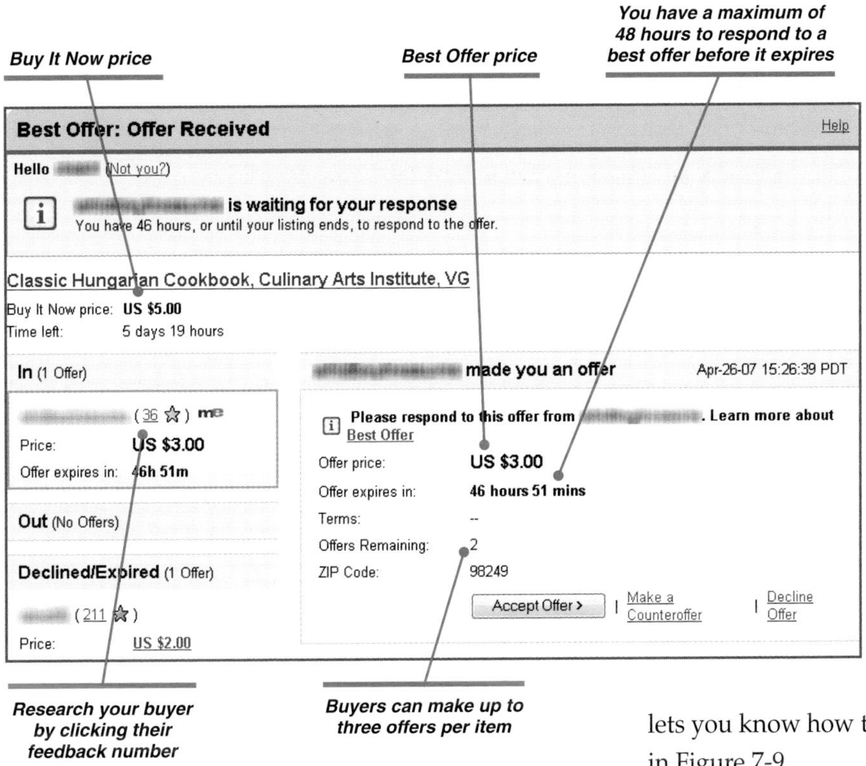

Figure 7-8 callouts

Buy It Now price

Best Offer price

You have a maximum of 48 hours to respond to a best offer before it expires

Best Offer: Offer Received

Hello ■■■■ (Not you?)

[i] ■■■■■■■■■■ is waiting for your response
You have 46 hours, or until your listing ends, to respond to the offer.

Classic Hungarian Cookbook, Culinary Arts Institute, VG

Buy It Now price: **US $5.00**
Time left: 5 days 19 hours

In (1 Offer)

■■■■■■■■ (36 ☆) **me**
Price: **US $3.00**
Offer expires in: 46h 51m

Out (No Offers)

Declined/Expired (1 Offer)

■■■■■ (211 ☆)
Price: US $2.00

■■■■■■■■ **made you an offer**   Apr-26-07 15:26:39 PDT

[i] **Please respond to this offer from** ■■■■■■■. **Learn more about Best Offer**

Offer price: **US $3.00**
Offer expires in: **46 hours 51 mins**
Terms: --
Offers Remaining: 2
ZIP Code: 98249

[Accept Offer >] | Make a Counteroffer | Decline Offer

Research your buyer by clicking their feedback number

Buyers can make up to three offers per item

Figure 7-8: **You can manage your best offers and respond to potential buyers in one location.**

Click **Make A Counteroffer** to provide a price greater than the buyer's offer but less than your Buy It Now price.

–Or–

Click **Decline Offer** to not accept the offer.

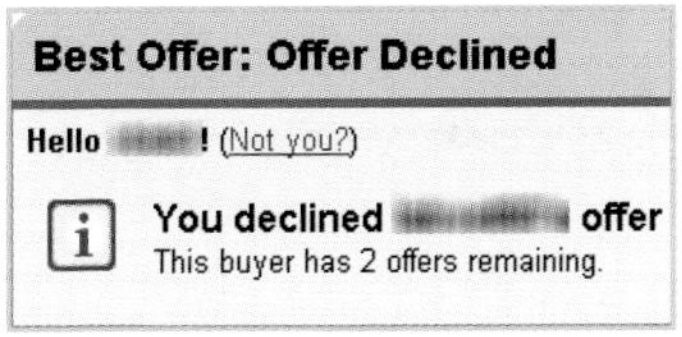

Best Offer: Offer Declined

Hello ■■■■ ! (Not you?)

[i] **You declined** ■■■■■■■ **offer**
This buyer has 2 offers remaining.

(In the latter two cases, you have the opportunity to add comments back to the buyer.)

–Or–

Do nothing and allow the offer to expire within 48 hours of its submittal.

Get Daily E-Mail

To assist you in keeping track of your current auctions, you can have eBay send you a daily status e-mail that lets you know how things are going with your sales (and purchases), as shown in Figure 7-9.

1. Click **My eBay** on the eBay header. On the My eBay Views sidebar, under My Account, click **Preferences**.

2. In the Notification Preferences section, click **Show** to the right of Selling Notifications to display your current settings.

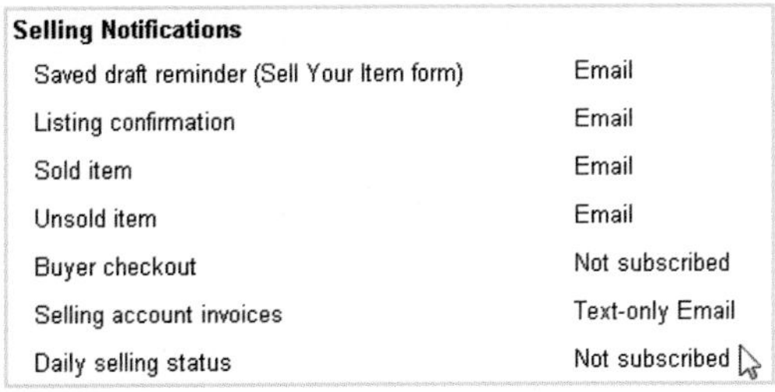

Selling Notifications

Selling Notifications	
Saved draft reminder (Sell Your Item form)	Email
Listing confirmation	Email
Sold item	Email
Unsold item	Email
Buyer checkout	Not subscribed
Selling account invoices	Text-only Email
Daily selling status	Not subscribed

3. Click **Edit** to display the Selling Notification Preference page. Scroll to the bottom of the page, and select the **Send Me A Daily Email Of The Items I Am Selling** check box.

> Daily selling status
> Send me a daily email of the items I am selling.   ☑

4. Click **Save** when finished.

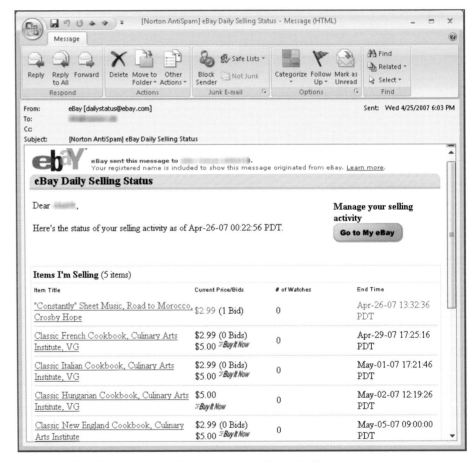

Figure 7-9: Let eBay keep you informed of your selling activities.

The Items I'm Selling view provides key information about listings that have items currently for sale or bid, as shown in Figure 7-10. Display the Items I'm Selling view by clicking any of these links on the My eBay Views sidebar: My Summary, All Selling, or Selling. (See Chapter 1 for more information on using the basic features of My eBay, such as creating notes.)

Sort your listings in ascending or descending quantities or by selling format

Filter your list of items for sale based on several criteria

Gauge interest in your item

Create another listing with the fields already filled in with the current item's options

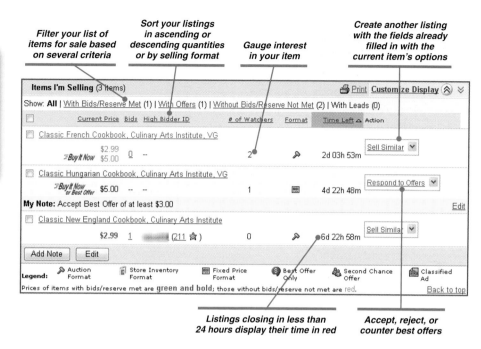

*Figure 7-10: **The Items I'm Selling view is your best place to monitor and manage listings that are currently for sale.***

Listings closing in less than 24 hours display their time in red

Accept, reject, or counter best offers

You only have two hours from a listing's start time to change its duration.

The easiest way to try and figure out what you can or cannot change in a listing is simply to follow the step to revise or edit it. eBay will only allow you to perform the changes that are allowed (unavailable fields are grayed out in the Sell: Revise Your Listing page).

Change a Listing

You can revise (or edit) most elements of a listing after you click List Your Item, though what you can change depends on three factors:

- The listing format—that is, whether your listing is an auction, Buy It Now sale, eBay Store sale, or classified ad.

- The time remaining before the listing ends. You can make significantly fewer changes when the listing is within 12 hours of closing.

- Whether a bid has been submitted for auction listings or a sale has been made for Buy It Now listings selling multiple items.

As an example, Table 7-1 shows the situations that dictate to what extent you can make changes when modifying an auction listing. Also, you can change each listing individually (using two methods) or, if you want to make the same change to multiple listings, you can do so based on listing format.

	NOT WITHIN 12 HOURS OF AUCTION CLOSING (NO BIDS)	NOT WITHIN 12 HOURS OF AUCTION CLOSING (RECEIVED A BID)	WITHIN 12 HOURS OF AUCTION CLOSING (NO BIDS)	WITHIN 12 HOURS OF AUCTION CLOSING (RECEIVED A BID)
Revise anything (except change selling format and duration less than 10 days)	X			
Add a second category	X	X		
Add pictures using eBay Picture Services	X	X	X	
Add or change a Gallery picture	X	X	X	X
Add to the item description	X	X	X	
Add counters	X	X	X	
Reduce the reserve price	X	X		
Add payment methods and shipping locations	X	X	X	
Adding selling upgrades ($$$)	X	X	X	X

Table 7-1: **Allowed Auction Listing Revisions**

REVISE INDIVIDUAL LISTINGS

To change individual listings by reviewing the options in the format of the Sell Your Item form (see "Add to the Item Description" in this chapter for information on how to add to it):

1. In My eBay, on the My eBay Views sidebar, click **Selling**.

2. Click the check box of the item you want to change, click the **Action** column down arrow for the item you want to change, and click **Revise**.

3. On the Sell: Revise Your Listing page, make any change that is available to you. Click **Save And Continue** at the bottom of the page when finished.

Sell: Revise Your Listing

Tell buyers about your item.
- To get help: Click ⑦
- To show or hide optional features, e.g. International Shipping, on this page, click the Show/Hide Options link.

⑦ Help   Show/Hide Options

160   eBay QuickSteps   *Managing Your Sale*

QUICKSTEPS

FINDING CURRENT LISTINGS WITH NO ACTIVITY

You can quickly see which auctions have yet to be bid on in the Items I'm Selling view.

1. Click **My eBay** on the eBay header.

2. On the My eBay Views sidebar, click **Selling**.

3. Click **Without Bids/Reserve Not Met** in the filter bar below the Items I'm Selling title bar to view only listings with no bidders.

> Without Bids/Reserve Not Met (2)

–Or–

Click **Bids** in the column headers row. Click once to sort all current listings with the greatest number of bids listed first (ascending sort); click a second time to sort all current listings with the least number of bids listed first (descending sort).

> Current Price   Bids   High Bidder ID

4. On the Sell: Promote And Review Your Listing page, add listing upgrades or click **Edit Listing** to return to the Sell: Revise Your Listing page to make other changes. Review your fees and preview the new listing.

5. Click **Save Changes** at the bottom of the page when you are finished. You are congratulated on your revision.

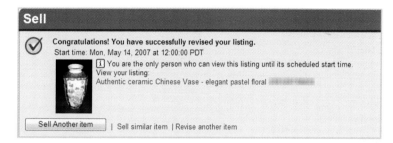

MAKE EDITS TO MULTIPLE LISTINGS

You can easily change the value of a Sell Your Item form feature separately in multiple listings, or you can make the same change across selected listings within the same listing format.

1. In My eBay, on the My eBay Views sidebar, click **Selling**.

2. Select the listings you want to change by clicking their respective check boxes to the left of the item title.

3. Click **Edit** [Edit] at the bottom of the Items I'm Selling view.

4. On the Edit Listings: Listing Information page, under Select Edit Method, click **Edit Listings Individually** to view a condensed Sell Your Item form for each selected listing, as shown in Figure 7-11.

> **Select edit method**
> ● Edit listings individually.
> ○ Edit listings in bulk.

–Or–

Click **Edit Listings In Bulk** to made a change that will affect all selected listings.

> **Edit Listings: Edit Listings in Bulk**
>
> Use this page to edit information for listings in bulk. When you are finished, click the **Continue** button.
>
> **Online Auction (1 listings)**
>
> | | | |
> |---|---|---|
> | Subtitle: ($0.50) | No Change ▾ | |
> | Item description | No Change ▾ | |
> | Starting Price | Edit ▾ | $ 4.99 |

In either case, click **Continue** at the bottom of the page.

Edit individual listings (2 listings)

Edit listings in bulk and apply the same changes to multiple listings at once.

Classic French Cookbook, Culinary Arts Institute, VG | Auction   Remove

Subtitle

55 characters left.

Add to description

Starting price *Required   Reserve price (fee varies)   Buy It Now price (fee varies)

$ 2.99 $ $ 5.00

Payment method

☑ PayPal accepted   Email address for receiving payment: cbts@verizon.net

Domestic Handling Time

Select a time period ▾   ☐ *Get It Fast*

☑ Gallery ($0.35)   ☐ Gallery Plus ($0.75)   ☐ Bold ($1.00)   ☐ Border ($3.00)

☐ Highlight ($5.00)   ☐ Featured Plus! ($19.95)   ☐ Home Page Featured ($39.95 for 1 item / $79.95 for 2 items)

Classic Hungarian Cookbook, Culinary Arts Institute, VG | Fixed Price   Remove

Subtitle

55 characters left.

*Figure 7-11: **You can quickly make individual changes to several listings.***

NOTE

eBay creates a special category of changes that take you directly to the upgrade options (and additional fees) for your listing. What we would call just another listing change (see "Change a Listing"), eBay calls "promote your item." To "promote" your listing, use My eBay to find the listing, and click its title to display it. On the View Item page, click **Promote Your Item** under the item's title bar. On the Promote Your Item: Picture & Item Details page, make your upgrade choices, and click **Continue**. Click **Submit** after reviewing the summary of upgrades.

5. In the respective Edit Listings pages, make the changes you want, and click **Continue**.

6. On the Edit Listings: Review & Submit page, review your changes and click **Submit** when finished.

Add to the Item Description

Once you have bidders or are within 12 hours of a listing closing, you cannot change a description—you can only add to it. The bidder or buyer will see the original description, and added text will be shown in a separate area on the listing. To change the item description:

1. Click **My eBay** on the eBay header. On the My eBay Views sidebar, click **Selling**.

2. Click the **Action** column down arrow in the listing whose description you want to annotate, and click **Revise**. (Alternatively, you can click **Add To Description** if that's all you want to do.)

3. On the Sell: Revise Your Listing page, scroll down to the Description area, and change the original description, if you are allowed to do so.

   –Or–

   Type or paste changes in the Add To Description area (see Chapter 6 for information on adding a description to the Sell Your Item form.

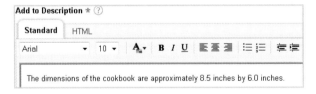

In either case, click **Save And Continue** at the bottom of the page.

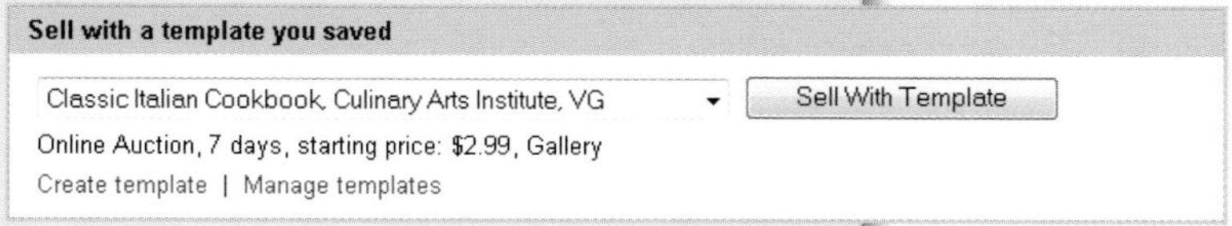

4. Review your changes and make any other changes on the Sell: Promote And Review Your Listing page. Click **Save Changes** at the bottom of the page when finished. Buyers will see a summary of your changes if you changed your description, as shown in Figure 7-12.

–Or–

Buyers will see your added description below your original description (note that added revisions to the description are date- and time-stamped).

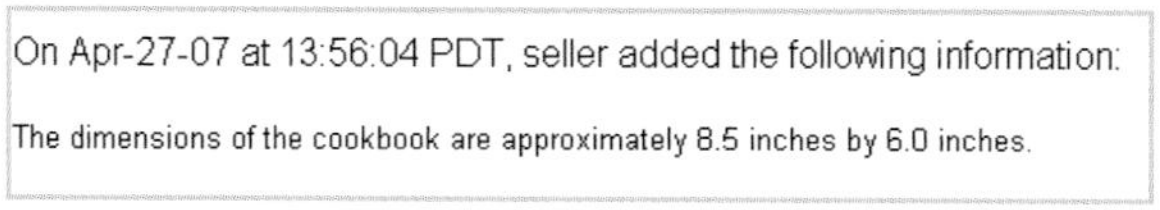

> On Apr-27-07 at 13:56:04 PDT, seller added the following information:
>
> The dimensions of the cookbook are approximately 8.5 inches by 6.0 inches.

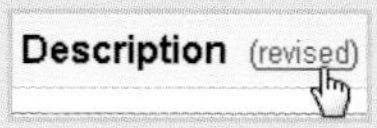

Item Revisions summary for item #270113684063

The seller has revised the following item information:

Date	Time	Revised Information
Apr-25-07	12:23:10 PDT	Details **Item Specifics:** - Nonfiction Books Changed Sub-Category from **Italian** to **French** Changed Publication Year from **1956** to **1955**
Apr-27-07	13:57:56 PDT	Description

*Figure 7-12: **When changing an item description, item-specific changes are detailed, but other changes are masked.***

Sell Similar Items

eBay provides a few slick features to keep you from having to re-create a Sell Your Item form scratch when selling items that share common details. For example, if you are selling anything in a series where the only thing that changes is the issue or series number, you only have to update that particular number instead of slogging through the steps of the selling form. To quickly sell an item similar to one currently for sale:

1. In My eBay, display the **Items I'm Selling** view from the My Summary, All Selling, or Selling pages.

2. Scroll through your list of items that are currently for sale, and locate the item whose details you want to use in another listing.

3. Click **Sell Similar** under the item's Action column. (If Sell Similar isn't shown in the item's Action column, click the **Action** column down arrow, and choose it from the drop-down list.)

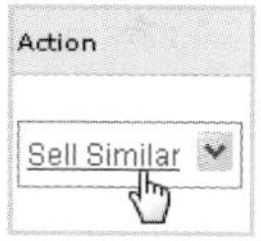

Action

Sell Similar ☑

4. A Create Your Listing page that is identical to the one you used for your original listing displays. Make any desired changes (see Chapter 6 for information on any of the fields on the page), and click **Save And Continue** at the bottom of the page.

5. On the Review Your Listing page, make any additional changes, review and preview your listing, and click **List Your Item** at the bottom of the page when finished.

Continued . . .

QUICKSTEPS

CHECKING ON YOUR BIDS AND BIDDERS

The Bid History page, shown in Figure 7-13, provides access to a wealth of information on the progress of your auction, as well as information on your bidders. As the seller of the item, you can also obtain the e-mail addresses of your bidders.

- To open the Bid History page, click the number of bids link in the Bids column in the My eBay Items I'm Selling view.

There are several sleuthing techniques you can employ to feel comfortable with the people you are about to do business with.

1. In the Bidding History section, click a bidder's **User ID**. On the member's My World page:

   - In the Feedback Score section, review the recent feedback statistics and note any bid retractions.

   - Note how long the bidder has been an eBay member.

   - Review any negative feedback to see if there is a trend.

   - See if a **New ID** icon 👤 or **Changed ID** icon 🔄 is displayed next to the bidder's User ID. (The New ID icon signifies that the bidder has been a registered eBay member for fewer than 30 days. Multiple changes of a User ID could mean someone is trying to bury his or her past.)

Listing summary

Bid History	Item number: 270113688713

Email to a friend | **Watch this item** in My eBay

Item title: Classic New England Cookbook, Culinary Arts Institute (revised)
Time left: 6 days, 20 hours 19 minutes 20 seconds

Only actual bids (not automatic bids generated up to a bidder's maximum) are shown. Automatic bids may be placed days or hours before a listing ends. Learn more about bidding.

Bidder	**Bid Amount**	**Date of bid**
labvet80 (211 ☆)	US $2.99	Apr-27-07 13:31:04 PDT

Bidder User ID and feedback links provide access to bidder details

Bidding details

Figure 7-13: *The Bid History page provides a snapshot of the bidding on your item and acts as a gateway to other bidder information.*

Cancel a Bid

Why would you want to take potential money out of your pocket? Typically, you wouldn't, but there are a few instances where you might have to—for example, you might find a bidder's feedback record to be questionable or his or her identity unverifiable. Also, a

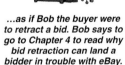

bidder might ask you to retract his or her bid. Furthermore, if you need to cancel an auction, you will need to cancel all outstanding bids, unless you're willing to sell to the current high bidder (see "End a Listing Early" later in this chapter).

...as if Bob the buyer were to retract a bid. Bob says to go to Chapter 4 to read why bid retraction can land a bidder in trouble with eBay.

Sally the seller canceling a bid doesn't have the same negativity attached to it...

1. Click **My eBay** on the eBay header, and then, under All Selling, click **Selling**.

2. In the Items I'm Selling view, click the number of bids link for the listing that contains the bidder you want to cancel.

3. On the Bid History page, select and copy the item number by selecting it and pressing **CTRL+C**, and note the bidder's User ID.

QUICKSTEPS

CHECKING ON YOUR BIDS AND BIDDERS *(Continued)*

2. Click **See All Feedback** to view the bidder's Member Profile page:

   - Review the full feedback history of the bidder.

   - Click the **ID History** link to see if the bidder has a high number of identity changes.

Don't take any individual piece of potentially negative data as reason to cancel a bid. There can be legitimate reasons for just about anything, and one or two disgruntled persons leaving negative feedback among hundreds of transactions shouldn't necessarily raise a red flag unless it's coupled with other warning signs.

CAUTION

eBay policy limits the circumstances under which you can contact a bidder to those specifically involving completion of a current or recent transaction. You cannot, for example, maintain a list of e-mail addresses you've gotten from past auctions and send e-mails offering non-eBay items for sale. eBay uses terms like "transactional interference" and "spam" to describe these actions, and might suspend an offender.

4. At the bottom of the Bid History page, click **Cancel Bids**.

> See how to cancel bids if you need to.

5. On the next page, scroll down to the Canceling Bids section, and click **Canceling Bids Placed On Your Listing**.

> **To cancel a bidders bid:**
> 1. Go to the Canceling bids placed on your listing page.
> 2. Enter the Item Number, the User ID of the bid you are canceling, and the reason you are canceling the bid.
> 3. Click the **Cancel Bid** button.

6. On the Canceling Bids page, shown in Figure 7-14, paste the item number in the Item Number box. (Copying and pasting is faster and less prone to typing mistakes.) Type the User ID of the bidder in the text box provided, and type your explanation for the bid cancellation in the Reason For Cancellation text box. eBay's legitimate reasons are when a bidder asks you to remove his or her bid, when you need to close a listing early, or when you cannot verify the identity of the bidder (though you can type any reason you want).

7. Click **Cancel Bid** when finished.

Bar Bidders and Buyers from a Listing

You can limit who can buy from you in two ways: You can create a set of buying rules to filter out buyers who don't meet your standards (see Chapter 6 for

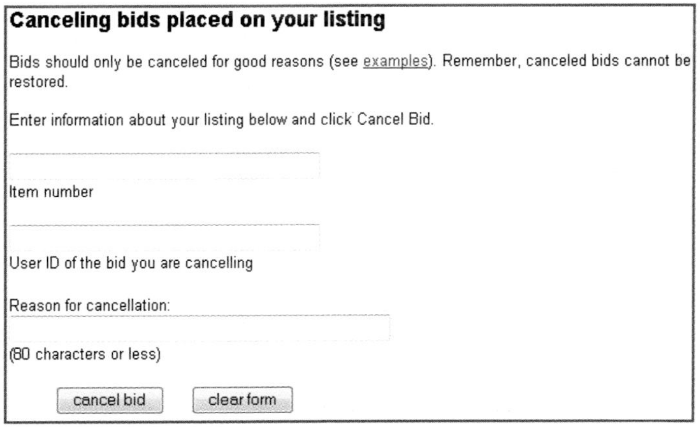

Canceling bids placed on your listing

Bids should only be canceled for good reasons (see examples). Remember, canceled bids cannot be restored.

Enter information about your listing below and click Cancel Bid.

_____

Item number

_____

User ID of the bid you are cancelling

Reason for cancellation:

_____

(80 characters or less)

[cancel bid]   [clear form]

*Figure 7-14: **It takes a bit to reach the Canceling Bids page, but canceling the bid is quite easy.***

TIP

Despite creating rules to limit buyers and bidders, you can allow select members to "blast through" your rules and bid or buy your items. On the Buyer/Bidder Management page (see step 2 in "Bar Bidders and Buyers from a Listing"), click **Add A Buyer To My Buyer Block Exemption List**. On the Buyer Requirements Exemption List page, type the User IDs you want ignored by buyer rules you've set, and click **Submit**.

NOTE

If you receive notification from eBay that a bidder was removed due to an *administrative cancellation*, count your blessings. The bidder had run afoul of eBay policies and was suspended. (You'll never know why the bidder was suspended, as eBay only communicates the reason to the offender.)

QUICKSTEPS

CANCELING A SCHEDULED LISTING

You can cancel a listing you've scheduled to start at a future time without incurring any listing fees.

1. Click **My eBay** on the eBay header, and then click **All Selling | Scheduled** on the sidebar.

2. Under Scheduled Items, select the check box to the left of the listing(s) you want to cancel, and click **Delete**.

---

information on establishing buyer requirements), and you can create a list of User IDs for buyers and bidders with whom you will not do business.

1. Click **Site Map** on the eBay header, and under Sell | Selling Activities, click **Block Bidder/Buyer List**.

2. On the Buyer/Bidder Management page, click **Add An eBay User To My Blocked Bidder/Buyer List**.

3. On the Blocking A Bidder/Buyer page, add the User IDs you want to block to the Blocked Bidder/Buyer List text box. Type a comma after an entry, or press **ENTER** to separate the User IDs.

–Or–

To remove a previously blocked User ID, select the User ID from the text box and press **DEL**.

4. Click **Submit** when finished.

End a Listing Early

There are several legitimate reasons why you might need to end a listing before its natural conclusion (item is no longer for sale, item is broken, family emergency prevents shipping, you discovered the item is a fake, and so on), and there are many illegitimate or unethical reasons to stop a sale (a buyer contacts you and offers to buy the item off eBay, you're just "testing the market" to relist at a higher price, and so on). There is no penalty for ending a listing early (eBay cannot force you to sell an item), but repeated premature endings will get bidders' attention and ultimately eBay's. Early endings are differentiated on

End My Listing Early

Select a reason for ending your listing early. The reason will appear on the Closed Item page.

○ The item is no longer available for sale.
◉ There was an error in the starting price or reserve amount.
○ There was an error in the listing.
○ The item was lost or broken.

[End My Listing]

CAUTION

You are not the only one who can cancel a listing. If eBay finds one of your listings in violation of its policies, it will cancel the listing and send a cryptic message to any member involved with the transaction (see Figure 7-15). Chapter 5 discusses how to avoid running afoul of eBay policies.

whether a bid has been made and whether you want to sell to the current high bidder.

1. Click **My eBay** on the eBay header. On the My eBay Views sidebar, click **Selling**.

2. Click the **Action** column down arrow in the listing you want to end early, and click **End Item**.

3. The action you need to take depends on one of four scenarios you can choose from. Select your reason and click **End My Listing**.

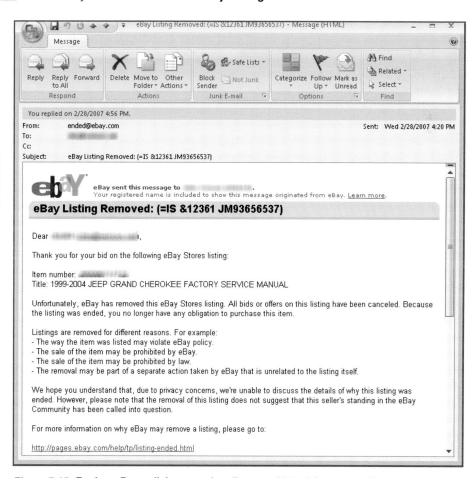

Figure 7-15: *Review eBay policies occasionally to avoid trashing your selling reputation.*

Chapter 8
Closing Out Your Sale

In this chapter you will learn how to close out a sale. After the sale is completed, there are still many things to do (or at least monitor), including following up with the winning bidder or buyer with payment instructions, receiving payment, shipping the item, taking actions to avoid future issues with problem bidders, and relisting items that didn't produce a sale the first time around.

Fortunately, eBay—and to a large degree PayPal (owned by eBay)—provide several features and tools to help you along the way and make the process typically painless. Some of these features and tools come at a cost, however, so it will be up to you to decide if convenience and some built-in degree of safety are worth the added expense.

Evaluate the Sale

After a sale ends, it's worthwhile to take a few minutes and review the specifics of the sale that were unknown until the highest bidder won at auction or a buyer purchased a Buy It Now item. For example, you can now determine the full amount you owe eBay for listing an auction item, as its winning bid amount (or final value) is now known. Also, you now know the winning bidder or buyer and can research his or her eBay standing to help you make possible decisions on receiving payment (see Chapter 3 for information on researching bidders and buyers). To help manage the overall process of closing out the sale, the Items I've Sold view in My eBay, as well as associated selling reminders, provide great tools to guide you along the way.

Determine Final Value Costs

In addition to the insertion and possible upgrade fees you incurred when listing an item, eBay charges an additional fee based on the closing bid of the auction or sale price, known as the *final value fee* (the fee is charged whether or not you and the buyer actually consummate the sale). The fee is cumulative, based on the following tiers (for Dutch auctions, use the final value fee for the lowest successful bid and multiply it times the total number of items you sold):

- Items with a closing bid price up to $25 are charged 5.25 percent of the closing price.
- Items between $25 and $1,000 are charged:
    - 5.25 percent on the first $25 (or $1.31); and
    - 3.25 percent of the closing price above $25.
- Items over $1,000 are charged:
    - 5.25 percent on the first $25 (or $1.31); and
    - 3.25 percent of the closing price between $25 and $1,000 (or $26.81); and
    - 1.50 percent of the closing price above $1,000.

Not all sales incur final value fees. For example, you are not charged a fee if no bid was made or if no bid met your reserve price, or if you listed a *non-binding* real estate item other than timeshares, manufactured homes, or property.

COMPLETING A SUCCESSFUL SALE STEP BY STEP (Continued)

ENSURE THE BUYER KNOWS WHAT IS OWED

Monetary information includes such details as shipping/handling and insurance costs, the final value cost of the item, applicable tax, and a total of all costs. Send the buyer an e-mail invoice after the auction. (See "Invoice the Buyer" later in this chapter.)

ENSURE THE BUYER KNOWS HOW TO PAY YOU

Include the payment types you accept, how the buyer can most easily accomplish them, and where to send paper-based instruments. For example, remind the buyer to click the Pay Now button on the winning confirmation he or she receives from eBay (if you accept PayPal and have chosen to display it), and, if you accept checks and money orders, reiterate your billing address. (See Chapter 6 for information on preparing payment instructions in the Sell Your Item form.)

PROVIDE POSITIVE FEEDBACK

Be sure to give positive feedback when you're satisfied payment is received. Remember: You get paid first and the buyer gets the item last. Don't expect a glowing feedback report from your buyer if you haven't done the same for him or her. (See Chapter 4 for more information on how to give feedback.)

PROVIDE SHIPPING DETAILS

Let the buyer know when the item is on its way. Provide the shipping service used; tracking information, if available; and estimated delivery time. (See "Ship the Item" in this chapter.)

Continued . . .

(The final value fee for these categories, $35, is referred to as a *notice fee*, which is charged whether or not you finalize a sale, assuming there was a bid and your reserve was met.)

View Your Sales Fees

You can see how much eBay is charging you for each current or sold listing.

1. Click **My eBay** on the eBay header. On the My eBay Views sidebar, under My Account, click **Seller Account**.

2. Under My Seller Account Summary, click **View Account Status**.

My Seller Account Summary

Account Activity

Previous invoice amount (12/31/05): (View invoices)

Payments and credits since last invoice:

Fees since last invoice: (View account status)

3. On the Account Status page, shown in Figure 8-1, view a snapshot for your current payments, fees, account balance, and account information—such as your eBay account number, account status, and how you pay your fees to eBay. Below the account status area you can view up to four months of your account activities:

- Click one of the **Sort By** links to sort and combine the account activity by date, fee type, or item number. Sorting by item number provides subtotals for each item.

Subtotal for Item#			**$1.31**
Apr-24-07 17:21:47 PDT	Classic Italian Cookbook, Culinary Arts Institute, VG	Gallery Fee	$0.35
Apr-24-07 17:21:47 PDT	Classic Italian Cookbook, Culinary Arts Institute, VG	Buy It Now Listing Fee	$0.05
Apr-24-07 17:21:47 PDT	Classic Italian Cookbook, Culinary Arts Institute, VG	Insertion Fee	$0.20
Apr-26-07 19:35:24 PDT	Classic Italian Cookbook, Culinary Arts Institute, VG Final price: $5.00 (Auction)	Final Value Fee	$0.26

- Click the **Date** column header (or the Item Number or Fee Type header) to sort the transactions in ascending order (earliest dates first). Click it again to sort in descending order (latest dates first).

- Click **Download** to receive a text file (comma-separated value) of your activity that you can import to auction management systems or spreadsheet programs such as Microsoft Excel.

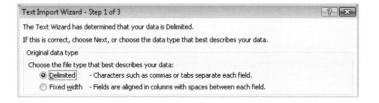

QUICKFACTS

COMPLETING A SUCCESSFUL SALE STEP BY STEP *(Continued)*

CLOSE OUT THE TRANSACTION

Send a final e-mail letting the buyer know you appreciate the business. Inform him or her that you left feedback, and ask if the item arrived satisfactorily and if there's anything you can do to improve the experience.

Manage Completed Sales from My eBay

You can monitor the status of completed sales from one of the several selling views available within My eBay. The Items I've Sold view in My eBay, shown in Figure 8-2, provides a great overview of your recently completed sales. Key features of the view include:

- Sort listings by column headings.

- Group listings by progress status (All, Awaiting Payment, Awaiting Shipment, Awaiting Feedback).

- Display durations of listings varying from 24 hours up to 60 days.

- Look at status icons for completed checkout, payment, shipping, and feedback (both provided to others and received from others). See Chapter 2 for an explanation of the icons.

- Use menu options to quickly change a listing's status or perform actions on listings that did not sell.

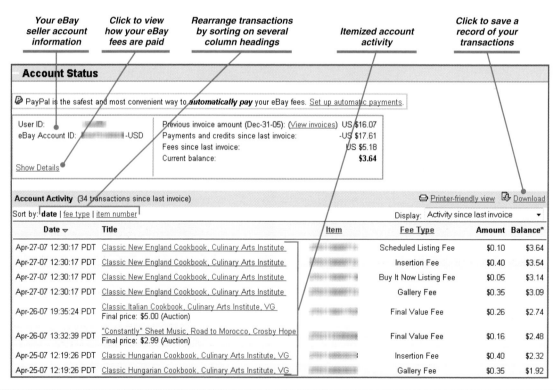

Figure 8-1: **You can view your eBay account details, and view and download a record of your eBay costs.**

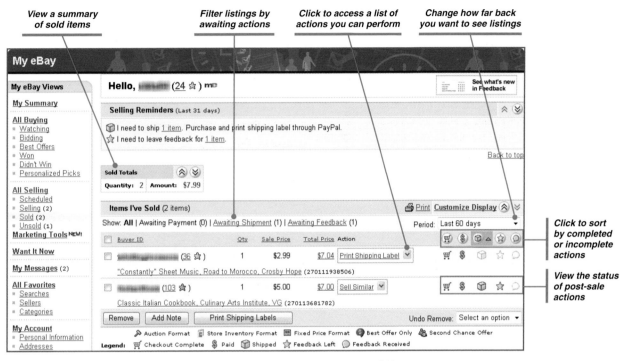

View a summary
of sold items

Filter listings by
awaiting actions

Click to access a list of
actions you can perform

Change how far back
you want to see listings

Click to sort
by completed
or incomplete
actions

View the status
of post-sale
actions

Figure 8-2: *The Items I've Sold view in My eBay is a great way to manage sold items.*

NOTE

The payment options a buyer has are determined by
you when filling out the Sell Your Item form and in
your Payment From Buyers settings in your My eBay
Preferences page (click **Preferences** on the My eBay
Views sidebar).

Receive Payment

When the auction ends, both the seller (shown in Figure 8-3) and the buyer
receive automated e-mails from eBay that let each know who the other party
is, restate the closing price and any fixed shipping costs, and start the end-of-
auction process. What happens next depends on two factors:

- **Is your payment amount final?** That is, are your shipping costs predetermined by
  a fixed cost or a calculated amount, or have you chosen for the buyer to contact you
  after the sale to negotiate shipping costs? If the latter, can the buyer pay immediately
  through PayPal or let you know an alternative payment method is on its way? If the
  final amount isn't known to the buyer, you will have to let him or her know the details
  by sending an invoice.

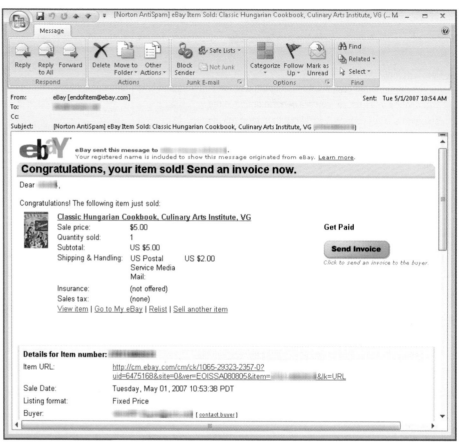

Figure 8-3: *eBay sends the seller an end-of-listing e-mail providing the final sales price and links to send an invoice through either eBay or private e-mail.*

- **Who's quicker to the draw?** Has the buyer or bidder clicked the Pay Now button Pay Now > that appears in his or her end-of-auction e-mail in the completed listing form and acknowledged payment using PayPal or one of your other accepted payment means? Do you need to send an invoice to request payment (or reminder the buyer with a second invoice)? (You can still send an invoice after a buyer acknowledges payment, but it's not necessary if all payment details are known and correct.) See Chapter 4 for details on the buyer's side of the end-of-auction experience.

QUICKSTEPS

COMBINING PURCHASES ON AN INVOICE

You can offer to combine multiple purchases from a buyer into one invoice and offer a shipping discount. If you choose this feature, you will see the option in the shipping area of your next Sell Your Item form (giving you the choice of excluding certain items). Successful bidders and buyers will see the other items you have for sale on the congratulatory e-mail they receive from eBay.

1. From My eBay, click **Preferences** on the My eBay Views sidebar.

2. Under Selling Preferences, click **Show** to the right of Combined Payments And Shipping Discounts, and then click **Edit**.

3. On the Combined Payments And Shipping Discounts page, under Combined Payments, click **Edit**.

4. In the Combined Payments window (see Figure 8-4), select the **Allow Buyers To Send One Combined Payment For All Items Purchased** check box, and click the down arrow to select how many days you want to provide the offer.

5. Click **Save** when finished.

6. In the Combined Shipping Discounts area, apply the shipping discounts you want to offer.

NOTE

Buyers will see the Checkout feature Pay Now button in various eBay interfaces, including in the listings they've won and have ended, the buyer's Items I've Won view in My eBay, and in e-mail invoices.

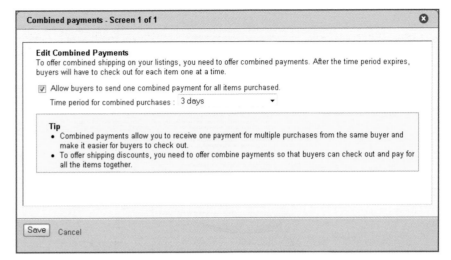

Combined payments - Screen 1 of 1

Edit Combined Payments
To offer combined shipping on your listings, you need to offer combined payments. After the time period expires, buyers will have to check out for each item one at a time.

☑ Allow buyers to send one combined payment for all items purchased.
Time period for combined purchases : 3 days

Tip
- Combined payments allow you to receive one payment for multiple purchases from the same buyer and make it easier for buyers to check out.
- To offer shipping discounts, you need to offer combine payments so that buyers can check out and pay for all the items together.

Save   Cancel

Figure 8-4: **When buyers purchase multiple items from you, combining the payments into one transaction saves them time and money.**

Invoice the Buyer

An invoice is a document sent by you, the seller, stating the amount owed by the buyer who is receiving the goods or services. Invoicing used to be a personal e-mail from the seller directly to the buyer (and still can be) in which payment and shipping details were reiterated; however, the ease-of-use features in the eBay and PayPal system-generated invoices make the automated process hard to beat.

USE CHECKOUT TO SEND AN INVOICE

By default, when you set up a seller account, eBay's Checkout feature is enabled and provides the winning bidder or buyer a Pay Now button that, when clicked, will make an instant PayPal transfer if that is the only payment you offer (see Figure 8-5).

Or, eBay provides notification to the buyer for payment by your acceptable methods, including PayPal, when offered with other payment methods. You will receive from the buyer an intent e-mail to pay your final value fee, shipping and handling, and insurance costs.

Item #	Item Title	Qty.	Price
270114082633	Classic Hungarian Cookbook, Culinary Arts Institute, VG	1	US $5.00
	Subtotal:		US $5.00
	Shipping and handling via US Postal Service Media Mail:		US $2.00
	Shipping insurance (not offered):		--
	Total:		**US $7.00**

I will be sending payment of US $7.00 for my item.

Dear ____,

I will be sending payment of **US $7.00** via **Personal Check** shortly.

Goulash...here I come!!!

Print postage for this shipment online

You can easily print postage or a label for US Postal Service and UPS.

Print Shipping Label

If you do not want to offer your bidders and buyers an immediate payment means, you can disable the Checkout feature and remove the Pay Now button from eBay notifications. The onus will then be on you to ensure that your buyers are provided with the information they need to pay you. To disable the Checkout feature (which is not recommended):

1. In My eBay, click **Preferences** on the My eBay Views sidebar.

2. Under Selling Preferences, click **Show** to the right of Payment From Buyers, and then click **Edit**.

3. On the Payment Preferences page, under Checkout Preference, clear the **User Checkout** check box. ☐ Use Checkout (recommended)

4. Click **Submit** when finished.

Figure 8-5: **When your buyers pay with PayPal, you receive an e-mail notifying you of the instant payment.**

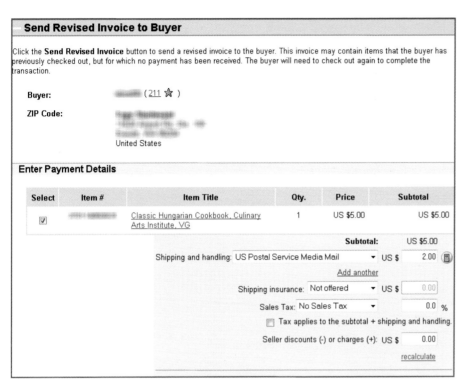

Send Revised Invoice to Buyer

Click the **Send Revised Invoice** button to send a revised invoice to the buyer. This invoice may contain items that the buyer has previously checked out, but for which no payment has been received. The buyer will need to check out again to complete the transaction.

Buyer: (211 ☆)

ZIP Code:

United States

Enter Payment Details

Select	Item #	Item Title	Qty.	Price	Subtotal
☑		Classic Hungarian Cookbook, Culinary Arts Institute, VG	1	US $5.00	US $5.00

Subtotal: US $5.00

Shipping and handling: US Postal Service Media Mail ▾ US $ 2.00

Add another

Shipping insurance: Not offered ▾ US $ 0.00

Sales Tax: No Sales Tax ▾ 0.0 %

☐ Tax applies to the subtotal + shipping and handling.

Seller discounts (-) or charges (+): US $ 0.00

recalculate

*Figure 8-6: **You can send revised invoices to your buyers after they receive an initial automated invoice from eBay.***

USE eBAY TO SEND A REVISED INVOICE

After eBay sends an automated invoice using the Checkout feature, you can easily send a follow-up, semi-automatic invoice to provide other pertinent details to the buyer.

1. Send a revised eBay invoice by clicking the **Send Invoice** button in the end-of-listing e-mail a seller receives (see Figure 8-5).

   –Or–

   In the Items I've Sold view in My eBay, click the **Action** column down arrow for the listing in question, and click **Send Revised Invoice**.

Print Shipping Label ✖
Mark As Payment Received
Mark As Shipped
Leave Feedback
View Order Details
Contact Buyer
Send Revised Invoice
Send Reminder Invoice

2. On the Send Revised Invoice To Buyer page, shown in Figure 8-6, make any changes to your Shipping And Handling, Insurance, Sales Tax, or Payment Instructions/ Personal Message settings. Select **Copy Me On This Invoice** at the bottom of the page to get a copy of the invoice e-mail, and click **Send Invoice**.

CUSTOMIZE YOUR PAYPAL INVOICE

You can create a custom message to be included in the automated invoice buyers receive when you offer PayPal as a payment method.

1. Type www.paypal.com in your browser's address bar, and log in when prompted.

2. On your PayPal account page, under the Enhance Your Account sidebar, click **Invoice Your Winning Buyers**.

Enhance Account
PayPal Plus Credit Card
Money Market
PayPal Preferred
ATM/Debit Card - Get 1% Cashback
Invoice your winning buyers

TIP

What if you send an invoice and then nothing happens? No need to panic—simply send a reminder invoice to "gently nudge" your buyer to pay up. From the Items I've Sold view in My eBay, click the **Action** down arrow for the listing in question, and click **Send Reminder Invoice**.

Here's the invoice for your item, ! ebaY

Dear
This is an invoice reminder. Thank you for your purchase. The total for your item below is **US $7.00**.

Pay Now

Click **Pay Now** to confirm shipping, get total price, and arrange payment through: PayPal; personal check; money order.

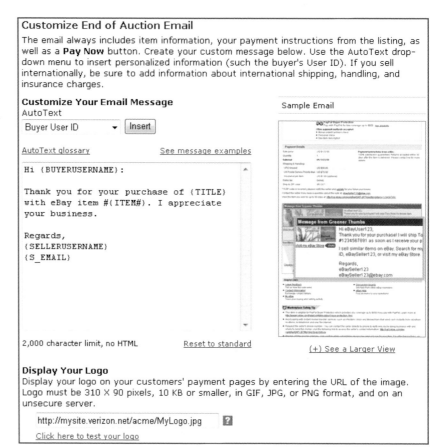

Figure 8-7: **Customize the invoice buyers receive when using PayPal as a payment method.**

Customize End of Auction Email

The email always includes item information, your payment instructions from the listing, as well as a **Pay Now** button. Create your custom message below. Use the AutoText drop-down menu to insert personalized information (such the buyer's User ID). If you sell internationally, be sure to add information about international shipping, handling, and insurance charges.

Customize Your Email Message   Sample Email
AutoText

[Buyer User ID ▾] [Insert]

AutoText glossary   See message examples

Hi {BUYERUSERNAME}:

Thank you for your purchase of {TITLE}
with eBay item #{ITEM#}. I appreciate
your business.

Regards,
{SELLERUSERNAME}
{S_EMAIL}

2,000 character limit, no HTML   Reset to standard

(+) See a Larger View

Display Your Logo
Display your logo on your customers' payment pages by entering the URL of the image. Logo must be 310 X 90 pixels, 10 KB or smaller, in GIF, JPG, or PNG format, and on an unsecure server.

[http://mysite.verizon.net/acme/MyLogo.jpg] [?]

Click here to test your logo

CAUTION

To avoid confusing your buyers with multiple invoices, ensure that you disable the Checkout feature if you plan on sending your own invoices. See "Use Checkout to Send an Invoice" earlier in the chapter.

TIP

If you want to get more creative with your invoice than your e-mail program allows, you can use more advanced formatting features in your word processor and attach the invoice as a file attachment to the e-mail you send the buyer. You do run the risk, however, that a small number of buyers might have problems opening the file, either because they have their security settings set up to block attachments or because they don't have a compatible word-processing program on their computer. Have a toned-down version of your invoice available to send just in case.

3. On the End Of Auction Email page, scroll down to the Customize End Of Auction Email area, shown in Figure 8-7. Use a combination of AutoText (fields of information drawn from the listing and from eBay and PayPal settings) and free text to customize a message to the buyer, provide a Uniform Resource Locator (URL) to a 310 × 90 pixel logo (if you want to include one), and click **Submit**.

SEND YOUR OWN INVOICE

To create a more personal feel to your transaction, you can create your own invoice and have complete control over what you say to your buyer. Also, an invoice of your own is a more flexible tool if you have left shipping costs and other details open for negotiation until after the sale is completed.

TIP

Let buyers know that you have received payment by dropping them a quick e-mail. Even when paying through secure methods, such as credit cards and PayPal, it's a nice touch to let the buyer know that his or her part of the transaction has gone through successfully. Also, this is a good time to indicate that you'll be leaving him or her feedback and remind the buyer to do the same for you after the item arrives. Don't pass up the chance to solicit positive feedback for yourself!

QUICKSTEPS

RECEIVING SELLING FUNDS FROM YOUR PAYPAL ACCOUNT

You can obtain use of your PayPal balance in a variety of ways: transfer money electronically to your checking account, receive a paper check, use a PayPal debit card, make ATM withdrawals, or shop at PayPal Shops. To make use of your PayPal funds:

1. Open PayPal (from the Account Guard menu on the eBay Toolbar, the Related Links sidebar from My eBay, or directly from www.paypal.com).

2. Log in using your e-mail address and PayPal password.

3. From your Account Overview page, click the **Withdraw** tab.

4. On the Withdraw Funds page, shown in Figure 8-8, click the link for how you want to use your funds.

1. Create the text of your invoice in a word-processing program, such as Microsoft Word. Include at a minimum:

   ● A description of what was bought and its item number

   ● Your mailing address if you accept paper currency, such as checks or money orders

   ● A reiteration of the payment and shipping instructions that appear in the listing (make sure the two sets of instructions are the same), including shipping method, insurance costs, when you expect to be paid, and when you will send the item

   ● A mention that you will leave feedback when paid (recommended) and you would appreciate the same from the buyer when the item is received

   ● A "thank you" for the opportunity to do business with the buyer

2. Copy and paste the text into your e-mail program, and send the invoice. (Ensure you have the buyer's e-mail address correctly spelled in the To field of the e-mail!)

3. Save the word-processing document for use in future sales.

4. In My eBay, update the item's status when you get paid. In the Items I've Sold view, in the item's Action column drop-down list, select **Mark As Payment Received**.

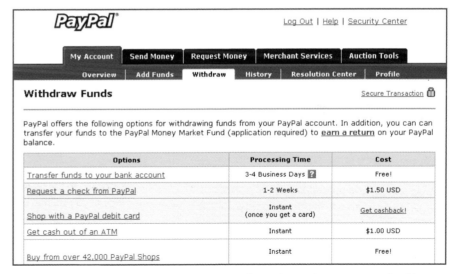

Figure 8-8: **You have several options to choose from when using money received from your sold items in your PayPal account.**

Leave Buyers and Bidders Feedback

eBay has a social contract between buyers/bidders and sellers based on the feedback concept that helps ensure the integrity of the overall system. Consider providing feedback to buyers after a transaction is completed as a mandatory part of the sale. eBay recognizes that we are all busy people and makes the action as easy as possible for us. (See Chapter 3 for information on writing feedback for both good and bad experiences.)

Selling Reminders (Last 31 days)

$ I am awaiting payment for 1 item.
📦 I need to ship 1 item. Purchase and print shipping label through PayPal.
☆ I need to leave feedback for 2 items.

1. To quickly find sales that need feedback, check the Selling Reminders view on My Summary to see if you have any recent sales for which you haven't submitted feedback. Click the link to open the Items I've Sold view with only those listings awaiting feedback displayed.

2. Click the **Action** column down arrow in a listing, and click **Leave Feedback**. The Feedback Forum: Leave Feedback page is displayed (see Figure 8-9), where you can assign a rating and type comments. Click **Leave Feedback** when finished.

–Or–

1. To leave feedback for several listings at once, click **Feedback** on the My eBay View sidebar. The Items Awaiting Feedback view opens, displaying listings that need feedback either by the seller or buyer. Click the **Leave Feedback** button.

[Leave Feedback]

2. On this version of the Feedback Forum: Leave Feedback page, each listing you have that is missing feedback is displayed. Assign ratings and type comments. Click **Leave Feedback** when finished.

Feedback Forum: Leave Feedback   help

Rating other members by leaving Feedback is a very important part of transactions on eBay.

Please note:
- Once left, you cannot edit or retract Feedback; you are solely responsible for the content.
- It's always best to keep your Feedback factual; avoid making personal remarks.
- Feedback can be left for at least 90 days following a transaction.
- If you have a dispute, contact your trading partner to try and resolve the dispute before leaving Feedback.

User ID:			Show all transactions
Item Number:			

Rating: ○ Positive ○ Neutral ○ Negative ⦿ I will leave feedback later

Comment:

80 characters left.

[Leave Feedback] Cancel

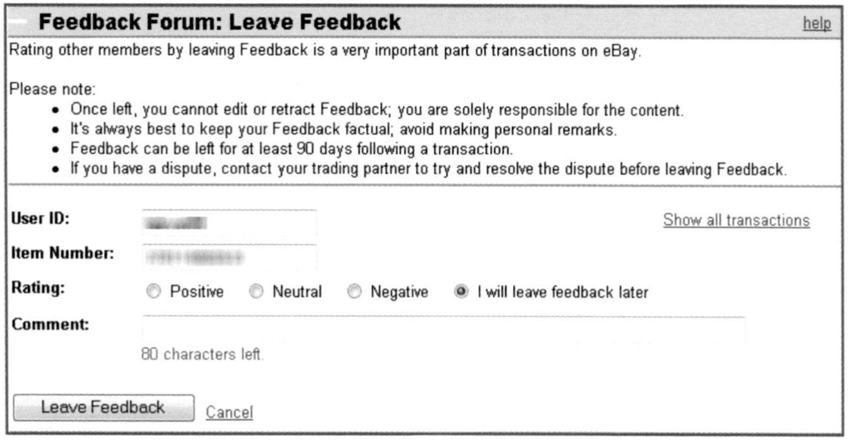

Figure 8-9: **You can display feedback fields for one listing at a time or list all items that require feedback and handle them all at once.**

Ship the Item

The most critical phase of the eBay transaction is moving the sold item from the custody of the seller to the buyer. Not only are you giving up complete control to a third party (the shipper), but you also are putting faith in your buyers that they will be reasonable people and accept the delivered item despite any number of potential problems: unforeseen delays in delivery, misinterpretations as to shipping instructions, or good-faith assumptions on

TIP

There is a way out of potential shipping nightmares—don't offer shipping! When you list an item, you can choose **No Shipping: Local Pickup Only** in the Shipping section of the Sell Your Item form. Typically, this option is only used when selling larger or fragile items for which shipping can be problematic.

Domestic shipping ⑦ ⑥ Shipping Wizard
Flat: same cost to all buyers ▾
Flat: same cost to all buyers
Calculated: Cost varies by buyer location
Freight: Large items over 150 lbs.
No shipping: Local pickup only

CAUTION

Do not use cord or string as a substitute for tape when sealing a package. Modern shipping companies use delivery-processing equipment that could become entangled with exposed, loose-fitting materials (and they typically won't accept the package).

NOTE

There are any number of shippers you can use to transport items to your buyers, and depending on several factors—such as cost, convenience, and delivery speed—you can probably find one that is a better choice for a given transaction. Unless you are doing volume shipping, convenience wins out in most cases (the top-tier shippers are quite competitive, and you will usually find their cost and delivery times comparable for common-sized items). eBay provides integrated features to use the shipping services of USPS and UPS (and www.freightquote.com for larger and heavier items). Unless you have an overriding reason to use another shipper, these should accomplish your needs.

your part. By performing the actions you do have control over (for example, using sound packaging and choosing tracking features your shippers offer), you will alleviate many headaches (and late-night e-mails).

Package the Item

As the saying goes, you only have one shot at a first impression. For your buyer, the appearance of the packaging he or she receives from you generally qualifies as that one opportunity. Even if your item arrives undamaged, an obviously poorly packaged item will leave a bad impression in the buyer's mind; whereas even when an item arrives damaged, if it's obvious you took all necessary precautions in your packaging to prevent it, the buyer will generally only be interested in getting a refund and will vent his or her angst toward the shipper instead of you. The do's and don'ts of packaging include the following:

- If you don't want to turn your house into a shipping center, pay a commercial packing outfit, such as the UPS Store, to do the packaging (and mitigate your responsibility in any insurance claims that might arise).

- Use only sturdy, clean boxes with old labeling and markings removed or covered. Don't exceed the maximum gross weight a box is designed for (this is often indicated on a bottom flap), especially when reusing a box.

- When in doubt, double-box. It's really quite amazing that outfits like Dell could ship relatively fragile items, such as computers and monitors, through normal channels without major breakage problems. Their secret to success (besides custom-fit Styrofoam) is to suspend the item in a well-packaged box of its own within a larger box full of cushioning material (allow at least three inches on all sides).

- Use packing tape (clear tape is the most common; the United States Postal Service recommends two-inch), not that roll of leftover masking tape from last summer's painting efforts. Think about getting a tape gun if you are planning on doing more than a few items a year. Tape all seams for added protection.

- Fill hollow items with packing material (Styrofoam or biodegradable peanuts, bubble wrap, crumpled paper, foam, or cardboard) to provide added structural integrity.

- Save quality packing material you receive. As most eBay sellers are also eBay buyers, you should have access to a lot of free boxes, bubble wrap, and Styrofoam peanuts. (A good measure of your buying-to-selling ratio might be whether your packing material inventory is losing or gaining volume.)

Access Shipper Services

eBay provides a great clearinghouse for links on all the current shipping rates and services provided by USPS, UPS, and www.freightquote.com.

1. Click **Site Map** on the eBay header, and under Selling Resources, click **Shipping Center**.

2. On the Helpful Links sidebar:

   - Click **USPS Shipping Zone** to access links to use the USPS as your shipper, shown in Figure 8-10.

   - Click **UPS Shipping Zone** to access links to use UPS as your shipper, shown in Figure 8-11.

Helpful Links

Save Time Watch this video!

USPS Shipping Zone

UPS Shipping Zone

Review shipping tips and hints

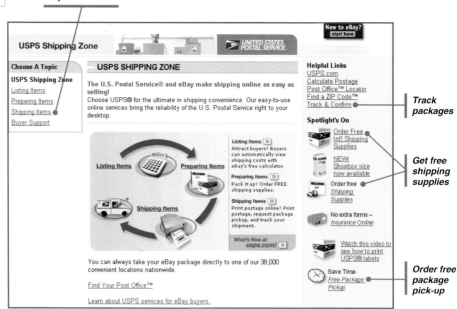

Track packages

Get free shipping supplies

Order free package pick-up

*Figure 8-10: **The combined eBay and USPS Shipping Center is a great time-saver for finding the postal service you want.***

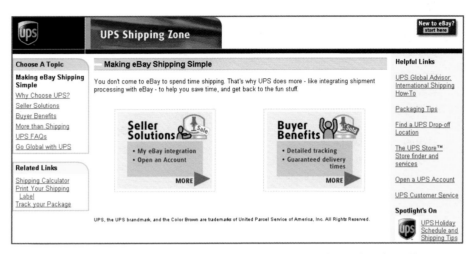

Figure 8-11: The UPS Shipping Center page offers access to basic services for sellers and buyers.

–Or–

On the Spotlight's On sidebar on the Shipping Center page, click **Freight Resource Center** to access links to set up a calculator buyers can use in your listing for heavier items (similar to the eBay Shipping Calculator described in Chapter 6), ship the item online, and track its progress.

Create Shipping Labels Online

This feature, whether you do it from the shipper's Web site or use the integrated eBay-PayPal–USPS/UPS method, is arguably the Eighth Wonder of the World. You can create USPS shipping labels, with or without postage, from the comfort of your home and drop off packages at a drop box or outlet near you. (You can also simply hand the package to your mailperson—a free pickup service that UPS and FedEx charge for.)

SIMPLIFYING SHIPPING COSTS

The costs involved in getting an item from seller to buyer provide much fertile ground for discussion and debate among eBayers. The $64 question is: who pays? If you, the seller, pay, it simplifies things immensely, as there's no need to discuss how to inform the buyer of the costs (however, most sellers do pass the shipping cost on to the buyer). Consider offering free or discounted shipping in the following cases:

- For more expensive items; the relative cost of shipping is diminished

- For multiple purchases from the same buyer (see the "Combining Purchases on an Invoice" QuickSteps earlier in the chapter)

- To eliminate e-mail traffic with buyers concerning shipping details and issues

- To avoid any impression that you are hitting your profit target through shipping and handling charges

TIP

Don't tape over bar codes on shipping labels. The tape can interfere with the scanners shippers use to track packages.

PRINT MAILING LABELS DIRECTLY FROM USPS

You can print domestic (Express Mail or Priority Mail) or international (Global Express Guaranteed or Global Express Mail) mailing labels, with or without postage (you need to establish an account to print mailing labels with postage).

1. Access the USPS home page at www.usps.com.

2. Click **Print A Shipping Label** along the links bar at the top of the home page.

3. On the Print Shipping Labels page, note that you may have to download software to print the labels. Click **Sign In** in the Domestic And International shipping area. Sign in using your USPS user name and password, or create a new account.

4. You need to go through five pages to print a label:

   - **Label Information** is used to provide return and delivery address information.

   - **Service & Postage Options** lets you choose the level of delivery service and decide if you want to add postage (mailing labels with postage require you to add a credit card to your account).

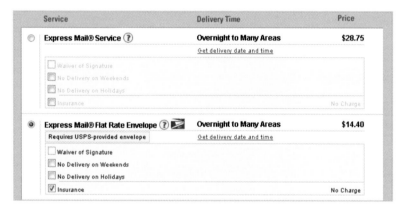

   - **Shipping Cart** lets you change and review any labels you have set up to print.

   - **Billing Information** is used to pay for postage-due mailing labels.

   - **Print Label** shows you a sample of the label to be printed, as shown in Figure 8-12.

5. Click **Pay And Print** to print a label with postage.

   –Or–

   Click **Print** to print a label without postage.

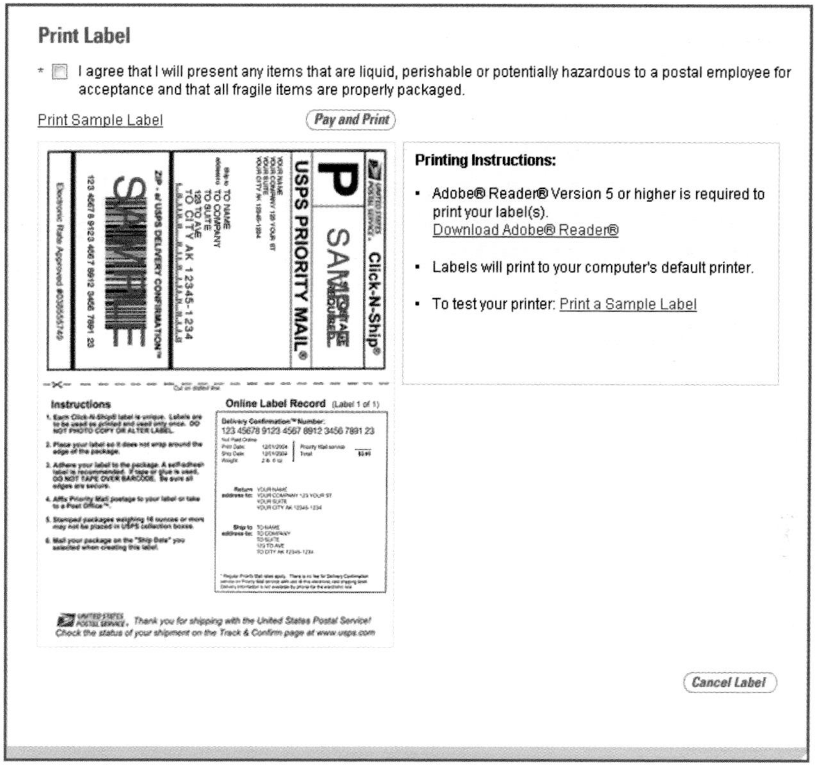

Print Label

* ☐ I agree that I will present any items that are liquid, perishable or potentially hazardous to a postal employee for acceptance and that all fragile items are properly packaged.

Print Sample Label   (*Pay and Print*)

Printing Instructions:

- Adobe® Reader® Version 5 or higher is required to print your label(s).
  Download Adobe® Reader®

- Labels will print to your computer's default printer.

- To test your printer: Print a Sample Label

Instructions   **Online Label Record** (Label 1 of 1)

UNITED STATES POSTAL SERVICE. Thank you for shipping with the United States Postal Service!
Check the status of your shipment on the Track & Confirm page at www.usps.com

(*Cancel Label*)

*Figure 8-12: **USPS provides online printing of mailing labels, with or without postage.***

PRINT SHIPPING LABELS FROM eBAY AND PAYPAL

You can print USPS or UPS mailing labels and pay for them from your PayPal account.

1. Open My eBay and display the Items I've Sold view.

2. Click **Print Shipping Labels** in the Action column for the item you want to print a shipping label.

3. Log in to PayPal, and the shipping options for your default shipping service are displayed (if you want to use an alternate shipping service, click **Choose A Different Carrier** in the Shipment Information section).

NOTE

You can only use the PayPal shipping tool with UPS when shipping to a street address. You cannot ship to a P.O. Box.

TIP

A free feature PayPal provides when creating shipping labels through their service is a packing slip you can print and include in the package to your buyer.

PayPal®

Packing Slip

Ship To: [redacted]   Ship From: John Cronan

4. Choose your shipping options, and click **Continue**.

5. Confirm your shipping service and cost. Click **Pay And Continue** to finish the process and print your label. Shipping confirmation and tracking data is provided to you by e-mail (see Figure 8-13) and is available on your PayPal Account Overview page.

Recent Activity | All Activity | Items Won **ebY**

File	Type	To/From	Name/Email/Phone	Date	Status	Details	Action	Amount ($)	Fee
☐	PayPal Services	To	US Postal Service	Apr. 30, 2007	Completed	Details	Check Shipment	-$1.73 USD	$0.00 USD

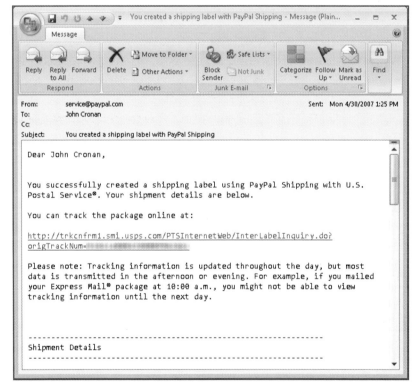

Figure 8-13: *After you create a mailing label, you receive an e-mail that confirms the transaction and provides tracking and other instructions.*

Resolve Non-Sales

Much like the salesperson's mantra, "A sale starts when the customer says no," you cannot give up on an eBay listing that completed but didn't provide a sale. You have two powerful eBay features at your disposal: relisting and Second Chance Offer. Relisting an item allows you to try selling the item again at a reduced cost. Second Chance Offer comes into play when you and the highest bidder cannot come to terms and the item is offered to other auction bidders (it can also be used in a few other situations). See Chapter 9 for information on actions you can take when a transaction really starts going south.

Relist an Item

eBay provides a 90-day window of opportunity to relist an item that did not sell or did not receive a bid and receive an insertion fee refund. (The same deal applies to an unpaid item, or UPI. See Chapter 9 for more information on actions to

take for UPIs.) There are several stipulations you must satisfy when it comes to relisting an item:

- You are only allowed one relisting for a refund—the first time you relist.
- The relisting starting price must be less than or equal to the first listing.
- Only single-quantity online auction and fixed-price selling formats are eligible.
- You cannot add a reserve if the original listing didn't have one. If a reserve was used the first time around, the relisted reserve must be less than or equal to it.
- The item must sell to receive the refund.

To relist an item:

1. Open My eBay.
2. On the My eBay Views sidebar, under All Selling, click **Unsold**.
3. In the Action column of the listing you want to relist, click **Relist**.
4. On the Review Your Listing page (identical to the page with the same name in the Sell Your Item form), click any of the **Edit Listing** links or add upgrades to the selling form that you want to change, and review any eBay recommendations.
5. Click **List Your Item** at the bottom of the page when you've completed any changes to the original listing.

Get a Second Chance Offer

"It ain't over 'til it's over" can certainly apply to an eBay sale. If you and your winning bidder cannot come to terms to complete the sale, you can offer the item to a non-winning bidder. The Second Chance Offer is free (you pay a final value fee only when the offer is accepted), but must be selected within 60 days of a completed sale and you must have at least one non-winning bidder.

1. Open My eBay.
2. On the My eBay Views sidebar, under All Selling, click **Sold**.
3. Click the **Action** column down arrow for the item you want to offer to another bidder, and click **Second Chance Offer**.

4. On the first Second Chance Offer page, review the feature specifics, and click **Continue**.

5. On the second page, shown in Figure 8-14, select a duration for the offer and the bidder to whom you want to offer the item (if you have duplicate items for sale, choose as many bidders as you have items left for sale). Click **Continue**.

6. On the last Second Chance Offer page, review the offer and click **Send**. Your bidder will receive an offer notification in Buying Reminders, My Messages, and an e-mail similar to that shown in Figure 8-15.

Choose how long the offer is good for

If you have multiple items for sale, you can offer second chances to the same number of buyers

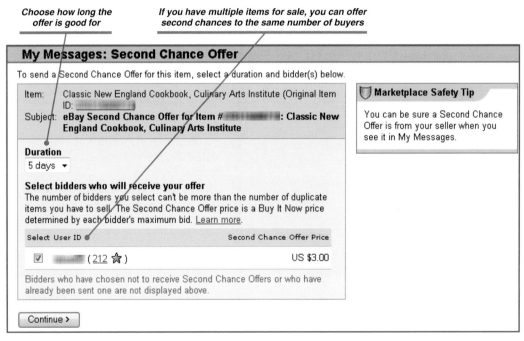

My Messages: Second Chance Offer

To send a Second Chance Offer for this item, select a duration and bidder(s) below.

Item: Classic New England Cookbook, Culinary Arts Institute (Original Item ID: ▓▓▓▓▓▓▓▓

Subject: **eBay Second Chance Offer for Item # ▓▓▓▓▓▓▓▓: Classic New England Cookbook, Culinary Arts Institute**

Duration

5 days ▾

Select bidders who will receive your offer
The number of bidders you select can't be more than the number of duplicate items you have to sell. The Second Chance Offer price is a Buy It Now price determined by each bidder's maximum bid. Learn more.

Select User ID	Second Chance Offer Price
☑ ▓▓▓▓ (212 ☆)	US $3.00

Bidders who have chosen not to receive Second Chance Offers or who have already been sent one are not displayed above.

Continue >

Marketplace Safety Tip

You can be sure a Second Chance Offer is from your seller when you see it in My Messages.

Figure 8-14: *You can offer an item to non-winning bidders if the winning bidder doesn't buy it, you have duplicate items for sale, or your reserve price wasn't met.*

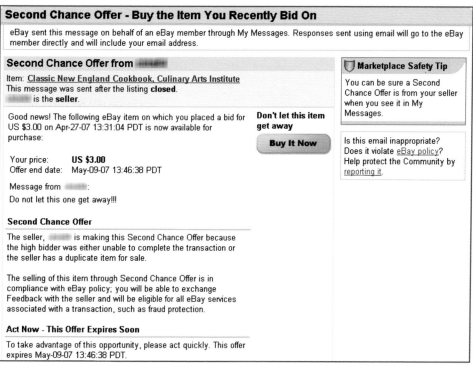

Figure 8-15: *Non-winning bidders selected for a Second Chance Offer receive messages that encourages them to buy the item now.*

How to...

Chapter 9

Protecting Yourself and Handling Abuses

This chapter addresses how you can protect yourself as a buyer or seller in how you set up your eBay account and handle it. From the very first step of signing on to eBay, you begin that process, first by researching your business partner and the item to be bought or sold as well as you can, and then with clear communication and straightforward transactions, always documenting your transaction activities. The second part of the chapter deals with how to handle problems when they do arise. This ranges from simply contacting the other party, to arbitration, to filing charges of fraudulent behavior against the other party. The most important part of protecting yourself is making sure you are doing your homework and communicating with the other party.

Do Your Homework and Communicate

Misunderstandings about what you are buying or selling rests on the shoulders of both the buyer and the seller. Both are responsible for making clear what is being bought or sold. The buyer can't claim, "I didn't know" if a transaction goes badly, and the seller can't claim, "I didn't think she'd be interested in that!"

Communicate Clearly with Buyers

It pays for the seller to be crystal clear in describing what is being sold and under what conditions. It costs time and money to deal with misunderstandings and irate customers, and you can lose future customers as well. Your bottom line as a seller demands that you be clear and precise. Questions to consider include the following:

Sally the seller works hard at communicating with her buyer—she loves green feedback ratings.

- Does the description clearly describe the item, its condition, prior history, color, brand, size, and any other significant things about it? Is there anything about the item you are trying to hide or deemphasize that will be misleading to a buyer? If so, clarify it.

- Have you represented the item fairly as to its condition and value? Are you trying to make it sound like something it is not?

- Does the photo clearly show all parts of the item, its blemishes as well as its strengths? Does it show only the items being sold? Is the photo potentially misleading? See Figure 9-1 for an example of a good photo and description.

- Is your return policy clearly stated?

- How much do you charge for shipping and handling? Do you require insurance? Do you ship overseas? How much do you charge for international shipping? Figure 9-2 shows an example of a shipping and payment policy. Is yours as clear?

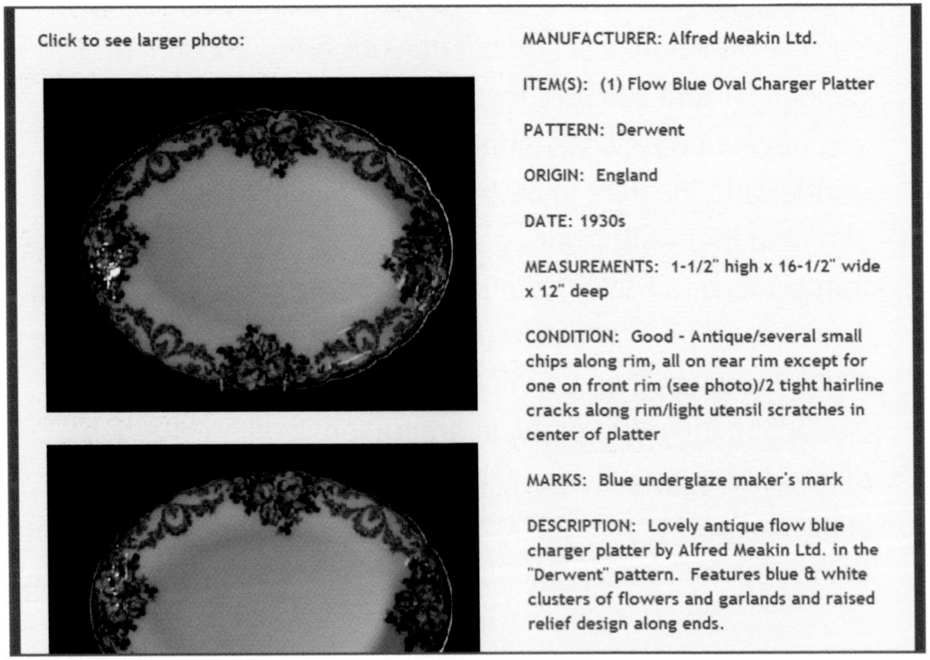

Click to see larger photo:

MANUFACTURER: Alfred Meakin Ltd.

ITEM(S): (1) Flow Blue Oval Charger Platter

PATTERN: Derwent

ORIGIN: England

DATE: 1930s

MEASUREMENTS: 1-1/2" high x 16-1/2" wide x 12" deep

CONDITION: Good - Antique/several small chips along rim, all on rear rim except for one on front rim (see photo)/2 tight hairline cracks along rim/light utensil scratches in center of platter

MARKS: Blue underglaze maker's mark

DESCRIPTION: Lovely antique flow blue charger platter by Alfred Meakin Ltd. in the "Derwent" pattern. Features blue & white clusters of flowers and garlands and raised relief design along ends.

*Figure 9-1: **This is an example of how you use a good photo in your View Item page.***

◄►PAYMENT OPTIONS◄►

PLEASE RESPOND to winning bid notification within 3 days of auction's end. Payment is due within 7 days. Acceptable payment methods include Paypal, cashier's check, money order or personal check.

◄►USA SHIPPING◄►

We take extra care in packaging your item(s) with brand new packing materials and therefore a small handling fee is included in our shipping costs. This helps ensure your item(s) will be safely delivered to you. Our preferred shipping method is USPS Priority Mail which includes delivery confirmation and insurance. We require insurance on all of our shipments to protect both buyer and seller in case of loss or damage. In special circumstances we will offer alternative shipping methods on large or heavy items. Any REFUNDS or RETURNS are for purchase price only! Shipping costs are not refundable.

◄►INTL SHIPPING◄►

Our preferred shipping methods are USPS Global Express Mail or Air Parcel Post with insurance. Under certain circumstances, Air Letter Post or

*Figure 9-2: **This payment policy is an example of how you can make it easy for the reader to follow and understand your terms.***

NOTE

The Sell Your Item form helps to inform the buyer about your shipping and handling terms by letting you select options (such as payment choices, return times, buyer filters, etc.) and then placing them in the View Item page the buyers will see.

- Is your payment policy clearly stated? Have you told the buyer exactly what payment methods you accept?

- Have you stated clearly which bidders you will accept (those with 98 percent positive feedback ratings, for instance)?

- Do you require something different for new buyers with limited feedback comments?

Communicate Clearly with Sellers

The buyer, too, is responsible for the transaction. Not having enough information is not an excuse for buying something you didn't want. Ask yourself these questions:

- Do I really know what I'm buying? Is this a prohibited or borderline product? If so, avoid it. Do I know everything I need to know about this product's history and its current condition?

- If I have questions, have I contacted the seller? Have I gotten a response? Has the response reassured me or raised more questions? (See Chapters 2 and 3.)

- Have I looked at the seller's feedback rating? What does it tell me? What are the customer comments?

- Do I really know how much I should be paying for this item? Have I researched what other similar products have sold for recently? (See Chapter 2.)

- Is this an unsolicited offer? Avoid it.

- How am I paying for it? Am I using a safe technique, such as PayPal? Keep a record of all your purchases.

Bob the buyer wants to know that the seller is a real person who will take the time to communicate.

eBay QuickSteps   *Protecting Yourself and Handling Abuses*   193

USING FEEDBACK

eBay's feedback system helps you by providing the transaction histories of others and enabling you to build your own reputation so that others may know you. See Chapters 4 and 8 to see how to leave feedback as a buyer or seller. This chapter describes how to use feedback to prevent mistakes in judgment about doing business with someone.

BUILD A REPUTATION

Other buyers or sellers will know you by how you have performed in the past. See Figure 9-3 for an example of a seller with ideal feedback ratings. If past buyers or sellers have had good experiences doing business with you, you will get good feedback comments. If you have provided bad experiences, your feedback comments will reflect that. Feedback ratings are like money in the bank. They are a real currency in this cyber-economy, where you can't shake hands with a business partner face-to-face. Protect your feedback rating by going out of your way to be fair and accountable.

PROVIDE FEEDBACK—GOOD, BAD, OR INDIFFERENT

Part of being a responsible buyer or seller is to give feedback. Do it fairly and in a timely manner. If the buyer or seller, however, is hard to deal with and you can't resolve the issue, be specific about how you were disappointed. Do not just say, "This guy is a bum!" Be more constructive, saying something like, "Two months late in shipping. Does not answer e-mail." Keep in mind that the other person can answer your negative e-mail, leaving his or her own interpretation of the experience as well as feedback for you, so be fair and accurate.

○ Could not fulfill order.

Continued . . .

Take Protective Actions as a Seller

There are some tasks you can do as a seller to reduce your risk—keeping proper paperwork is high on the list. Other actions include:

● Answer queries from a buyer immediately and fully. Always disclose anything that was not in the description. Keep the questions and answers where you can find them.

● Always save your shipping records, and ship with a tracking number and insurance (UPS provides free insurance for up to $100 in value). You want to be able to prove that you shipped the item, and if it arrives broken or the buyer claims it is damaged, you won't be out any money. Pack the item carefully.

● If you have records on the authenticity or appraised value of your item, be sure to keep a copy for your own records in case the buyer disputes the value or authenticity.

● Contact the winning bidder and be clear again about how you accept payment and how long you will wait before you consider the sale void.

Protect the Transaction Summary

In addition to your communications with the buyer or seller and your attention to feedback and the item itself, there are some other practical ways you can protect the actual transaction:

● **Protect your account** by changing your password periodically. Keep your password and personal information private.

● **Insure the item** to protect you and your buyer in case the item is damaged, broken, or lost while shipping.

*Figure 9-3: **An ideal feedback rating, one in the high 90s, reassures buyers and sellers of your reliability.***

USING FEEDBACK *(Continued)*

HANDLING NEGATIVE FEEDBACK

If you receive negative feedback, always reply to it and explain what happened. Be clear about why the transaction was handled as it was, such as, "Tried to e-mail to explain delay, but buyer's firewall protection refused delivery." Sometimes it's easy to get carried away with indignation. If the other party was at fault, explain in a nonaggressive manner.

> Perfect condition? Two 6-inch age stained cracks. Didn't answer 3 emails
> - Reply by ▓▓▓_▓▓▓_ (Oct-30-06 17:55):
>   Buyer was moving and broke piece I never received any emails - please disregard
> - Follow-up by ▓▓▓▓▓▓ (Oct-31-06 14:27):
>   Reply is all untrue. Leaves retaliatory feedback, ruins my perfect record!

In some cases, negative feedback comments can be removed. To do this, both parties must agree that the comments are no longer appropriate. Both parties then seek to have the negative feedback withdrawn with a process called *mutual feedback withdrawal*.

1. To see whether this applies to you, click **Security Center** in the second footer on the eBay home page.

2. In the Security & Resolution Center, click **Report Problem**. The option Report Another Problem should be selected by default.

3. Under Contact Us, click **Feedback** and click **Continue**.

4. In the Contact Us: Feedback page, in Step 1, click **Feedback Concerns**. Then in Step 2, click **Review A Negative Feedback Comment For Removal**. Click **Continue**.

5. In the Contact Us page, click **Can I Have An Unfair Negative Feedback Comment Removed?**. You will see the procedure you need to follow to get negative feedback mutually withdrawn and links to further action.

> - Rating mutually withdrawn
>   Buyer and seller mutually agreed to withdraw feedback for this item. Learn more

Continued . . .

- **Use PayPal** to pay for items or refund money.

- **Use ID Verify** to give others confidence in you. Look for other buyers and sellers who have been ID Verified.

- **Use credit cards** for the easiest and simplest transactions. Most credit card companies issue insurance against fraudulent transactions for additional protection.

- **Use an escrow service** for items of high value, usually over $500. The escrow service will make sure that the item is received and approved before releasing the money to the seller. If there is any question, or if the buyer is dissatisfied with the item, the escrow service continues to hold the money until the item is returned to the seller. Be aware, however, that there are fraudulent escrow services out there. Use www.escrow.com, which is recommended by eBay.

Deal with Buyer Problems

As a buyer, you may find several forms of fraud on eBay. Someone may pretend to be from eBay in order to access your personal information, or sellers may be fraudulent in their item descriptions. If, as a buyer, you have not been able to resolve the issue by contacting the seller and you still have not received your item after paying for it, or if the item is significantly different from what you expected, you have other choices available to you. This section addresses some of the problems you may encounter and how to resolve them.

Detect and Report Account Theft

Account theft can happen when someone else learns of your User ID or password and uses that information to steal your identity on eBay. He or she might purchase items on your credit cards, even going so far as to change your password so that you can no longer monitor your own account.

USING FEEDBACK (Continued)

EVALUATE OTHERS' FEEDBACK

Figure 9-4 contains an example of a seller with a good rating in spite of negative and neutral feedback. In this case, you can tell that some of the negative ratings were from the same person—feedback from the same person only counts as one feedback comment. Figure 9-5 shows what can happen if even one person feels he or she has been unfairly treated. For a seller with a high feedback rating, a few negative comments resulting from multiple sales to one individual are not a terrible thing. For a relatively small seller, however, it can be disastrous. In this case, since the issue was shipping charges, you can look through the feedback comments and determine if this is a consistent problem or one that just occurred with this particular buyer. You might see neutral comments that echo the same sentiment but with less passion. Or, perhaps you will just see glowing comments, as seen in Figure 9-6. In this case, you can see that the sellers have given some favorable feedback to a buyer.

Things to consider when evaluating feedback ratings include:

- Become familiar with the stars, colors, and meanings (see Chapter 2).

- The rating is calculated on unique persons: +1 point for each positive comment, 0 points for neutral comments, and –1 point for each negative comment.

- Feedback comments can indicate a trend, either positive or negative.

Continued . . .

This is the overall feedback for the past 12 months, showing how it is distributed over the year

This shows the breakdown of unique ratings

Some of these are from the same person

Figure 9-4: **Negative feedback is considered along with positive and neutral comments.**

PREVENT ACCOUNT THEFT

Ways to protect your account include:

- Never give out your eBay password, credit card information, or other personal information in response to an e-mail claiming to be from eBay. eBay promises never to ask for it in an e-mail, only online on their secure site.

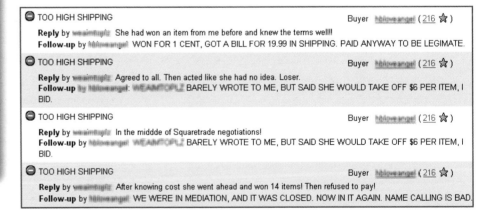

Figure 9-5: **One bad experience can have big repercussions in negative feedback ratings.**

USING FEEDBACK *(Continued)*

- Check the time that negative comments were placed—recently or in the past.

- If the negative comments indicate a problem with the item, you can check the item listing to see if it is described clearly and fully.

- Do the ratings reflect the seriousness of the negative comments? That is, does the seller or buyer have too few ratings so that the results are skewed? Conversely, does the seller or buyer have so many ratings that the results are unaffected by a serious charge? Be aware of these patterns.

Figure 9-6: *All green comments tell you this seller or buyer has had good experiences.*

- Check your account regularly to see if there are any purchases on it that you have not made.

- Change your password regularly, making it a maintenance routine, like brushing your teeth.

- Use the eBay Toolbar Account Guard feature. Account Guard warns you if you might be on a fraudulent Web site. (See the "Using Account Guard" QuickSteps.)

SECURE YOUR ACCOUNT

You may be the victim of account theft if you cannot log on to your account because your password no longer works, you have unfamiliar charges, your PayPal account does not reflect your own activity, or you get e-mail from eBay confirming that you have purchased something you know nothing about. If any of these things happen to you, first secure your account:

- Change your password to contain both letters and numbers, and to be different from your User ID. (See Chapter 1 for information on creating strong passwords.)

- Change your secret question and answer on your eBay account.

- Verify that your address information is correct.

- Verify that your listings, purchases, and bids are yours or belong to someone who is authorized to use your eBay account (such as a spouse).

NOTE

You have 90 days from the end of the transaction to leave feedback. After that, eBay may remove it from the system.

REPORT TO eBAY

If you cannot access your account, or if you find unauthorized entry to your account:

1. Click **Security Center** from the second footer links bar on the eBay home page. (You can also click the **Account Guard** down arrow on the eBay Toolbar, and click **eBay Security Center**.)

2. In the area entitled "Have A Problem? We Can Help," click **Report Another Problem**, and then click **Report Problem**.

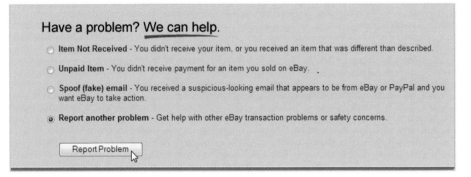

3. The Contact Us form is displayed. Select **Account Security** and click **Continue**.

4. On the Contact Us: Account Security page, select your topic:

   - In Step 1, click a subtopic. For instance, if you no longer have access to your account because you opened and responded to a fake eBay e-mail, click **Email Abuse**. If the subtopic is not immediately apparent, click each one and see how the subtopics in Step 2 relate to what you want to report.

   - When Step 1 is selected, click the subtopic in Step 2.

5. When your subtopics are selected, click **Continue**.

6. On the Contact Us page, see if the related Help pages resolve your problem. If not, click **Email Us With Your Question Or Concern**.

7. On the My Messages: Contact eBay Customer Support page, shown in Figure 9-7, fill in any relevant fields and your question or problem. The fields may vary according to the nature of the problem reported. Then click **Send**.

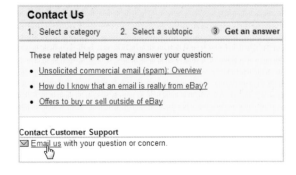

NOTE

Another method of reporting account theft is to use eBay's Live Help. To access it, click **Live Help** on the eBay home page header. There are two paths to finding advice here. Clicking the **Account Security** link will lead you to finding advice. Just follow the prompts. You can also chat directly with an agent online. Type your e-mail address or User ID. Click the **Subject** down arrow, and click **Other**. Click **Send**. When the agent appears, type your message in the lower box and click **Send** to send your message. Continue to chat with the agent until you know the solution to your problem. Chapter 1 contains additional information on using the Live Help feature.

QUICKSTEPS

USING ACCOUNT GUARD

Account Guard is a feature on the eBay Toolbar that helps to guard your access to the eBay and PayPal sites and warns you when you may be on a fraudulent Web site or one impersonating eBay or PayPal.

READ ACCOUNT GUARD WARNINGS

The Account Guard button changes color to verify accounts:

- **Green** indicates that you are signed in to your eBay or PayPal account.
Account Guard
- **Gray** indicates that you are no longer on eBay's protected Web site. This may be simply another Web site you commonly use or one claiming to be eBay.
Account Guard
- **Red** indicates that you might be on a spoof site.

Account Guard
Potential Spoof Site

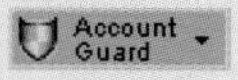

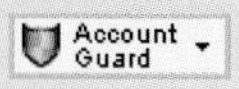

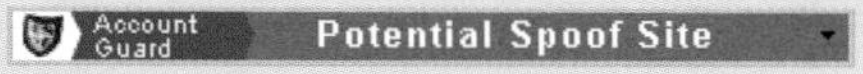

SET ACCOUNT GUARD PREFERENCES

1. Click **Account Guard** and click **Account Guard Options**. If the Account Guard tab is not displayed, click it, as seen in Figure 9-8.

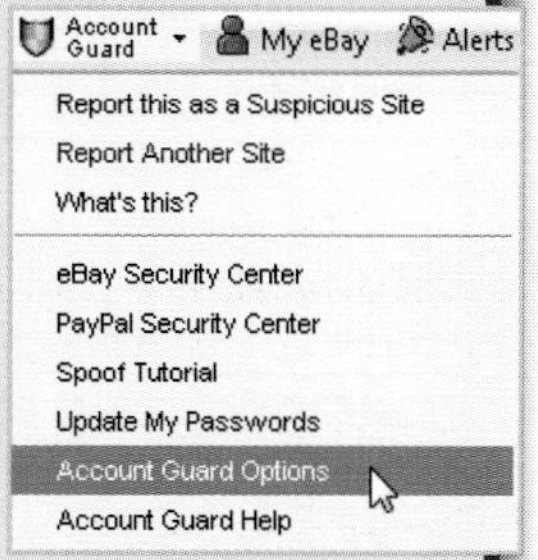

Account Guard
My eBay
Alerts
Report this as a Suspicious Site
Report Another Site
What's this?
eBay Security Center
PayPal Security Center
Spoof Tutorial
Update My Passwords
Account Guard Options
Account Guard Help

2. Since the default is to inform you if your password is used on another site, you must click **Inform Me If I Enter My eBay Password On Other Sites** to clear it.

Continued . . .

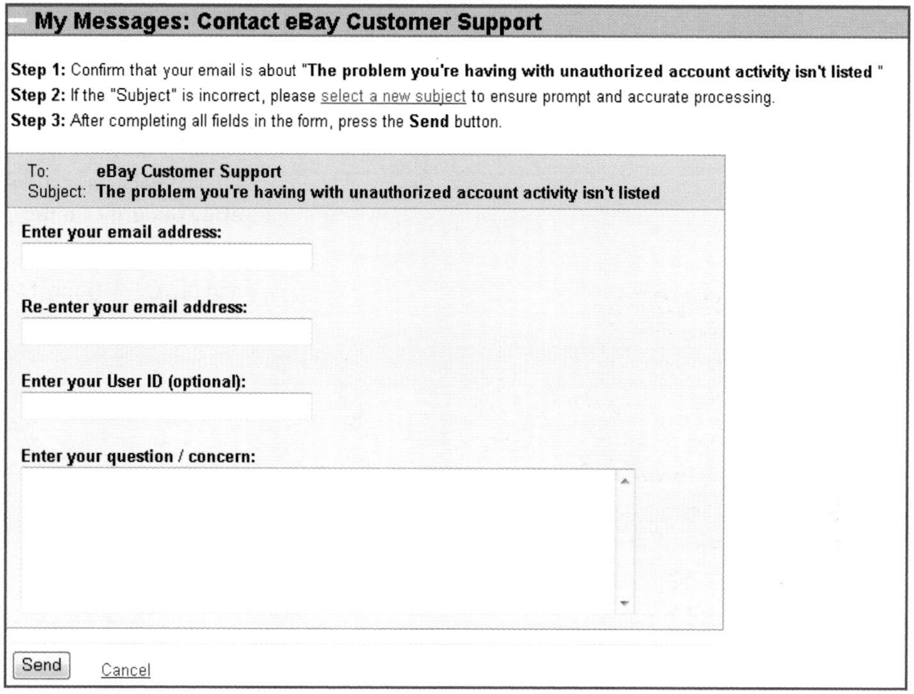

My Messages: Contact eBay Customer Support
Step 1: Confirm that your email is about "The problem you're having with unauthorized account activity isn't listed "
Step 2: If the "Subject" is incorrect, please select a new subject to ensure prompt and accurate processing.
Step 3: After completing all fields in the form, press the Send button.
To: eBay Customer Support
Subject: The problem you're having with unauthorized account activity isn't listed
Enter your email address:
Re-enter your email address:
Enter your User ID (optional):
Enter your question / concern:
Send
Cancel

Figure 9-7: ***Send your security problem or concern to eBay.***

Use Fraud Protection Measures for Buyers

If you think you have been defrauded by a seller, you have some choices. Table 9-1 explains the critical timing in any official disputes. If you have paid for an item and have not received it, have received an item that is significantly different from what you thought you had ordered, received an item that was counterfeit, or returned an item but did not get the refund, you'll want to proceed in this order:

- First, within the first ten days after the listing ends, try connecting with the seller by e-mail to resolve the issue between the two of you.
- Second, if that does not work, request the seller's contact information from eBay. eBay will send you the seller's telephone number and address, and your contact information will also be given to the seller.

QUICKSTEPS

USING ACCOUNT GUARD *(Continued)*

3. When the checkbox is selected, a warning message will be displayed when you enter your password on another site. (If the option is not selected, you will not be warned while using the eBay password in a non-eBay site.)

USE THE ACCOUNT GUARD REPORT FORM

To report a suspicious Web site or one clearly impersonating eBay, click **Account Guard** and click either **Report This As A Suspicious Site** or **Report Another Site**. An e-mail form is displayed in which you can type the circumstances for your suspicion.

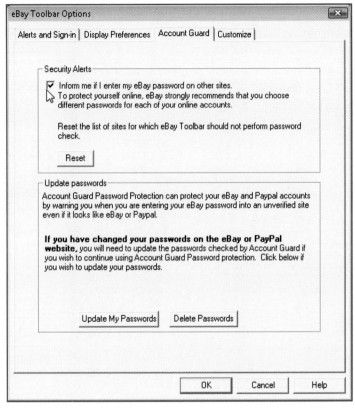

Figure 9-8: *Decide if you want to be warned or not when using your eBay password on other sites.*

NOTE

eBay facilitates communication between the buyer and seller by providing contact information, by providing a Dispute Console where communications can be easily tracked by both parties, and by structuring the feedback system to be so evident to future buyers or sellers. However, eBay cannot make a buyer pay for an item or a seller send the item as promised. You will have to do your own communicating with the other party. If you use PayPal or a credit card, you might be able to get reimbursed for legitimate abuses.

DESCRIPTION OF DAYS	NUMBER OF DAYS
Number of days before a dispute can be opened	10
Number of days by which a dispute *must* be opened	60
Number of days a seller has to respond before the dispute can be escalated into a claim	10
Number of days a buyer has to wait before a dispute can be escalated	40 (30 days after the listing ends, and 10 days for the seller to respond)
Number of days before a PayPal claim can be filed	20 days after a dispute is opened
Number of days by which a dispute must be settled	90

Table 9-1: *Item Not Received or Significantly Different Timing Considerations*

NOTE

If a seller refuses to sell the promised item to the buyer, he or she risks a range of penalties, from cancelling a listing to having an account suspended. A PowerSeller can lose that status, and selling fees may be increased. The exact penalties depend on how often and how badly the seller is abusing the system.

QUICKSTEPS

DEALING WITH SPOOF E-MAIL

Spoof e-mail is e-mail claiming to be from eBay when it is not. These are fraudulent e-mails often seeking your User ID, password, credit card information, Social Security number, or other private and sensitive personal information.

DETECT SPOOF E-MAIL

A spoof e-mail may have these characteristics:

- A legitimate look, with the appropriate logos and official-sounding names
- A claim that your account must be updated or changed in some way or your personal information reentered
- A request that you enter your private information (User ID and password, checking account or credit card information, or Social Security number), either within a response to the e-mail or to a Web site for that purpose
- Some type of threat that your account will no longer be accessible or that your ability to use eBay depends on your response

Continued . . .

- Third, within 45 days, contact the PayPal Resolution Center if you have paid for the item with PayPal.
- Fourth, within 60 days, use eBay's Item Not Received Or Significantly Not As Described process.
- Finally, file a claim to have your payment removed from your credit card company if you paid with a credit card. (If you used a credit card through PayPal, you should first contact PayPal.)

USE eBAY'S ITEM NOT RECEIVED OR SIGNIFICANTLY NOT AS DESCRIBED PROCESS

Between 10 to 60 days after a listing has been ended, and after you have exhausted efforts to contact the seller individually, you can open a dispute with the seller. In this procedure, eBay facilitates communication between the buyer and seller by giving them choices each step of the way. If the dispute is not resolved within 90 days, the dispute is closed and the buyer can no longer file a Trust And Safety complaint with eBay.

1. Click **My eBay** on the eBay header.
2. In the My eBay Views sidebar, scroll down and click **Dispute Console**.
3. On the Dispute Console page, click **Report An Item Not Received Or Not As Described**.
4. On the Report An Item Not Received page, shown in Figure 9-9, you see an explanation of the process. Type the item number of the disputed item in the Item Number text box, and click **Continue**. Follow the prompts until the report is finalized.
5. At this point, the dispute has been opened, and eBay now contacts the seller to tell them about your dispute. The seller replies to the complaint, and most disputes end at this point.
6. The seller can respond by indicating one of the following choices:
   - The seller wants to communicate with the buyer, and a message will be posted.
   - The seller indicates the item has not yet been paid for.
   - The item has been shipped, but seems not to have been received yet. This is where insuring an item becomes worthwhile for the seller in order to prove that the item has been sent.
   - The seller will offer a full or partial refund.

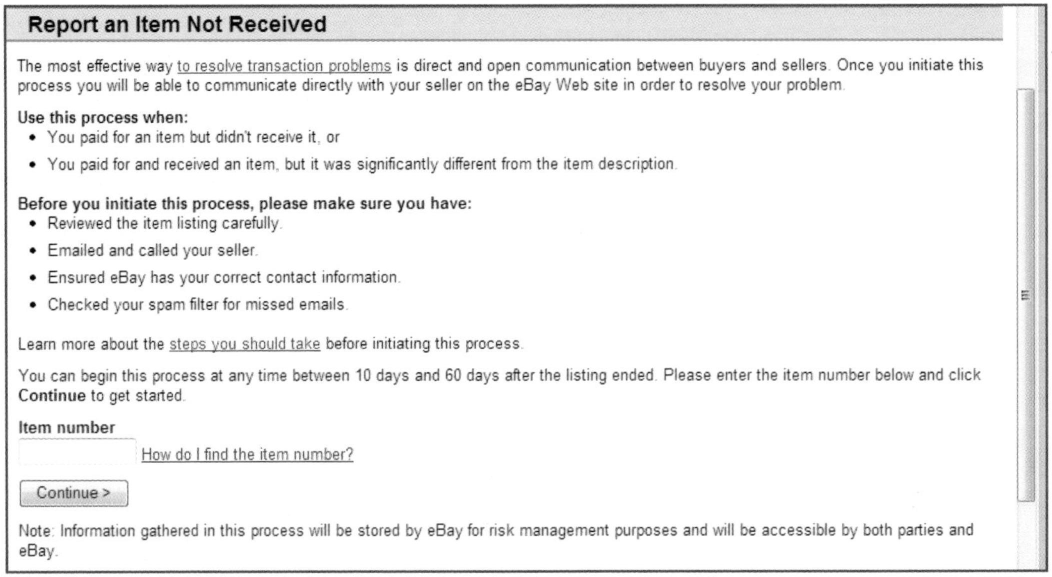

Figure 9-9: *If you do not receive the item, or if it is significantly not as described, you can open an official dispute with the seller.*

Report an Item Not Received

The most effective way to resolve transaction problems is direct and open communication between buyers and sellers. Once you initiate this process you will be able to communicate directly with your seller on the eBay Web site in order to resolve your problem.

Use this process when:
- You paid for an item but didn't receive it, or
- You paid for and received an item, but it was significantly different from the item description.

Before you initiate this process, please make sure you have:
- Reviewed the item listing carefully.
- Emailed and called your seller.
- Ensured eBay has your correct contact information.
- Checked your spam filter for missed emails.

Learn more about the steps you should take before initiating this process.

You can begin this process at any time between 10 days and 60 days after the listing ended. Please enter the item number below and click **Continue** to get started.

Item number

_____ How do I find the item number?

[Continue >]

Note: Information gathered in this process will be stored by eBay for risk management purposes and will be accessible by both parties and eBay.

QUICKSTEPS

DEALING WITH SPOOF E-MAIL

(Continued)

- The link address that you click to get to the site (which looks correct) and the Uniform Resource Locator (URL) of the site itself do not match (eBay's URL will always have an "eBay.com" before the first slash (/), such as http://pages .**ebay.com**/education/spooftutorial/spoof_3html; international sites may be slightly different)

- The Account Guard on the eBay Toolbar will turn gray or red

REPORT SPOOF E-MAIL

If you receive an e-mail that claims to be from eBay or PayPal or one of their related sites and you don't think it is, forward the e-mail to eBay using your e-mail

Continued . . .

7. The buyer and seller now are communicating. The Dispute Console now becomes the way by which the seller and buyer track communication.

8. At some point, the dispute will be closed, either because the dispute has been resolved or because it has not been. In this case, the buyer can choose to report the seller to the eBay Trust and Safety Team. The team will determine if the seller has abused the system and take appropriate action. The buyer can put in a claim to PayPal to be reimbursed. If the dispute is not actively closed by the buyer, it will be automatically closed by eBay after 90 days. In this case, the seller will not be reported to the Trust and Safety Team.

FILE A CLAIM TO BE REIMBURSED

In some cases, after not being able to successfully resolve your dispute with the previously described procedure, you can file a claim to be reimbursed for purchases in which you have not received the item and have paid for it using PayPal's Buyer Protection feature. PayPal may pay up to $2,000 per claim. The circumstances under which you might be entitled to some protection include:

UICKSTEPS

DEALING WITH SPOOF E-MAIL

(Continued)

program's Forward button or command. (You'll find valid messages from eBay in My Messages in My eBay.)

1. In the To field of the e-mail, type spoof@ebay .com or spoof@paypal.com. Do not alter the subject line. Don't attach the e-mail to one you are sending to the security site since that destroys some of the detection capability that eBay has.

2. Delete the e-mail from your e-mail account or inbox.

FIND ADDITIONAL SPOOF INFORMATION

- From the Account Guard menu on the eBay Toolbar, click **Spoof Tutorial**.

  –Or–

- Click **Security Center** from the second footer links bar on the eBay home page, and on that page, scroll down to the Security & Resolution Center Tools links bar, and click **Stopping Spoof Emails And Web Sites**. You will be shown additional information.

⸬ Security & Resolution Center Tools

Marketplace Safety Tips | Stopping spoof emails and Web sites | eBay Account
Protection/Reporting Account Theft | eBay Tutorials | Privacy Central | Privacy Central | PayPal
Security Center | Need More Answers to Your Questions?

- A tangible item has been purchased on eBay. Items such as services or e-mailed information (such as e-books) are not included.

- A dispute must have been opened within 10 to 60 days of the PayPal payment being made.

- PayPal Buyer Protection only covers payments made with PayPal. The program does not cover cash or instant money transfers, since they cannot be proved.

- You are limited to six claims per year.

- The claim must be made within 20 days of the dispute opening.

In addition to the protections offered by PayPal, you may also be protected by your credit card policies, such as Visa, MasterCard, Discover, or American Express.

FILE WITH PAYPAL

In order to file for reimbursement from PayPal, you must file within 20 days of the dispute being opened and the item must be PayPal-protected.

To file a claim with PayPal Buyer Protection:

1. Verify that the item is protected by PayPal and that you paid using PayPal. The following logo will be displayed beneath the Meet The Seller area in the View Item page.

   PayPal Up to $2,000 in buyer protection. See eligibility

2. In PayPal, sign in and click the **My Account** tab.

   My Account

3. Click **Resolution Center** on the menu bar.

   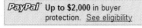

4. On the Resolution Center page, click **Report A Problem**.

   Report a Problem
   - Address a problem transaction with your seller
   - Report unauthorized account activity

5. On the Report A Problem page, click **Item Dispute**. Click **Continue**.

6. On the Resolution Center – Open A Dispute page, scroll down, set the date ranges for the transactions you want to see, and if you do not know the transaction ID, click **Select Transaction ID**. You will be shown the history of your transactions. Click the Transaction ID you want to dispute, as shown in Figure 9-10.

7. The transaction ID will be displayed in the PayPal Transaction ID text box. Click **Continue**.

8. You will be asked to specify the reason for the transaction. Click the applicable reason under Reason For Opening Dispute, and click **Continue**.

9. You will be asked for further information. Continue to fill in the form as you are prompted. At the end, your dispute will be opened and you will be able to track the dispute as you continue through the process.

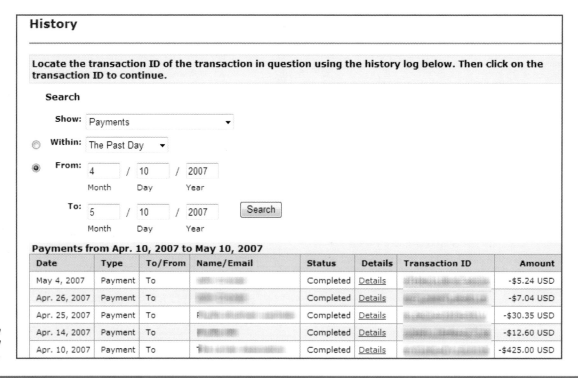

Figure 9-10: **PayPal will find a transaction ID for you if you do not know it offhand.**

Solve Problems for Sellers

Sellers have special problems with nonpaid items. eBay considers nonpaying a serious violation of its policy and prohibits buyers from not following through with payment for items they have won in a bid or Buy It Now purchase. Sellers have several options: they can block buyers from bidding on their sales, they can relist an item not paid for, they can make Second Chance Offers to other bidders, or they can request a refund on the costs of relisting items. A Bidder Alert may be placed on a nonpaying bidder, which is a serious thing. See Table 9-2 for timing considerations.

File an Unpaid Item Dispute

To enter into a dispute with a buyer who has not paid for an item you have sent to them, you must notify eBay by opening a dispute.

1. Click **My eBay** on the eBay header. Find and copy the item number for the unpaid item by highlighting it and pressing **CTRL+C**, or write it down where you can remember it.

2. In the My eBay Views sidebar, scroll down and click **Dispute Console**.

3. On the Dispute Console page, click **Report An Unpaid Item**.

4. On the Report An Unpaid Item Dispute page, read the overview of the process, and type or paste (by pressing **CTRL+V**) the item number into the Item Number text box.

5. Click **Continue**. The Report An Unpaid Item Dispute page will open.

Have a problem? We can help.
Report an Unpaid Item | Report

DESCRIPTION OF DAYS	NUMBER OF DAYS
Number of days before a dispute can be opened	7
Number of days by which a dispute *must* be opened	45
Number of days a buyer has to respond before the seller can receive a final value fee credit	8
Number of days before the dispute is automatically closed	60

*Table 9-2: **Unpaid Item Timing Considerations***

QUICKFACTS

UNDERSTANDING THE UNPAID ITEMS PROCESS *(Continued)*

To help avoid unpaid items, you can clearly include all information about an item in the description, including shipping and handling costs. You can make it easy for the bidder/buyer to check out and pay for the item, including PayPal as an option. You can ship using insurance to prove the item has been received, and maintain records about all transactions. Be careful when dealing with international buyers.

TIP

If a buyer does not pay for an item, eBay will issue an *unpaid item strike* against the buyer, which tells future sellers about this buyer. If a buyer accumulates too many unpaid item strikes, their account can be suspended or limits placed on their buying ability.

6. Click the **Why Are You Reporting This Unpaid Item** down arrow, and click an option.

7. Click the **What Has Happened So Far In The Dispute** down arrow, and click an option.

8. On the Send The Unpaid Item Reminder page, click the button, as shown in Figure 9-11.

9. At this point, the dispute has been opened, and eBay now contacts the buyer to tell him or her about your dispute. The buyer replies to the complaint, and most disputes end at this point.

10. The buyer can respond by indicating one of the following choices:
    - The buyer has already paid.
    - The buyer will pay now.
    - There needs to be further communication between the buyer and seller.

11. The buyer and seller now are communicating. The Dispute Console now becomes the way by which the seller and buyer track communication.

12. At some point, the dispute will be closed. If it is closed because both parties are now satisfied, the seller will not receive a final value fee credit. If the transaction is mutually determined to be voided, the seller receives the final value fee credit. If no resolution can be reached, the seller can receive a final value fee credit and can relist the item.

Verify a Final Value Fee Credit

A final value fee tells you the total cost of a listing, including the fees you paid to eBay. Before you can file a final value fee credit, however, you must have filed

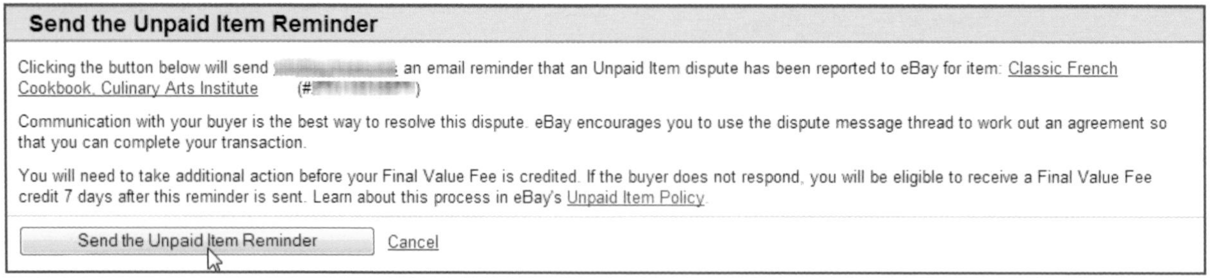

Send the Unpaid Item Reminder

Clicking the button below will send ██████████ an email reminder that an Unpaid Item dispute has been reported to eBay for item: Classic French Cookbook, Culinary Arts Institute   (#█████████)

Communication with your buyer is the best way to resolve this dispute. eBay encourages you to use the dispute message thread to work out an agreement so that you can complete your transaction.

You will need to take additional action before your Final Value Fee is credited. If the buyer does not respond, you will be eligible to receive a Final Value Fee credit 7 days after this reminder is sent. Learn about this process in eBay's Unpaid Item Policy.

    Send the Unpaid Item Reminder   Cancel

*Figure 9-11: **If your buyer does not pay for an item, you can open an official dispute with the buyer by first sending an eBay reminder.***

an unpaid item dispute within 45 days of the listing end. You must have tried for at least seven days to resolve the problem with the buyer. You are eligible for a final value fee credit if you cannot work out a resolution with the buyer and close the dispute. The final value fee credit will be available without further processing, unless a seller has excessive unpaid item disputes.

To confirm if a credit has been paid:

1. Click **My eBay** on the eBay header, and in the sidebar, under My Account, click **Seller Account**.

2. Click **View Account Status**.

3. You will see whether you have a final value fee credit.

Block Bidders or Buyers

You can block certain people from bidding on or buying items from you. You would do this with nonpaying bidders or buyers, or if you have had a bad experience with a buyer. You can build a list of up to 1,000 blocked buyers. See Chapter 7 for how to do this.

Handle Shipping Concerns

If you have a problem with shipping—for instance, you shipped a package and it didn't arrive or it arrived damaged—you may have to deal with insurance concerns. If you did not insure the item, you cannot make a claim for it. If the item is insured, you may be reimbursed for all or part of the item's price. In that case, contact the carrier and make the claim according to their requirements. Some possibilities are:

- www.usps.com/welcome.htm for the United States Post Office (USPS)
- www.ups.com/content/us/en/resources/service/claims/index.html for United Parcel Service (UPS)
- www.fedex.com/us/customer/claims for Federal Express (FedEx)

NOTE

With nonpaying buyers, the seller can either relist the item and put it up for sale again or use Second Chance Offers. With a Second Chance Offer, the seller contacts a losing bidder and asks if he or she wants to buy the item. (See Chapter 8 for how to relist an item or use Second Chance Offers.)

CAUTION

If the item is damaged and it has not been packaged correctly, or if the seller charges for insurance but does not secure it from the carrier, the carrier's insurance may pay only a part of the costs (in the case of damage) or none at all. The seller is responsible for reimbursing the buyer. If the seller does not do so, the buyer may be able to claim reimbursement through the Buyer Protection Program.

QUICKSTEPS

REPORTING OTHER PROBLEMS

There are other concerns that eBay users may have to deal with other than unpaid items, items not delivered, or items delivered that were significantly differently from what you expected. These have to do with illegal listings, illegal solicitations, off-eBay transactions, and more. To report problems such as these:

1. Click **Security Center** in the second footer links bar and click **Report Problem.** Identify the category of your problem. Click **Continue.**

2. Select a subtopic in both Step 1 and Step 2, click **Continue**.

3. Click **Email Us** on the third Contact Us page. Type the e-mail message, and click **Send**.

REPORT ILLEGAL ITEMS

- Select **Listing Violations** as the category.

- Click **Prohibited (Banned Items)** in Step 1.

- Click the type of prohibited item in Step 2 and Step 3 if needed (see Figure 9-12).

REPORT ILLEGAL SOLICITATIONS

- Select **Selling And Managing Your Item** as the category.

- Click **Fraud And Transaction Problems** in Step 1.

- Click **Buyer Offered To Purchase Item From You Outside eBay** in Step 2.

REPORT INTELLECTUAL PROPERTY RIGHTS INFRINGEMENTS

- Select **Listing Violations** as the category.

- Click **Counterfeits And Copyright Violations** in Step 1.

Continued . . .

Report Unwelcome Buyers

It's hard to imagine that there are buyers you may want to avoid, but it happens. For example, you may find buyers that are:

- **Failing to meet your terms**. Perhaps they are international buyers and you state that you will ship to your home country only, or you clearly state that you do not accept buyers with negative feedback ratings and you get a bid from a buyer with a negative feedback rating.

- **Using techniques that are meant to disrupt your sale**. For example, someone might be bidding with no intent to pay or trying to bid even though he or she is blocked from bidding on your site or placing a bid that is so high that no one else will bid and then not paying.

Step 1: Select a subtopic
Copying of your listing
Counterfeits and copyright violations
Prohibited (banned items)
Listing policy violations (improper keywords, outside links, excessive shipping, etc)
eBay Motors or vehicle related
Fraudulent listings (illegal seller demands, you didn't receive item, etc)
Stolen property

Step 2: Select a subtopic
Alcohol, tobacco, drugs and drug paraphernalia
Animals, plants, and wildlife
Artifacts
Electronic equipment
Event tickets
Firearms, weapons, and knives
Government and transit IDs, licenses and uniforms
Hazardous items
Items with a face value (currency, coupons, etc.)
Law enforcement items
Medical and prescription items
Travel
Offensive and potentially offensive items
Teacher's edition textbooks
Mature audience items
Other prohibited (banned) items

Step 3
Travel related items listed in an inappropriate category
Travel items listed without appropriate verification/certification
Listings that require additional fees, charges or purchases
Travel club memberships and "choice travel" certificates

Figure 9-12: **To report a listing violation, identify it using the multileveled menu of possibilities.**

QUICKSTEPS

REPORTING OTHER PROBLEMS

(Continued)

- Select **eBay Item Infringes Your Intellectual Property Rights** in Step 2.

- Step 3 will display: **Contact eBay's VeRO Program** (Verified Rights Owner Program). To learn about VeRO, click **Security Center** on the footer links bar, and under Resources, click **Protection Programs**. Under What eBay Can Do, click **Protecting Intellectual Property (VeRO)**.

To report unwelcome buyers:

1. From the second footer links bar on the eBay home page, click **Security Center**. The Security & Resolution Center page is displayed. Click **Report Another Problem**, and then click **Report Problem**. The Contact Us page is displayed

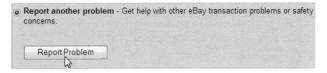

2. Click **Selling And Managing Your Item** to report problems with a buyer. Click **Continue**. The Contact Us – Selling and Managing Your Item page is displayed:

- In Step 1, click **Problems With Buyers**.

- In Step 2, select the reason you want to report the buyer, such as **User Is Bidding/Buying To Harass Seller Or Prevent Sale**, as shown in Figure 9-13.

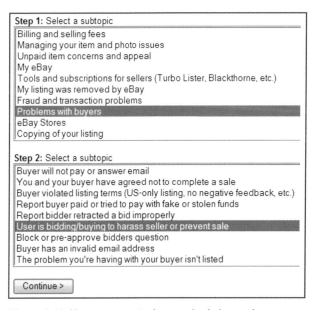

Figure 9-13: You can report a buyer who is harassing you or trying to prevent a sale.

3. Click **Continue**. On the second Contact Us page, click **Email Us**. The e-mail form shown in Figure 9-14 is displayed.

Contact Customer Support

✉ Email us with your question or concern.

4. Complete the form and click **Send**.

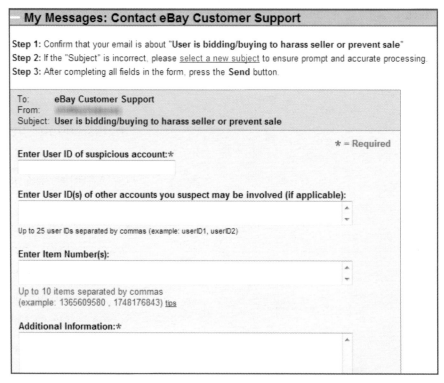

My Messages: Contact eBay Customer Support

Step 1: Confirm that your email is about "**User is bidding/buying to harass seller or prevent sale**"
Step 2: If the "Subject" is incorrect, please select a new subject to ensure prompt and accurate processing.
Step 3: After completing all fields in the form, press the **Send** button.

To: eBay Customer Support
From:
Subject: **User is bidding/buying to harass seller or prevent sale**

✻ = Required

Enter User ID of suspicious account:✻

Enter User ID(s) of other accounts you suspect may be involved (if applicable):

Up to 25 user IDs separated by commas (example: userID1, userID2)

Enter Item Number(s):

Up to 10 items separated by commas
(example: 1365609580 , 1748176843) tips

Additional Information:✻

Figure 9-14: *eBay will respond to an e-mail about unwelcome bidders/buyers.*

Chapter 10
Making eBay Your Business

In this chapter you will learn how to ramp up your selling on eBay beyond the casual sales designed to clear out a crowded cellar or garage. Selling on eBay as a business is very much both a traditional entrepreneurial undertaking and a totally unique venture. You follow basic steps, just as you would for starting any business. You will need to put together the necessary components of your online business, such as an accounting system, photo and shipping areas, and inventory (what you used to call "items to sell"). Once you have built the foundation of your business, you will need to actually run it—that is, decide how best to employ the programs, tools, and unique aspects of the eBay community to help you achieve your financial goals. This chapter helps you do this.

10

CREATING AN eBAY BUSINESS INFRASTRUCTURE

As an occasional seller on eBay, you can get away with temporary or otherwise cobbled-together "centers" to support your eBay selling. The increase in volume you can expect as your business takes off, however, will require a more formalized approach.

CHOOSE A BUSINESS ENTITY

When you establish a business, government entities at all levels will want to share in your success, from the $10 local municipality business license to the double hit the federal government imposes on collecting Social Security tax. The type of entity you choose will have serious tax, reporting, and legal consequences, so take the time to consult with professionals and businesspeople to see what makes the most sense for you (see the "Understanding Business Entities" QuickFacts later in the chapter).

SET UP YOUR BOOKS

Keeping accurate records of your inventory costs, selling prices, shipping and handling, overhead, and associated costs is the foundation to satisfying government reporting requirements, as well as to keeping on top of the financial health of your business. You can get professional help to set up your accounts, use an accounting program (a popular small-business accounting software is Intuit's QuickBooks Basic/Pro/Premier—www.intuit.com), use eBay and third-party tools tailored to selling on eBay, or set up your own spreadsheets, either paper-based or using a program such as Microsoft Excel.

SET UP PROCESSING AREAS

Henry Ford revolutionized manufacturing by introducing the assembly line. A hundred years later, you can benefit

Continued . . .

Set Up Your eBay Business

eBay has moved quite rapidly from being an "amateur hour," garage sale, Beanie Baby–selling dot-com to being a multibillion-a-year enterprise. If you want to play on this playground, you'll be going head to head with professionals, including Fortune 500 companies. The only way to compete is to play by the accepted rules of business.

Promote Your Product

You can conduct business on eBay without doing anything more than submitting Sell Your Item forms, as you've probably done several times already. To recognize and support those who want to ratchet up their involvement, eBay provides several programs that can help you take advantage of its powerful marketing and advertising engine. Promotion gets the word out about your product to your target audience. In eBay, you have several promotional upgrades and features you can apply to your listings (see Chapter 6). Examples of other promotional actions you can explore include the following:

- Cross-promote between your business Web site and your eBay listings (see "Link to eBay from Your Web Site" next).

- Utilize eBay specialty sites to leverage exposure to your listings. For example, your Half.com listing can automatically be displayed on eBay Express, and you can take advantage of cross-promotional tools by having your eBay Store listings appear in item listings. (See Chapter 5 for more information on selling in eBay specialty sites such as Half.com and eBay Express; see "Open an eBay Store" later in this chapter for steps to set up an eBay Store.)

- Create an About Me page (see "Create an About Me Page" later in the chapter) to provide information about you, your company, and your products (see Figure10-1).

- Create an eBay My World page to provide links to your listings and further tell buyers about yourself and your business. Chapter 1 directs you to where you can create an eBay My World page.

10

CREATING AN EBAY BUSINESS INFRASTRUCTURE *(Continued)*

from his wisdom by applying the same principle to move your product quickly from inventory to shipment by devoting dedicated centers to the eBay sales process. An item's typical journey through your business might include:

- **Purchasing center** logs a new item into your inventory database (it can be a simple notebook or a database program, such as Microsoft Access) and includes sales cost, date of acquisition, and source.

- **Photo center** photographs the item using a studio that's set up to quickly introduce the item into a neutral background with adequate lighting. Enhance pictures to accentuate features. Pictures are uploaded to a local computer system for ready use by your hosting method.

- **Listing center** describes the item, researches similar items for pricing and category selection (see Chapter 5 for information on determining the price of items) and enters the listing directly into eBay or your auction-management system. Listings are monitored for bidding activity and bidder/buyer inquiries (see Chapter 7 for more information on managing listings).

- **Accounting center** processes incoming payments and releases items to shipping when funds have cleared.

- **Shipping center** provides materials and equipment for easy and professional packaging (see Figure 10-2). Liaison and accounts with shippers are established to maximize convenience (daily pickups) and minimize costs.

Figure 10-1: An About Me page is a great tool for promoting yourself, your listings, and your eBay business.

- Use Google Base, a tool that lets you publish your eBay Store listings to Froogle, a search component of Google for items for sale. Go to http://base.google.com, click **Learn More**, and research information on connecting your eBay Store listings.

10

Bubble wrap rolls | Boxes in various sizes | Styrofoam peanut dispenser | Tape guns and extra tape | Packing paper rolls

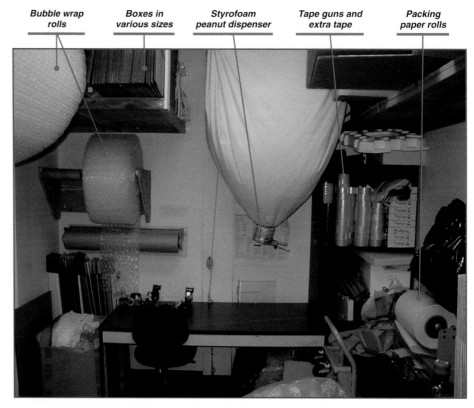

Figure 10-2: *Utilize the efficiencies of workflow, space, and location of materials the professional packers use when setting up your own packing area.*

LINK TO eBAY FROM YOUR WEB SITE

Having a Web site is almost a given for anyone who does business today, online or offline. Even if only providing informational and customer service-oriented material, a Web site adds credibility to your eBay business. Simple Web sites are generally provided by your Internet service provider (ISP), and you can easily create your own with a Web site creation program, such as Microsoft FrontPage. Your ISP typically provides free Web server storage space as part of your Internet connection subscription, so cost is low or minimal. To drive "outsiders"

10

to your eBay listings, use the eBay logo to provide links to the eBay home page and your listings.

1. Click **Site Map** at the top of any eBay page.

2. Under Sell | Selling Activities, click **Promote Your Listings With Link Buttons**.

3. Select the links you want on your Web site (for example, to the eBay home page and to your listings).

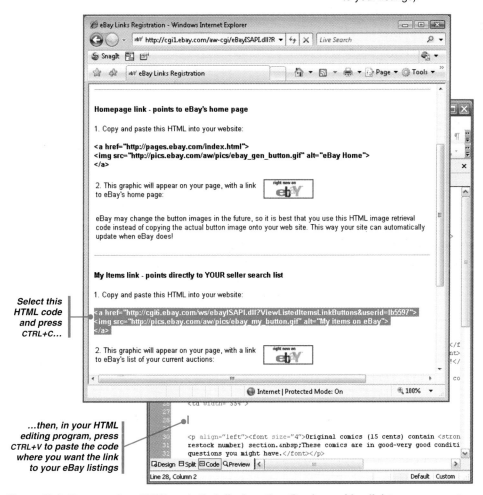

4. Type the Uniform Resource Locators (URLs) of your Web pages that will contain the links.

5. Read the eBay Link License Agreement, and click **I Agree** (if you don't agree, you won't be able to continue).

6. On the Instructions For Installing Buttons On Your Site page, copy the Hypertext Markup Language (HTML) code for the link you want, as shown in Figure 10-3, and paste it onto your Web page. When buyers click the eBay logo, they will go to an eBay page that lists your items for sale.

CREATE AN ABOUT ME PAGE

You can create a page about your business (or self) that others can reference when they are researching your eBay activities. You can insert text or pictures of yourself or of items you're selling. You can give other sellers or buyers information that they can

Figure 10-3: You can place HTML code that displays the eBay logo with a link to your current listing on your own Web site.

use to judge what kind of a business partner you will be. When you create an About Me page, an icon is inserted into your User ID, such as seen here, and in your eBay Store header.

1. From the My eBay Views sidebar, scroll down to My Account, and click **Personal Information**.

2. Under Account Information, click the About Me Page **Edit** link. The page shown in Figure 10-4 is displayed.

3. The About Me introductory page will introduce what the page is used for. Click the **Create Your Page** button.

4. On the About Me: Choose Page Creation Option page, choose between creating a page using a step-by-step process, where you are led through the process, or by entering your own HTML text. Click **Continue**.

5. If you have chosen the HTML route, type your text with the appropriate HTML tags, or paste code created in an HTML editor.

–Or–

If you choose the step-by-step process, follow the prompts (you can also add your own paragraph and picture hosting HTML):

- Add text to your page. Type a page title and paragraph text in the Paragraph 1 and Paragraph 2 text boxes provided. Be creative and give information about yourself and your business that you think others would want to know.

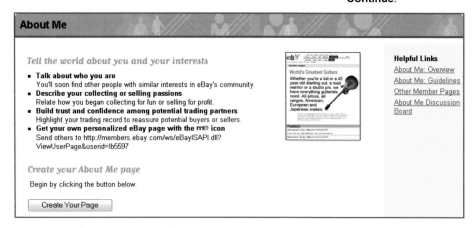

Figure 10-4: Creating an About Me page lets you tell others who you are and what you sell.

- Use the Font Name, Size, and other character and paragraph formatting tools on the toolbar to format your text.

- To add a picture to your page, type a label in the Label For Picture text box. Click **Browse** to find and select the picture file you want using eBay Picture Services (see Chapter 6 for more information on adding pictures to eBay listings and other pages).

- To show your feedback on your page, click the **Show Feedback You've Received** down arrow, and select the number of feedbacks you want to display.

- To show a product list, type a heading in the Label Your Listings text box, click the **Show Your Current Listing** down arrow, and select the number of items you want to show in your listing.

- To add links to your page, type a name in the text box, and then type the corresponding URL for the Web page you want. You can have up to three addresses.

6. Click **Continue** to see a preview of the page.

7. Choose a page layout. Scroll down to see the preview of the page layout, shown in Figure 10-5. If you want to make changes, click **Back**. If the preview displays the edits the way you want them, click **Submit**.

8. You will see a message about your About Me page being successfully edited. Click a link, such as to My eBay, where you want to go next.

Figure 10-5: Start building your About Me page, and preview changes as you make them.

USE CROSS-PROMOTION

eBay can help you sell more items by displaying, or *cross-promoting*, other items you have for sale when a buyer bids on or buys an item ("Start an eBay Store," later in this chapter, describes the cross promotions in eBay Stores). eBay has a default set of rules it uses to pick which items to display. You can create rules to customize which items are displayed and whether you want work with other sellers to display each other's items.

Thoroughbred Horse Legends Ltd Ed Cantrell Starlite	Seabiscuit Thoroughbred Horse Legends Ltd Ed Starlite	Secretariat Thoroughbred Horse Legends Ltd Ed Starlite	Ruffian Thoroughbred Horse Legends Ltd Ed Starlite
Buy It Now price: **US $67.49** Original price: US $89.99	**0** bids: **US $99.99** *Buy It Now* US $124.99 Time left: 1d 21h 9m	**1** bids: **US $99.99** Time left: 1d 20h 59m	**1** bids: **US $99.99** Time left: 1d 21h 16m

All Selling
- Scheduled
- Selling
- Sold
- Unsold

Marketing Tools

Want It Now

1. In the My eBay Views sidebar, in the All Selling section, click **Marketing Tools**.

2. On the Marketing Tools sidebar, under Item Promotion:

   - Click **Defaults** to establish rules that tell eBay which of your for-sale items you want displayed (based on category) for given listings (also based on category).

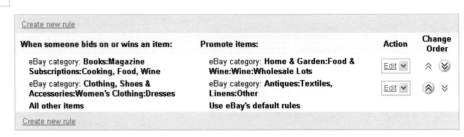

Create new rule

When someone bids on or wins an item:	Promote items:	Action	Change Order
eBay category: **Books:Magazine Subscriptions:Cooking, Food, Wine**	eBay category: **Home & Garden:Food & Wine:Wine:Wholesale Lots**	Edit ▾	⌃ ⌄
eBay category: **Clothing, Shoes & Accessories:Women's Clothing:Dresses**	eBay category: **Antiques:Textiles, Linens:Other**	Edit ▾	⌃ ⌄
All other items	**Use eBay's default rules**		

Create new rule

- Click **Settings** to select whether you want to cross-promote and where it's applicable, as well as whether you want to create cross-promotion connections with other sellers to display each other's items that match your criteria (see Figure 10-6).

- Click **Connections** to establish cross-promotion connections with other sellers.

UNDERSTANDING BUSINESS ENTITIES

The typical business entities that are recognized by local, state, and federal authorities are described in the following sections.

SOLE PROPRIETORSHIP

This is the simplest entity to establish for a single owner, typically requiring only state fees to obtain a business license to get going and few, if any, recurring fees. Tax preparation is relatively easy, as all income is treated as personal income. Easy setup and maintenance is offset, however, by lack of incorporated income tax benefits and exposure of personal assets to business liabilities—for example, if your business is sued, so are you!

PARTNERSHIP

Easy to set up and maintain, a partnership agreement should be crafted to consider all eventualities, including dissolution, departure of a partner (this can be tricky; it's good to think things through early), and management control. The main difference between general and limited partnerships is the classification and liability of members:

- **General partnerships** are comprised of two or more members who share individual responsibility for taxes and liability of the business concern.

- **Limited partnerships** provide for two classes of partners: general and limited. General partners share similar responsibilities to those in a general partnership. Limited partners do not share in the management of the partnership and are not personally liable for any more than their individual investments in the company.

Continued . . .

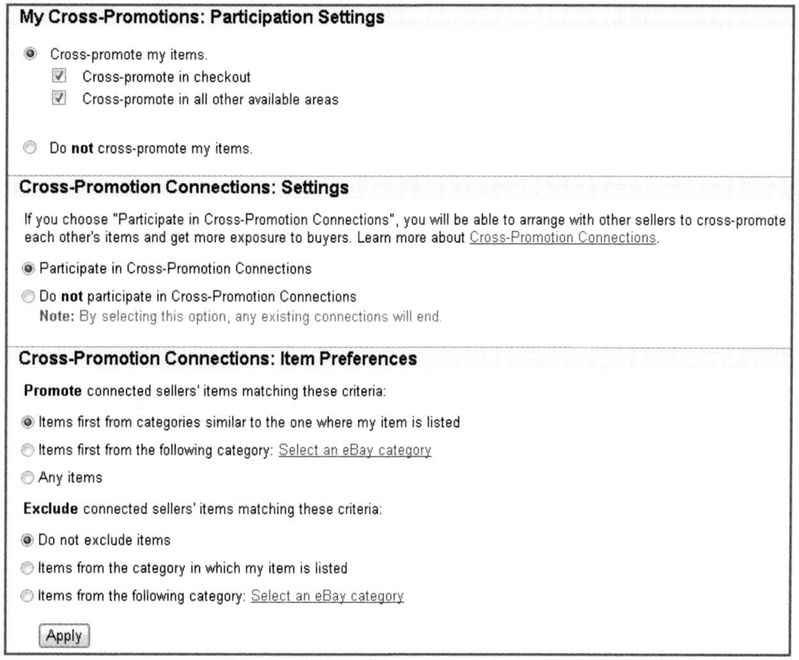

My Cross-Promotions: Participation Settings

◉ Cross-promote my items.
    ☑ Cross-promote in checkout
    ☑ Cross-promote in all other available areas

◯ Do **not** cross-promote my items.

Cross-Promotion Connections: Settings

If you choose "Participate in Cross-Promotion Connections", you will be able to arrange with other sellers to cross-promote each other's items and get more exposure to buyers. Learn more about <u>Cross-Promotion Connections</u>.

◉ Participate in Cross-Promotion Connections
◯ Do **not** participate in Cross-Promotion Connections
    Note: By selecting this option, any existing connections will end.

Cross-Promotion Connections: Item Preferences

Promote connected sellers' items matching these criteria:

◉ Items first from categories similar to the one where my item is listed
◯ Items first from the following category: <u>Select an eBay category</u>
◯ Any items

Exclude connected sellers' items matching these criteria:

◉ Do not exclude items
◯ Items from the category in which my item is listed
◯ Items from the following category: <u>Select an eBay category</u>

[Apply]

Figure 10-6: You have several options on how you establish cross-promotions in your listings.

SELECT ITEMS AS A FAVORITE SELLER

Buyers can subscribe to you as a Favorite Seller, view a page (see Figure 10-7), and receive e-mail notifications of your Top Pick items you have for sale (Chapter 2 describes how buyers subscribe to Favorite Sellers). To set up how you want your Favorite Seller items selected:

1. In the My eBay Views sidebar, in the All Selling section, click **Marketing Tools**.

2. On the Marketing Tools sidebar, under Item Promotion, click **Favorite Seller Top Picks**.

3. On the Favorite Seller Top Picks page, under Item Selection, click **Change To Manual Selection** to choose the items you want buyers to see.

–Or–

UNDERSTANDING BUSINESS ENTITIES *(Continued)*

CORPORATION

Corporations are the most expensive entities to create and maintain (think board meetings, minutes, issuance of stock, and so on), but can be bought and sold, either privately or publicly (although this is not really practical for an S corporation due to a limit on the number of stockholders), and enjoy some favorable tax treatment. Corporations are a separate legal entity and generally shield owners (called shareholders) from personal liability:

- **C corporations** are what govern the largest companies in corporate America. Not generally associated with small startups, these corporations are taxed at the entity level, and shareholders are also individually taxed on dividends.

- **S corporations** provide the personal liability protection of a C corporation, but "pass through" the corporation's income to the shareholders' personal tax obligation, avoiding the "double tax" issue. This is usually a better option for most small businesses.

LIMITED LIABILITY COMPANY

A limited liability company (LLC) combines many of the favorable tax treatments of a corporation with personal liability protection and the management structure of a partnership. The rules governing LLCs vary from state to state, so check with a tax or business professional in your area to see if an LLC might be a better option in your case than an S corporation. Key differences between the two are that an LLC can be owned by non-U.S. citizens and nonresident aliens, while an S corporation can be owned only by U.S. citizens or permanent resident aliens; in addition, an LLC may have any number of shareholders, while an S corporation is limited to 75.

Figure 10-7: **You can select the listings you want to display as Top Picks or let eBay automatically choose them.**

Click **Edit Criteria** to change how eBay automatically selects which items to display. Click **Save Criteria**.

4. Click **Apply** at the bottom of the Favorite Seller Top Picks page when finished.

Target Selling with Your Sales Data

To assist you in analyzing your sales data so that you can make listing decisions, such as which sales format to use (bidding or fixed-price), what listing durations and ending times seem most effective, which categories are doing best, and several other sales metrics, you can receive Sales Reports from eBay. The basic Sales Report is free (your seller's account must be in good standing, must have sold at least one item in the last four months, and must have a feedback rating of at least 10). The more robust Sales Report Plus is also free on a trial basis and doesn't have minimum requirements to subscribe (also, it's included when you open an eBay Store).

	Sales Reports Sign Up Now!	Sales Reports Plus Sign Up Now!
Description	See a high-level view of your most recent activity, including a summary of your: • Sales • Ended Listings • Successful Listings % • Average Sale Price • eBay and Paypal fees	See in-depth views of your most recent activity. Sales Reports Plus offers everything in the basic product PLUS: • Metrics by Category • Metrics by Format (e.g, Fixed Price) • Metrics by Category & Format • Metrics by Ending Day or Time for all formats • Buyer counts • Detailed eBay fees • Unpaid Item Credits Requested • Ability to show or hide sections • Download capabilities
Subscription Fee	FREE !	FREE !
Requirements	Sales Reports	Sales Reports Plus

Figure 10-8: Sales Reports provide you additional selling metrics to those available in My eBay.

1. Click **Site Map** on the eBay header.

2. Under Sell | Selling Tools, click **Sales Reports**.

3. On the Sales Reports Overview page, view the side-by-side comparison of the products, as shown in Figure 10-8:

   ● To sign up for the basic Sales Report, click the Sales Report **Sign Up Now** button, click **Sales Reports (Free)**, and click **Continue**. If you don't meet the requirements for a free subscription, you will be offered only the Sales Reports Plus option.

   ● To sign up for Sales Reports Plus, click the Sales Reports Plus **Sign Up Now** button. Accept the terms and conditions, and you'll receive a congratulatory page and an e-mail with welcome information.

4. View your report from My eBay (your initial report might take a few days to generate), as shown in Figure 10-9. Under My Subscriptions on the My eBay Views sidebar, click **Sales Reports**.

Figure 10-9: Sales Reports provide sections that detail your sales, fees, and unpaid items.

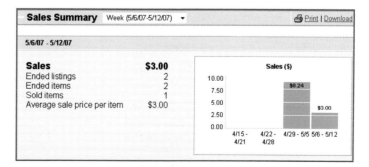

10

Conduct Your eBay Business

eBay provides several programs that can help you take advantage of its powerful marketing and advertising engine.

Sell for Others

You can leverage your experience and knowledge of eBay selling by offering to sell items for others. Selling on *consignment* pays you for your services (which can be anything you and the consignee agree upon) by collecting a fee or a percentage of the selling price or both.

QUICKSTEPS

SELLING LIVE

If you have an established auction business (licensed auction house or those auctions using a licensed auctioneer), you can partner with eBay and offer its members the opportunity to place absentee bids and even live bids during the conduct of your auction.

1. Visit www.ebayliveauctions.com and under Sellers Login, click **Sign Up As A Seller**.

2. Contact eBay by e-mail, or complete and submit an online form, as shown in Figure 10-10. (Chapter 4 describes how to bid on live eBay auctions.)

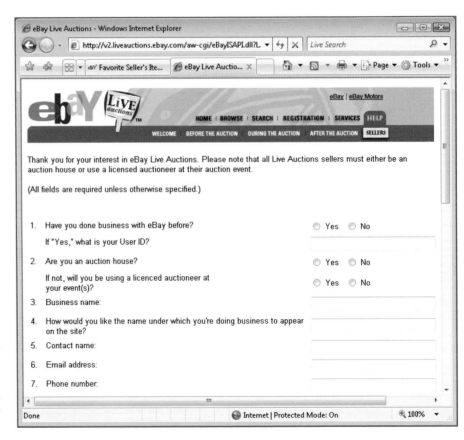

Figure 10-10: Leverage your auction business by offering eBay members a chance to place absentee bids.

NOTE

Announced at eBay Live! 2007 were several forthcoming changes to the PowerSeller program. Prominent among the changes was recognition to sellers who sell a lot but only for a short period, that is, seasonal sellers, and sellers who sell a lot of items but at lower dollar volumes. These and other feature changes to the program should be showing up in the fall of 2007.

CONSIGN ITEMS

One of the hottest trends for using eBay as a business is the concept of listing items for others; that is, becoming a *trading assistant*. Many folks don't care to join eBay, get involved with the mechanics of creating a Sell Your Item form, or deal with the customer service interaction of current and completed sales. You typically purchase a software program that allows you to set up accounts for multiple consignees and provides other related features, such as allowing each consignee to view his or her listings (under your eBay User ID). Trading assistants sell a myriad of items for a variety of clients, including:

- Individuals (best served with a retail outlet; see "Open a Drop-Off Store")
- Charitable and fundraising organizations
- Retail businesses that have excess inventory or returns
- Other eBay sellers who have just too many items to sell themselves

To become a trading assistant:

1. Set up your business infrastructure (see the "Creating an eBay Business Infrastructure" QuickFacts earlier in the chapter).

2. Procure suitable software (see the "Understanding eBay Listing Management Tools" QuickFacts later in the chapter).

3. Advertise your business by joining the eBay Trading Assistant Program (next) to gain potential exposure among the millions of eBay users.

JOIN THE eBAY TRADING ASSISTANT PROGRAM

eBay provides a clearinghouse for successful sellers and potential customers to come together, but doesn't get directly involved in the terms or arrangements—these are left to the participants to work out. Pricing, shipping, relisting decisions, and how you get paid are among the details that should be worked out before you list an item for someone. If you would like to offer your selling services to others (you can also offer to *buy* for others), you need to demonstrate some selling prowess and that you're a good eBay member:

- **Recent sales experience**. You must have sold an average of four or more items per month for the last three months.

- **eBay buying and selling track record**. Your feedback score must be 100 or better.

- **Good customer relations**. Your feedback ratings must have at least 97 percent positive comments.
- **Financial responsibility**. You must be in good standing with eBay.

To start the process of becoming an eBay trading assistant:

1. Click **Site Map** on the eBay header. Under Sell | Selling Resources, click **Trading Assistant Program**.

2. Under Choose A Topic, click **Become A Trading Assistant**.

3. On the Become A Trading Assistant page:
   - Read about the benefits of becoming a trading assistant.
   - Click the **eBay Trading Assistant User Agreement** link, and review the stipulations.
   - When ready, click **Create/Edit TA Profile** on the left sidebar or click ⬛ Click Here . If you are lacking qualifications, eBay will quickly let you know. If you do qualify, you will continue to set up the profile page that displays in the Trading Assistant Directory and advertises your services, as shown in Figure 10-11.

> Sorry, but you have not met all the requirements to become a Trading Assistant.

OPEN A DROP-OFF STORE

One idea for capitalizing on the eBay juggernaut is to open a brick-and-mortar storefront and accept items off the street to sell on eBay. Basically a consignment business, you typically charge an upfront insertion fee (different from and greater than eBay's fee) and then pay the consignee when the item sells, minus shipping costs and a commission fee. You can open your own store or join one of the national franchises, such as iSold It (www.i-soldit.com) and QuikDrop (www.quikdrop.com). However, eBay doesn't leave you completely on your own. You can aspire to become an eBay-sanctioned Trading Post 🐾, a drop-off store designation for trading assistants with a demonstrated sales record (a minimum of $25,000 in monthly eBay sales).

Figure 10-11: A well thought-out profile, along with PowerSeller status, will help drive customers to you.

Add a logo that distinguishes your business

The description provides a place to give buyers a sense of what items you have for sale

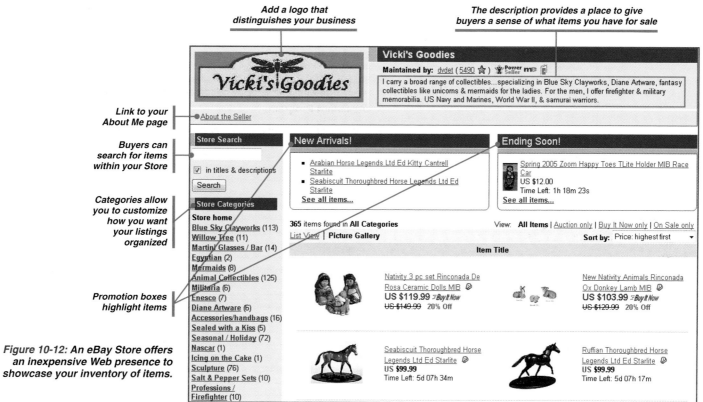

Link to your About Me page

Buyers can search for items within your Store

Categories allow you to customize how you want your listings organized

Promotion boxes highlight items

Figure 10-12: An eBay Store offers an inexpensive Web presence to showcase your inventory of items.

NOTE

eBay Store inventory listings do *not* appear when searching or browsing in the main section of eBay, www.eBay.com. They are restricted to searches within the eBay Stores arena. (Buyers can search eBay Stores from within the main section of eBay by clicking Advanced Search on the eBay header and clicking Items In Stores on the Search sidebar). However, a short list of Store inventory listings does appear when a search in the main section of eBay returns fewer than ten standard listings.

Open an eBay Store

eBay provides an easy-to-set-up, inexpensive feature that allows you to establish an eBay Store as a "home" within the eBay community (see Figure 10-12). If you maintain a few dozen or more listings, you may find that having a virtual storefront provides greater visibility to your listings by gathering them under one roof—yours.

Final value fees for eBay Store inventory items, as with standard auction and Buy It Now listings, are based on the selling price of the item. Selling prices up to $25 are charged 10 percent. Selling prices above that are progressively charged: Over $25 and upto $100, 7 percent is added; over $100 and upto $1,000, 5 percent is added; and over $1,000, 3 percent is added. For example, the final value fee for an item selling for $800 would be $42.75 ($2.50 plus $5.25 plus $35).

In your eBay Store, you can use the Markdown Manager to mark down the selling price of inventory listings—every buyer loves a sale! Create a sale by clicking **Marketing Tools** on the My eBay Views sidebar and clicking **Markdown Manager** on the Store Management sidebar.

Mr. Christmas World's Fair Ferris Wheel Musical MIB
US $86.24 *Buy It Now*
US $114.99 25% Off

DECIDE IF AN eBAY STORE IS FOR YOU

You can open an eBay Store under one of three subscription levels. Some of the basic benefits and features of opening an eBay Store include the following:

	Basic	Featured	Anchor
Monthly Subscription Fee	$15.95	$49.95	$499.95
No One-Time Set-Up Fee Many e-commerce providers charge a set-up fee, but not eBay Stores	$0	$0	$0
Sales Management Tools Selling efficiently in volume requires tools to save time-eBay Stores provides valuable FREE subscriptions to help you succeed.	$0 Selling Manager (reg. $4.99/month)	$0 Selling Manager Pro (reg. $15.99/month)	$0 Selling Manager Pro (reg. $15.99/month)

- **Creating eBay Store inventory listings** (Buy It Now–type format) that run for greater lengths of time than standard listings (30 days or Good 'Til Canceled) to help minimize relisting headaches.

- **Saving money** on eBay Store inventory listings—for example, the insertion fee for an item with a starting or reserve price that is less than $25 is only $0.05 every 30 days (final value fees and similar upgrade fees also apply).

- **Displaying standard auction and Buy It Now listings within your Store** along with your Store inventory listings.

- **Organizing your Store items** in custom categories.

- **Obtaining your own URL** that you can provide to potential buyers, both in and out of eBay.

- **Cross-promoting listings** by displaying similar or complementary listings that appear in the Sell Your Item form and in bidding and purchase e-mails your customers receive. (See "Use Cross-Promotion" earlier in the chapter.)

- **Customizing your Store's presence** by selecting themes or by using your own HTML design, inserting your own logo and graphics in the Store header, and including additional pages.

- **Obtaining monthly sales reports from eBay**, breaking out your sales into several categories, such as the number of unique buyers, how buyers got to your listing, and bids per listing (see "Target Selling with Your Sales Data" earlier in the chapter).

START AN eBAY STORE

To start an eBay Store:

1. Ensure that you meet the minimum requirements: maintain a seller's account with a credit card on file and have a feedback score of 20 or higher, be ID Verified, or have a PayPal account.

2. Click **Stores** on the eBay header.

3. On the eBay Stores page, follow the links to read additional information on Stores.

   –Or–

   Click **Open A Store**.

4. On the Subscribe To Stores: Choose Your Subscription Level page, click **Basic Store** (a good starting point from which you can upgrade as your business develops), type a name for the Store, and click **Continue**.

5. On the Subscribe To Stores: Select Additional Products page, select the offered products you want, and click **Continue**.

Subscribe to Stores: Select Additional Products
As a Basic Store subscriber, you qualify for discounts on the following products:
☑ Add Selling Manager **free**

6. On the Subscribe To Stores: Review & Submit page, shown in Figure 10-13, review your costs and the license agreement, click the **I Accept The User Agreement** check box, click the marketing down arrow, and select your applicable response. Click **Subscribe** when finished. You will then be able to manage your store by setting up its home page and creating categories for your listings.

Use Auction-Management Tools and Services

As your eBay business grows, you will quickly find yourself needing more auction-management features than those provided by My eBay.

TRY eBAY TOOLS

eBay provides several tools to assist you in listing and managing your sales. Though you can try many of them for free on a trial basis, it's quite

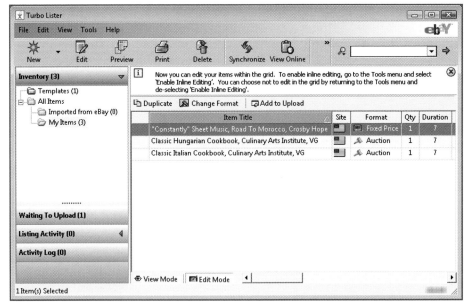

Figure 10-13: A basic eBay Store includes free tools and provides a potentially huge sales presence for $15.95 a month.

confusing trying to sort out which tool is best for your level of selling and recordkeeping needs (see the "Understanding eBay Listing Management Tools" QuickFacts). Fortunately, eBay provides a detailed comparison chart and a wizard that asks a few simple questions and steers you toward the tool you are most likely to be happy with.

1. Click **Site Map** on the eBay header. Under Sell | Selling Tools, click one of the tools, for example **Turbo Lister** (not specifically a management tool, the free Turbo Lister, shown in Figure 10-14, does ease your workload by allowing you to more easily create, organize, and submit multiple listings while working offline).

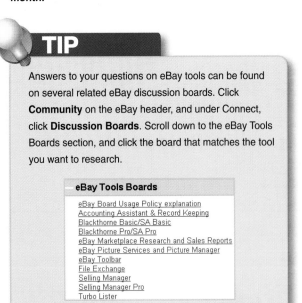

TIP

Answers to your questions on eBay tools can be found on several related eBay discussion boards. Click **Community** on the eBay header, and under Connect, click **Discussion Boards**. Scroll down to the eBay Tools Boards section, and click the board that matches the tool you want to research.

eBay Tools Boards

eBay Board Usage Policy explanation
Accounting Assistant & Record Keeping
Blackthorne Basic/SA Basic
Blackthorne Pro/SA Pro
eBay Marketplace Research and Sales Reports
eBay Picture Services and Picture Manager
eBay Toolbar
File Exchange
Selling Manager
Selling Manager Pro
Turbo Lister

Figure 10-14: Turbo Lister lets you create listings offline and upload them, singularly or in bulk, when you are ready.

10

UNDERSTANDING eBAY LISTING MANAGEMENT TOOLS

eBay listing and management tools are subscription, Web-based, or desktop applications that provide all the tools most sellers will need. There are no hidden fees, and you can easily cancel your subscription or upgrade:

- **eBay Selling Manager** ($4.99 per month and free with a Basic eBay Store) is an enhanced My eBay, although it offers greater post-sale support (Web-based).

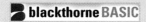

- **eBay Selling Manager Pro** (($15.99 per month and free with Premium or Anchor eBay Stores) is touted for "high volume and business sellers" (translation: PowerSellers) and includes bulk listing, reporting, and many automated features (Web-based).

☢ selling manager PRO

- **Blackthorne Basic (formerly called Seller's Assistant Basic)** ($9.99 per month), lets you create bulk listings, track sales, and manage correspondence with buyers. Recommended if you sell 25 items a month (desktop application).

▇ blackthorne BASIC

Continued . . .

---

2. On the Seller Tools page, on the Choose A Topic sidebar, click **Feature Comparison**. Review the features of the six tools, and click their respective headers to see details about each tool.

Feature	My eBay (Sell)	Turbo Lister & Selling Manager	Selling Manager Pro	Blackthorne Basic	Blackthorne Pro
Application Type					
Offline - Access through your desktop		✔TL		✔	✔
Online - Access through My eBay	✔	✔SM	✔		
Creating Listings					
List items on eBay in Bulk		✔TL	✔	✔	✔

–Or–

1. On the Seller Tools page, on the Choose A Topic sidebar, click **Tools Recommendations**.
2. On the Tools Recommendations page, answer the three questions, and then see which tools eBay recommends, as shown in Figure 10-15.
3. Select one of the eBay recommendations, and click **See My Choices** to get details on the tool.

EMPLOY SOLUTION PROVIDERS

When you've outgrown the capabilities provided by off-the-shelf programs and need a custom approach to your eBay sales, consider employing one of eBay's Solution Providers. These companies have been reviewed by eBay and provide complete solutions to your eBay business, including custom software development, auction management, hosting, order fulfillment, and complete system integration.

1. Click **Site Map** on the eBay header.
2. Under Sell | Selling Tools, click **eBay Solutions Directory**. On the Solutions Directory page, type keywords in the Search text box, and click **Search Directory**.

> Search Directory

–Or–

UNDERSTANDING eBAY LISTING MANAGEMENT TOOLS *(Continued)*

- **Blackthorne Pro (formerly called Seller's Assistant Pro)** ($24.99 per month), provides everything in Blackthorne Basic and adds inventory management, enhanced reporting and data retention, and multi-user profiles. Recommended for higher volume sellers and trading assistants (desktop application).

 **blackthorne** PRO

Use the Solution Finder to guide you to the providers that best match your needs.

Need help?
Use the **Solutions Finder** to guide you to selling solutions from Certified Providers and eBay.

GO

–Or–

Click one of the Solution categories to browse a list of providers.

3. Preview the providers, check out their user ratings, and contact one or more of them via e-mail, phone, or snail mail.

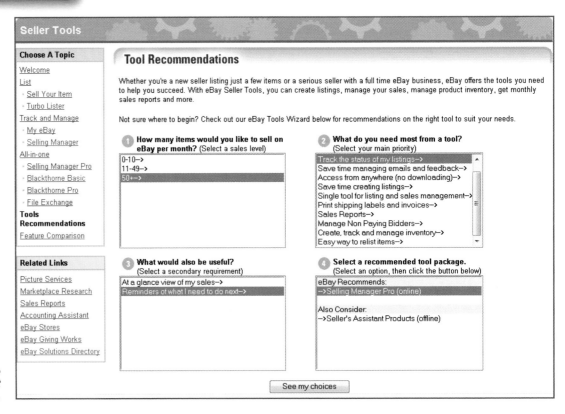

Figure 10-15: eBay can guide you to seller tools that best meet your needs.

Symbol

home page
  browsing, 4
  components of, 3
  selling view as, 152
Home Page Featured listing upgrade, cost and
  description of, 143
hot items
  finding, 9, 99–100
  watching, 68–70
HTF acronym, meaning of, 42
HTML
  formatting text with, 116–117
  using to add pictures, 117–118
HTML tags, using to format text, 129

I

icons
  beside seller's User ID, 50
  eBay icons, 26
  for eBay users, 39
  in listings, 32
ID history, finding, 39–40
ID Verify feature, using, 21–22
illegal items and solicitations, reporting, 208
IM (Instant Messaging), using, 64
inkjet printer, recommendations for, 93
insertion fees
  calculating, 103–105
  doubling by choosing multiple categories, 120
  viewing, 104–105
Install ActiveX Control option, using with
  pictures, 125–126
Instant Messaging (IM), using, 64
insurance, adding in PayPal, 83
insuring items, 194
intellectual property rights, reporting
  infringements of, 208–209
international shipping options, establishing, 139
Internet connection, recommendations for, 92–93

invoices
  combining purchases on, 175
  customizing in PayPal, 176–177
  formatting, 178
  personalizing, 178–179
  revising, 176
  sending, 178–179
  sending via Checkout feature, 175–176
IRS, position on online auction sites, 214
item descriptions
  adding to listings, 162–163
  customizing, 116–118
item listing, reviewing, 68
Item Not Received process, using, 201–202
Item Significantly Not as Described process,
  using, 201–202
item specifics, availability in Sell Your Item
  form, 125
item titles
  creating, 114–115
  entering for listings, 123–125
items. *See also* categories; closed items; products
  acronyms used with, 42
  budgeting, 52
  consigning, 222–223
  damage to and incorrect packaging of, 207
  deleting, 18
  deleting from searches, 31
  describing, 116, 129–131
  determining prices of, 102
  displaying in views, 18
  displaying locality for, 139–140
  disputes about, 200
  finding, 31
  finding completed items, 40
  finding with Search Options sidebar, 41
  grading, 59
  insuring, 194
  meaning of "new" items, 125
  packaging, 181

pricing, 132–134
receipt and difference concerns, 200
refusal of sale of, 201
relisting, 186–187
researching, 40–43
searching, 31–34
searching in stores, 37–39
searching stores with specific items, 38
selecting as Favorite Seller, 220–221
selling multiple items, 134
selling similar items, 163
unpaid items process, 205–206
watching, 68–70
items for selling, sources of, 95–96
Items I'm Selling view, displaying, 159
items in "play," selling, 151
Items I've Sold view
  choosing time frame for, 151
  managing completed sales from, 172
  removing listings from, 151

K

keyboard shortcuts
  Add To Favorites, 155
  copying item numbers, 164
  Refresh browser, 55
  splitting browser into two windows, 54
keywords
  entering for searches, 29
  listing for searches, 31
  using to search for categories, 119–122
Kijiji, description of, 8

L

layouts and themes, adding, 131–132
Level 4 category, explanation of, 99
limited liability company (LLC), explanation
  of, 220

themes and layouts, adding, 131–132

thrift stores, considering as sources of
items, 95

thumbnails, changing in Picture Services,
127–128

tickets, selling on StubHub, 110–112

time, finding for listings, 54

time format, setting, 52–53, 69

titles
creating for items, 114–115
entering for items, 123–125

Toolbar
installing, 60–61
removing and hiding, 63
setting options for, 69–70
tracking activity with, 70
using for bidding information, 62

Top Picks, displaying listings as, 219–220

Top Ten Reviews, displaying, 103

topics, browsing, 23

trading assistant, becoming, 223–224

transaction services fee (TSF) charging for vehicle
auctions, 170

transaction summaries, protecting, 194–195

transactions
closing out, 172
giving feedback on, 48–49
path of, 2
rearranging, 172
saving records of, 172
types of, 7

TSF (transaction services fee), charging for
vehicle auctions, 170

Turbo Lister, using, 228

U

unpaid item disputes, filing, 205–206

unpaid item strike, issuing, 206

unpaid items process, steps in, 205–206

Unsold Items view
choosing time frame for, 151
removing listings from, 151

upgrade options, accessing, 162

upgrades, combining for savings, 142

UPI acronym, meaning of, 42

UPS
contacting regarding shipping concerns, 207
free insurance offered by, 183
obtaining free packaging from, 182
using PayPal shipping tool with, 185

UPS acronym, meaning of, 43

UPS Shipping Zone option, selecting, 182

User Agreement, reviewing, 93

User ID
icons beside, 50
restriction on changing, 11
using, 10

USPS
contacting regarding shipping concerns, 207
obtaining free packaging from, 182
printing mailing labels from, 184

USPS acronym, meaning of, 43

USPS Shipping Zone option, selecting, 182

V

vehicles, selling in eBay Motors, 107–108

VF/VFC acronym, meaning of, 42

VHTF acronym, meaning of, 42

videos and pictures, adding, 126

View item page, getting details from, 48

views
displaying items in, 18
sorting, 18

visibility upgrades, using, 142–143

V/M/D acronym, meaning of, 43

VR acronym, meaning of, 42

W

Want It Now buyers, selling to, 105

Want It Now listings, reviewing, 100–101

Watch This Item feature, using, 89

Web sites, linking to eBay from, 214–215

Welcome page, components of, 3

What's Hot page, accessing, 99

wholesale, buying, 94–95

widescreen displays, limitation of, 92

wireless eBay alerts, receiving, 62–65

With Offers option, using, 156

WOB/WOC/WOF/WOR acronym, meaning
of, 42

words, finding, 31

WYSIWYG editors, using, 116